THE
SEER'S HANDBOOK

D1557107

THE
SEER'S HANDBOOK

A GUIDE
TO HIGHER PERCEPTION

Dennis Klocek

STEINERBOOKS

Copyright © 2005 Dennis Klocek

Published by SteinerBooks
P.O. Box 749, 610 S. Main Street
Great Barrington, MA 01245

www.steinerbooks.org

Book design by Will Marsh

Library of Congress Cataloging-in-Publication Data available.

ISBN 0-88010-548-8

All rights reserved. No part of this book may be reproduced or used in any
form without the written permission of the publisher.

10 9 8 7 6 5 4 3 2 1

Printed in the United States of America

CONTENTS

INTRODUCTION

In contemplating Nature's being
Know the one as many seeing
In and outer coinciding
Nothing in from out dividing
Open secret revelation
Grasp it without hesitation
Free of seeming truth's confusion
Revel in the serious game
Separateness is the illusion
One and many are the same
                              — Goethe, "Erirrhema"

IN THE ALCHEMICAL TRADITION, the highest goal a human being can aspire to is the fertilization, gestation, and birth of a higher person within the soul of the lower human personality. This second birth is known esoterically as the birth of the Spirit Embryo. The first birth is into a body of flesh. Given to us by nature working through our parents, the body of flesh is governed by the laws of nature and returns to nature when we die. This is the natural way of things. Alchemists, however, know of another birth, one that is, as Jung said, a work against nature (*opus contra naturam*). In the second birth a Spirit Embryo is fertilized and then brought to term by the conscious work of the student. This Spirit Embryo is called the "I Being" by Rudolf Steiner, the "True Self" by Carl Jung, and "the parent who would never lie to us" by the Kahunas of Hawaii. These names all relate to different functions of a being who resides in human consciousness as if asleep and is awakened only by conscious acts of will and rhythmical practices.

To understand this work, it is useful to think of the soul as a stage on which a cosmic drama is being unfolded. The human being has multiple sheaths or bodies that allow existence in both the sense world and higher realms, the world of the spirit behind the sense world. The problem is that human consciousness cannot easily be aware of both worlds simultaneously. For that to happen, special training is necessary in which the human being must build organs of cognition that can function both in the sense world and in the hidden world of the spirit. The link between the two polar worlds of the physical sense-imbued body and direct experience of the spirit is the world of the soul.

We could say that the spiritual part of the human being has the potential to live as a spiritual being among spiritual beings. The earthly part of the human being is imbedded in the laws of nature governing the functioning of the senses and of the physical body. The bodily part of the human must be overcome consciously through higher development for the soul to have a direct and unadulterated experience of itself as a spirit free of the body. The body is not denigrated, but placed in a context through which the soul can distinguish impulses arising solely from the body from those coming from the spirit, free of the desires and urges given to humans through the trial of living in a body of flesh prone to unconscious repetition of challenging patterns.

The human soul has latent abilities to focus conscious awareness into any number of levels. The ability to determine the focus of awareness is the great gift and the great challenge of humanity. It is a gift when we are focusing consciously, and it is a challenge when we are not. The shift from one mode to another is astonishingly rapid and counterintuitive. We can be simultaneously elated and guilty of horrible crime. We can laugh and cry at the same time. The part of the soul that is aware that the individual can control the focus of conscious awareness is the Witness. The Witness is a being that dwells in a more transcendent or cosmic human being linked to the individual human being. This transcendent human is the

True Human, a mysterious being living completely in the spiritual worlds. The Witness is a special capacity in the True Human capable of linking the spirit and the physical world. The only criterion is that the individual human must be aware of the level on which the consciousness is focused. This awareness is so important that the sole function of the Witness is to witness every shift and phase of consciousness; it is a constant monitor for the exact level of focus present in the soul at any given time, hence its name. It is actually a spiritual sheath of the True Human, with its own quality of being, its own personality.

In children and adolescents, who have immature souls, the Witness is not strongly present. The True Human has not yet established a focal point in the soul, and the Witness gives way to the promptings of the guardian angel. When a person reaches the age of twenty-one, the Witness enters the soul and establishes itself specifically within the individual's life. The guardian angel now retires, and the Witness begins to steer the ship of fate. Through time the Witness, observing the arising of consciousness in particular formations, gradually becomes aware of the difference between the portion of the soul linked directly to the body and the portion free of the body's pulls and urges. The Witness begins to intuit that there is another part of the soul that is not of this earth. That part is the True Human.

Most indigenous cultures believe the real human being comes from the stars and has deep connections to beings living there. In that realm there are no nouns: a name is a function. In the world of spirit, all beings are verbs. Our True Human is a process rather than a thing. As humans mature in deeper ways, the Witness comes more and more into contact with this higher being living in a nascent state within our soul being. With that increased contact comes the realization that the spiritual world is populated by spirit beings that are more like aware energetic processes than substantial bodies.

A deep yearning usually awakens to become more intimate with these beings who represent limitless energy and awareness. However, entering the realms where these beings have eternal life presents strong challenges to our relationship to our body. In a word, we must face death. To deal with these emotional challenges we need help to transform the parts of the soul linked only to sense experience into levels of consciousness that can make a bridge between the spirit and the sense world without a sense of discontinuity. The portion of our soul that can do this is the Spirit Embryo, which, because of its great potential for development, is like a seed force hidden within the soul of every human being. Working on this Spirit Embryo is like conceiving and being pregnant within the personality. Our sense experiences become transformed in varied and miraculous ways. But to conceive and bring the Spirit Embryo to birth, we must develop capacities that go against the natural or instinctual patterning in the body of flesh and the psychological patterning of the personality; we must face fears of death and self-doubt. This is the work against nature.

In many traditions this work is known as mystery training. Through a deeper perception of the True Human, the limitations imposed on the soul by the laws governing the working of the body of flesh are overcome. To work against nature in this way is not to desecrate nature, it is just to understand that the true human being is not really a product of nature. The True Human is a spiritual being living within the human soul as a being within a being. Its impulses, which are purely spiritual, are antagonistic to the forces of nature as they are found within the body. This antagonism of the spirit and the body must be tempered into a mood of cocreation with the hierarchies that stand behind nature if the True Human is to be a truly creative being. This tempering, or "alchemical marriage," sets the stage for the development of the Spirit Embryo and is filled with trials and tests for the developing human soul. The trials and tests are the mystery training.

Since mystery training is such a difficult and dangerous undertaking, the Great Spirits that guide humanity have provided teachers who, since ancient times, have served as guides for aspirants. Some of these guides have incarnated in human form as the great teachers of the mysteries. Others have been beings inhabiting more archetypal planes of existence than do human beings. These teachers, guardians, or doorkeepers help humans walk the dangerous path of self-awareness from instinctual patterning toward their Spirit Embryo. To do this work against nature, an aspirant must study nature in a systematic, yet humble and caring way, and then develop forces to overcome the patterned and unfree elements in the soul by tempering them with spiritual impulses.

 In esoteric language the term *seer* refers to persons who can "see" or perceive using higher sight. Normal seeing involves perceiving patterns of light in the eye, which are then interpreted as things in the world. Higher sight involves perceiving patterns and relationships that are not normally seen, yet are present within the things in the world. We can often recognize someone we know walking down the street three hundred yards away even though normal sight sees nothing that can be interpreted as a face. We "see" the person using faculties lying outside normal physiological seeing.

Most higher seeing has more understanding or cognitive experience coincident with it than normal seeing. In the example of seeing someone at a distance, our normal seeing and our higher seeing are separate functions, and with reflection we can experience the differences. When we understand the differences we say, "I see." In the day-to-day world, our normal seeing and higher seeing are blended seamlessly, but in unusual circumstances they can be experienced separately. We might see unusual colors on the face or moving lines of color surrounding the body of a person who is sick or has a high fever. The illness is pushing the subtle bodies of the person's life forces and feelings slightly apart and we can then see in a higher way. However, in this type of seeing much less understanding is available than is available to our awake consciousness. So while seeing colors hovering around a person or animal is higher seeing, not all higher seeing is beneficial to the seer or, indeed, accurate.

Those who see the colors of the human aura when no fevers and delirium are present, or who see beings in the air or elemental beings as forms in nature, are sometimes gifted with powers of seeing because of a subtle misalignment of the forces of their own subtle bodies. They can see a great deal with higher sight, but they do not necessarily know what they are seeing. If such naturally gifted seers find their way into a developed esoteric tradition or get a disciplined modern scientific training, then their gifts can develop safely. If they are not part of a tradition or have not trained themselves to think critically and the gift arises spontaneously through living, then it can lead to ego inflation and emotional imbalances. Modern people need to undergo a rigorous training in clear and sequential thinking in order to deal successfully with seeing as a gift. When this happens the gifted seer becomes an "exact seer."

Exact seers do not "see" as readily as gifted seers, but when they see they simultaneously know. They can experience the higher seeing almost constantly as a cognitive overlay of their normal seeing. They have a simultaneous knowing experience of hidden elements in what they are seeing that cognitively accompanies their normal seeing. Being able to tell the weather by watching cloud patterns and shifts in the wind is an entry-level example of this type of exact seeing. If you think you see something and make a prediction, the weather will come along and let you know if you were accurate in your cognitive seeing.

Contrary to common perceptions, the most advanced seers are the ones who do not so readily see visual phenomena like colored lights hovering around people. It is as if the development of their gift requires that they surrender it. This is hard to understand until we look at the most fundamental rule of seership – the rule of "give away." To see and simultaneously to know requires that the seer be willing to dissolve or give away what is seen outwardly in order to see it inwardly. To the seer this is alarmingly like losing the gift of seeing. It is easy to understand how many seers would balk at this, yet the fundamental rule of seership is that if we wish to transform our gifts into capacities we must transform them ourselves and not just use them as they are given to us. The exercises in this book are organized with this rule in mind.

There are three levels of training that can systematically transform a gift for seeing into a capacity for seeing. The first level is concentration. In concentration we can develop the ability to concentrate on an inner image for an extended period of time. It is  usually necessary first to "find" the place where we form our inner picture. We do this by concentrating our attention inwardly upon forms we consciously choose to see. It is important that we choose to see them and that we hold on to them for as long as we wish. When we practice this type of concentration we are actually entering our own physical body.

The second level of training is to practice rotating the pictures or transforming them, a capacity needed to be able to track images as they morph and shift in the spirit world. While rotating or transforming an image, we are entering our own etheric body or body of life forces. The body of life forces is roughly linked to the endocrine pathways and chemical feedback circuits governing the life forces and the life organs in human beings. This level of the work is known as contemplation.

The third level of the work involves systematically dissolving images and developing the capacity for thinking an image backward into a state of prolonged inner silence. This level is known as meditation. In meditation we are entering directly into our own body of feelings. The body of feelings consists of the unconscious messages we tell ourselves when things go wrong or when things go our way. We could call it the body of beliefs. The feelings and beliefs of this body are connected to patterns we receive from impulses arising from the life body composed of glands and life organs. Some would call the feeling body the unconscious; others would call it the soul. The feeling body has many levels, and the exercises in this book are aimed at bringing the various levels into focus in the awake state. The work on the feeling body is necessary in order to become a spiritual being among other spiritual beings while still maintaining the essential core of the awake consciousness. This is not so easy, since when we enter a higher consciousness our own awake consciousness is dimmed. This dimming is a protection and a challenge.

Concentration, contemplation, and meditation are the three levels of training the capacity for higher seeing.

In this book, the first level of training for seership is found in the form of the elemental mandala with its four stages of development. The elemental mandala can be thought of as a system for developing concentration. The second level of training is developing the system of the four chakras linked with the stages of the elemental mandala. The system of the chakras can be thought of as a method for developing contemplation. The third level of training is found in the teachings of the being the Rosicrucians called the Confidant Doorkeeper, and the teachings can be called the four lights. The four lights of the Confidant Doorkeeper can be thought of as a system for developing meditation.

In reality, these stages of development are not separate but are closely integrated. It is possible, for example, to fashion a very effective meditation on the four elements, but to do so certain requirements must be met. To work on our seeing, we must know where we are and where we want to go. Finding one's place in the context of the great work is the most fundamental and serious task for seers. Once a place is found, much good work is possible. My intention in this book is to present the systems for training the seeing in a way that will serve as a reference guide to the essential inner work for those starting on the path without the aid of a teacher. It is usually understood that when the student has sufficiently prepared, a teacher will appear.

The elemental mandala of earth, water, air, and fire is the system closest to the physical body. In working with this mandala, four questions are used. In earth mode we ask what is different. We get data ("dust" in alchemical language) as a result of that question. In water mode we ask what is changing. We get images of the flow or process level of the work from that question. In the air level we ask what has reversed. We see how a system that is changing can go through a reversal when in the air mode. In fire we ask what is the whole and get answers about destiny and the implications of the whole nexus of forces around the original phenomenon.

The system of the chakras is a higher octave of the elemental mandala. In studying the chakras, we are looking at the dynamics and energetic dialogues of the life organs in the body. At this level of seership, we practice relating experiences of the patterns of energy that flow in the body to images of the ways the soul flows in and out of situations in life. The brow chakra, or the two-petal lotus, is located in the head behind the eyes. It is concerned with the integration of sensory input and the forming of concepts. It corresponds to the earth element in the elemental mandala. The throat chakra, or the sixteen-petal lotus, is concerned with the perception of lawful patterns of motion that result in the forms of words or the creative motions behind the manifestation of objects in the sense world. It corresponds to the water level in the elemental mandala. The heart chakra, or the twelve-petal lotus, is an important center for the capacity to create and form lawful inner images. It corresponds to the air level of the elemental mandala, where everything must go through a reversal to achieve completeness. The forces of the heart chakra help the student to form and edit moving inner pictures that morph from one form to another in the course of the work. The next lower chakra, the spleen chakra, or the ten-petal lotus, aids us in perceiving patterns connected to the role of our individuality in the context of the role of humanity in general. Through it we can see the ways in which power and karma weave into life relationships with others. It corresponds to the fire level of the elemental mandala.

The questions of the Confidant Doorkeeper are another octave of these two systems. We have called these questions the four lights in the darkness of the abyss. The first light, awareness, is the condition of the consciousness of the human being who is living mostly in a stimulus-response mode. We could say the consciousness is off/on in these individuals. This light corresponds to the earth element and the brow chakra. The second light correspond to the water element and the throat chakra. Here the higher soul faculties of the individual become independent of sensory input, and we become aware within ourselves that we are aware. The third light, awareness of being, corresponds elementally to the air element of reversal and in the sheath of life forces to the heart chakra, which enables a seer to see selflessly (that is, as the other person sees things — reversed from our usual way of seeing things) into the spirit in an active way.

The last light, the light of surrender to being, corresponds to the fire pole in the elemental mandala and to the spleen chakra.

From the above descriptions we can see that the elemental mandala, the system of chakras and life organs, and the conversations with the Confidant Doorkeeper are linked to each other by corresponding moods and gestures. All of the forces involved deal with the eventual development of a perceptive capacity within the profound and utter silence of the spirit. To develop that capacity, we ask what is different (data), what is changing (process), what has reversed (reversal), and what is the whole (destiny). Unless we work on ourselves every day to build the mental flexibility to be able to withstand the resentment that can make life an emotional chaos, going inside ourselves can be like a descent into the deepest darkness imaginable. The capacity to perceive within the silence of the spirit is the root of inner development and the hallmark of exact seership. To be able to live devotedly and attentively for extended periods in that profound silence is the practice and the goal of the exact seer. All insights come from the silence and all images received in meditation are to be dissolved back into the silent, creative darkness from which all light of understanding flows.

The purpose of this book is to present a path that can be followed to develop higher seeing and the capacity to perceive and live within the profound silence of the spirit. Part one gives some of the philosophical background of the alchemical tradition that underlies the path. Part two presents exercises that can allow seekers and researchers to find out where they are in the great work and develop a rational and safe practice for reaching their goals. Part three takes us on a journey up the Alchemical Mountain to show how the exercises can be used to work with a seemingly mysterious image and lead us to heartfelt thinking.

Part One

The Alchemy
of
Transformation

1

AWAKENING

IN THE DREAM OF LIFE

THE STARRY HEAVENS SEEM SO FAR AWAY that an anxious loneliness can pervade a soul contemplating the limitless dark distances and cold vast expanses of space. A similar feeling of anxiety can arise when through sickness or the death of someone close the inner life comes to resemble a bitter pile of cold and caustic ashes rather than a bright and shining flame. For most people, the anxiety produced when contemplating the abyss between life and death brings out thoughts of the extreme vulnerability of human beings in the face of mysteries and polarities we can only dimly divine. Absurd and crushing paradox lies in the hidden depths of the inward looking human soul at the *intensive* pole of transcendent experience. At the other, *extensive,* pole the terrorizing loneliness of death in exile at a distant periphery lurks in silence for the outward looking soul. Is it any wonder then that human consciousness tends to wallow lazily in the warm, muddy shallows of soul life, afraid to rock the boat of contentment for fear of learning that, both *intensively* and *extensively,* in our True Self we are a riddle to the universe? We are a seeming something whose vital core of self stands ultimately revealed as exponentially less than nothing.

Actually, this reality is only a problem when we hold the unexamined belief that a great and incandescent vault of something must lie at the very core of our existence. The seemingly alien intuition that we are less than nothing at the very center of our self is not very affirming. As a result of this intuition the human soul is often desperately seeking to maintain the general human feeling that the self should, after all, be "something." In contrast to this general human feeling, Eastern religious teachings have always asserted emphatically that there really is no self at all. Self and all of its possible manifestations are illusion. The void, or the great less-than-nothing, is the true nature of human existence. The self and its attendant personality are best obliterated in meditative practices aimed at attaining oneness with all of creation.

To the Western soul caught up in the struggle for personal freedom as it is now manifesting in the popular deification of the struggling persona, the experience of a great transcendent void where the soul can lay down its burdens of striving and suffering is either a natural heavenly reward for being a righteous person or evidence of complete moral degeneracy. How unstriving to give up and surrender to the void! In the West, to surrender to a void seems threatening and somehow passive. Soul-wise, it feels more human to surrender to Christ.

However, in postmodern times the exotic nature of contemplation of the void seems particularly attractive to Western physicists. A great deal of serious thinking has arisen in attempts to marry the abstract void of Eastern religious experience and the abstract mindset of Western physics. And from one point of view there definitely seems to be a marriage. The experience of self within a human consciousness appears to the scientific observer to be a contradictory, void-like, paradox. An experience of self is impossible to measure scientifically.

In quantum mechanics the impossibility of measuring a something that defies measurement, or worse is changed by the attempt to measure it, is now a classic experience for physicists seeking to classify particles. When a particle meter is used to measure a photon, it appears to be a particle; when a wave meter is used, it appears to be a wave. Today some of the greatest Western minds are looking for an escape route from this paradox by seeking the door to higher perception in the abstract void, which is seen, as it was in the Eastern mystery schools, as composed simply of patterns of forces. In this view, all forces in the universe are alike in being units of consciousness, but none have the quality of self or independent being. This view of reality avoids the issue of an independent self by denying that a self exists. The self as a separate something is seen as an illusion, as maya. What appears as separate existence is simply a force among other forces, all composed of consciousness. A separate self existing independently would violate the feelings of oneness that sustain the mystical experience. Given this tendency for analogs from Eastern thought, it is highly interesting that the role of the observer is becoming the paramount issue in theoretical physics. Is an observer a part of the experiment (a consciousness among other patterns of consciousness) or a separate being independent of the experiment? To answer affirmatively to either of these questions is to maintain the split between the mystical abstractionists and the technical reductionists.

A possible solution would be to say, with the poet Goethe, that the experiment and the object are united or married in the act of observing, and that when the observing ceases the observer, the observation, and the observed all fall into separate existence. The true nature of the observer is fulfilled when the observed and the observer are united in the act of observing.

To most Western scientific thinking, such word play most likely seems decidedly speculative and ultimately unscientific. For the technician, the world is the reality, the void is the illusion, and the consciousness of the observer is irrelevant. In the Western reductionist worldview, to value the mystical experience of the oneness in the void and reject the reality of the outer world is to deny the necessity of entering the dark mystery hidden in the heart of matter itself as if it were in an abyss.

In the East, transcendence into the abstract void of absolute oneness without dealing with the problem of anything separate, whether it be the self or matter, allows a soul to avoid the descent into the abyss, the source of the contemporary widespread cultural alienation in the West. In the West the abyss, the separateness of self and world, is the alienating portal of initiation through which the self must pass in order to eventually divine the possibility of transcendence. St. Augustine said, "No salvation without temptation." Many Westerners are unconsciously entering the dark abyss of despair as materialism threatens to overwhelm human experience. For Eastern thinkers, this shows a fundamental flaw in Western thought. However, the social challenges in the West arising out of materialism hinge on a common unconscious intuition in many contemporary Western souls that there is a noble something in a human being. This something survives and transcends the forces of obliteration found in the hyped, annihilating daily contact with the world. To be sure, the powerful unconscious energies surrounding these daily survival events are messy and dangerously subjective. But social malaise is not scientific. The problems of Western society will probably not be resolved by a brilliant experimental breakthrough in theoretical physics.

How can we possibly come to some balance about these issues? We could simply ask meditators, both Eastern and Western, "What is the inner experience when a person actually awakens in the dark chasm between the humbling incongruity of the material human on one side of the abyss and the alarming elusiveness at the core of the spiritual human being living on the other shore?" Can a radically extensive or expanded consciousness experience itself as a separate being, or, most simply stated, does being deny oneness? Perhaps only the dead know for sure, but they are hard to survey with any reliability. It may be that only those who make a practice of daily dying into the True Self in meditative states can vouch for the integrity of beingness or the lack of it in the expanded state of unity. Can there be a difference in the meditative values of transcendence in the East and West? Can a person imbedded in a materialistic, egoistically driven society truly relinquish the sense of being a separate being in order to live in a more cosmic consciousness? Can cosmic consciousness allow the attention of a "separate" observer to be within it as a painful yet necessary developmental phase?

Perhaps, since this rambling appears to have finally yielded a few distilled questions, an analogy might be useful in an attempt to point to even better questions. In the life of every child a profound change happens around seven years of age at the time the milk teeth are changing into the adult teeth. Prior to this change, the inner life of the child centers on play that is stimulated by fantasy. In fantasy, the inner pictures of the child arise as a result of contact between the sense organs, as part of the organism, and sense objects, which are outside the organism. A block of wood becomes a boat, a box becomes a castle, a cloud becomes an animal. The child cannot form these fantasy pictures at will. They arise as an organic response to a sense stimulus. The pictures form around the unconscious core of the personality in temperamentally driven rhythms of ebb and flow. The fantasy pictures enable the child to participate responsively in a numinous, ever-changing dialogue with the world as it is presented to the senses.

For young children, beingness pours out of the sense world in creative torrents, and their inner life and the objects of the world all participate in the magical, transformative ritual of play. Each separate thing can easily become something else in a world held in the enchanting bosom of love and oneness. The Sun-like nature of children's instinctive vision draws to them constellations of objects and people that help their organism to find the proper forces for development.

However, this stage cannot continue unchanged, and at the change of the teeth the fantasy life must undergo a transformation. The child can no longer rely on the objects of the world to stimulate inner images. Inner images must come under the control of the individual consciousness so that they can be developed and manipulated at will. The spontaneous and magical mood of oneness evaporates, and what slowly takes its place is the capacity to develop inner images independent from the sensations given by the world. The advantage of this development is that the purely personal inner images arising in fantasy can now be corrected and objectified by the child and are not dependent upon subjective feelings that arise spontaneously under the instinctual influence of sensory stimulus. In short, forming inner images separate from sense experiences is the first sign of the potential for the human being to eventually attain freedom from the iron necessity of instinct. But there is a price to pay for this freedom. Coincident with the arising of the capacity to visualize inwardly is the loss of the feeling of oneness with all of creation. This loss eventually leads, in the ninth and tenth years, to the experience of the fall from Paradise, when children often experience the rise of a skeptical and critical mood that prevents free access to the mood of play so necessary for learning.

The analogy here is that the conflict about the nature of the self in the East-West dialogue is rooted in the demands made on the changing focus of consciousness as a human being develops biologically and socially, and this polarity is reflected in the two opposing contemporary scientific points of view. The first view is that the original magical consciousness is the most valid one for solving the present problems in the world because it obviously contains an abundance of feelings of love and connectedness. In this view, the creative spirit is really a transcendent, undifferentiated, nonpersonal field of force very much akin to who we are in our deepest meditative consciousness, and the only way to know this force is to drop any illusion of separateness. We then enter the limitless creative void of nature and all of creation as an integral part of this sublime force. Our experience is then that the All is composed of different vibrations of consciousness in which we are embedded in a seamless magical unity, transcendent in its quantum-mechanical perfection.

The other, polar scientific view is that we must awaken to the potential for human beings to master the forces of nature. To do this requires an inward separation from nature so that the forces can be seen objectively through the researcher's capacity to develop personally controlled objective inner pictures (hypotheses). Those who adhere to the technological worldview are rightfully suspicious of any attempt to include the researcher's level of consciousness as a parameter for an experiment, since by definition any interaction between the consciousness of the observer and the object of study would be a breach of objectivity and open the door to bad science.

It is interesting that the most physical of the sciences, physics, is just where the mystical pursuit of oneness in the void is posited as a scientific metaphor. Just as noteworthy is the fact that the introduction of cybernetic cognitive principles into cultural life has been done most effectively through the fantasy life of games and the entertainment media. In addition, both the cybernetic technical worldview and the scientific mystical worldview are united in a strong tendency toward forming an abstract metalanguage of signs and symbols. Both tendencies in science also share a fascination with the arcane and magical.

The scientific mystic seeks to explain the magical experience of the quantum domain by returning to ancient descriptions of the state of oneness; the poetic ambiguity of the ancient adepts helps to describe the feelings engendered in the observer by highly sophisticated technical experiments. The cybernetic technician seeks the magical forces released through the activity of playing with images and icons to relieve the uneasy feelings of alienation that can arise when fantasy is transcended and one lives exclusively in an inner world of preconditioned choices like those found in computer protocols. Cybernetic technologists do not usually seek a return to older spiritual practices except in the form of arcane games and puzzles as a diversion from the repetitive labors of exactitude.

But in the end science is not *life,* and neither a return to ancient terminology nor the technical application of rigorously organized images can prepare a person to solve the deeper questions in life. Developmentally, we could ask if, since in the child fantasy gives way to voluntary inner picturing, there is a stage of natural development that follows development of the capacity to form voluntary inner pictures. In the normal biological unfolding of an individual, the next step of adolescence brings to awareness many unresolved feelings rooted in the personality structure. Unlike the natural advance from fantasy to inner picturing that marks the school readiness of the younger child, nature has no clear cognitive gift for the adolescent as part of an automatic path of self-development. In fact, the onset of raging hormones often obscures any true cognition about the self from taking place. So simply paying greater attention to the biological patterns connected to the sense life becomes an appropriate developmental task for adolescence. Beginning in adolescence, any step taken toward inner development must be taken voluntarily, and usually at great expense to the natural appetites.

Ideally the next step in inner development for all stages after adolescence is never simply a return to a mystical worldview nor simply a diversion from the boredom brought on in reaction to overly complex abstract thought patterns. Esoterically, even mythologically, the next step always involves purification. The purging is brought about through giving away the treasures gained in the labors of the previous steps.

To summarize, in the young child the freeing of the life forces at the changing of the milk teeth provides for a more individualized use of the organism than the earlier conception-to-seven-year period can allow. After the change of teeth, the early intense focus of the life forces into biological necessity can be transcended, transforming biological life into thought life. When independence in the inner picturing process is finally attained at the ninth-year change, the feeling forces are the next to be liberated in adolescence. After that the thinking is never again directly addressed biologically as it is, for instance, in the myelinization of the neurons in the preschooler.

Comparing this to the dialogue in science, we could say that once mysticism has been transcended into analytical science, the search for a feeling metaphor to express what is experienced numinously in the physics laboratory has nowhere to go. The apparent result in a longing to go back to the precognitive fantasy language of mysticism full of portentous feelings of the sublime. By definition, feelings are not allowed in modern science. It is no wonder then that quantum physicists use Eastern mystical analogies, since these images are so connected to magical feelings.

Since the analytical capacities given to children by freeing the life forces for the processes of inner picturing seem to dim, if not actually dampen, the capacity for mystical transcendent experience, what is the purpose in the grand scheme of things for freedom in the inner picturing process? Why is it that the life forces in particular are transformed in the preschooler into the seeds of analytical thinking? What is it about the life forces that specifically support the independent inner picturing process? And finally, since there is a sequence from fantasy to inner picturing, is there a metamorphosis independent of the biology of the inner picturing capacity that can be developed beyond analytical thinking? And if there is, could it satisfy the feeling language requirements of mystical scientists and still be as rigorous as the analytical language of the technical sciences? All of these questions point to the development of what is known to esotericism as imaginal consciousness or Imagination with a capital "I."

The development of Imagination is not a biological given. That is, it is not simply part of a maturation process in the organism. Once the life forces are freed from the intense biological necessity of forming the physical organs, the greater part of the life forces in the organism can be devoted to the "free" part of the soul, the inner life. The soul uses the biological organ-forming forces to complete the biological task and then applies these *organizing* forces to create soul *organs* in the cognitive field of the individual. In the ancient schools these soul organs were called *chakras*. They allow the soul to breathe and digest the incoming rush of sensory and cognitive stimuli that can inundate the developing individual as the demands of schooling become more rigorous. The first indication of this development is the awakening of the intellect in the middle-school child. When the emotional forces are liberated from the sexual organs in adolescence, the individual is given the capacity to create life, but no accompanying cognitive development parallels the freeing of the emotional forces. The surging hormonal reasoning so prevalent in adolescence attests to this curious development. Why do we not by nature have wisdom along with the passion? The sad fact is that we do not, and therein hangs many a tale.

Esoterically, the free life forces in the budding intellect of the school-age child are seen as a seed in the thinking for developing imaginative cognition in the adult. The free feeling forces arising in adolescence must be purified in the young adult through willfully employing the newly arisen seedlike thinking capacities that are liberated in the school-age child. This task is further developed in the maturing postadolescent young adult through planting the seed of thinking developed at the change of teeth into the soil of *life*.

The cultivating of this seed can be accomplished a bit later by a mature adult through rigorous inner application of the capacity to form objective, logical inner pictures independent of sense impressions. The mature adult must then use this capacity to look consciously at the way the soul reacts to sense impressions. Finally, adepts who enter imaginative consciousness go consciously into their sense life in an attempt to see the sense world once again as a little child. This path leads back into the magical forces behind the sense world the individual leaves at the change of teeth. It is the path of development walked in the pursuit of imaginative consciousness.

Development first requires the freeing of the life forces from imperatives given by the organism. This freeing gives rise to stronger thinking forces ultimately related to the experience of the True Self. First, in the preschooler, thinking frees itself from the biological necessity of forming the life organs and becomes thinking that is independent of biological necessity. Then, during the school years, independent thinking must be gradually freed from the emotional demands of adolescence by developing the capacity to reason abstractly, free from any sense impressions.

At some later date, each individual needs to further purify and strengthen the thinking beyond abstraction into what Rudolf Steiner called morphological or living thinking. This purification is accomplished by working to transform the will forces in thinking. In reality this purification is the basis of the work on thinking even from an early stage of the inner work.

For instance, in adolescence the will impulses surrounding the reproductive urges must be purified through the realization of logical consequences and culturally realized moral ideals that temper the individual's motives for forming relationships. In the postadolescent development, the intellect and its logic pictures must be *further* purified so that they become capable of being a vessel for the later awakening and freeing of the True Self. In the first purification the ordering forces come from the outside in the form of culturally determined values that awaken the thinking to higher motives. To accomplish the *second* purification, individuals need to apply, out of their *own* inner moral imagination, the thinking capacity of the free intellect back onto their own feelings in an act of free willing. This purification must happen in the postadolescent adult and is difficult to do since the life forces and the feelings constellated within them by individual life experiences are the very basis of the instinctual life of the body. As such they are intimately connected to habitual patterns of personal feelings in the soul, such as basic drives to appease hunger or to survive. More profoundly, through the forces of karma present in the person's biography, these basic biological instincts and drives become connected to feelings of self-worth arising out of the fundamental need to be recognized as a worthy human being. To face these powerful forces at the root of the soul means to face food issues, self-image issues, fear, doubt, and the fundamental aggressive dislike of others who threaten our security. Through this inner work of will and purification, the thinking processes become more flexible and creative – in a word, more living. The thought life starts to be more integrated and whole, and it takes on the characteristics of an organism, hence Rudolf Steiner's term "morphological thinking."

Eventually, as an individual matures to his or her life work, the life forces begin to wane and bring with the later stages of development the clear presentiment that physical life and the temperamental personality dependent upon it are indeed terminal. This insight may or may not appear consciously. If it remains unconscious and unintegrated, the individual runs the risk of feeling resentful that the free life forces are beginning to radically ebb away. If the individual has undertaken inner development exercises to enter consciously into his or her own life forces and feeling forces in meditative states, then the higher person sleeping within every human being awakens as a witness of the great dreaming of the world. This is the morphological consciousness. It opens to researchers the possibility of awakening within their own dream states.

The meditative practice of awakening within the dream allows the soul to become a conscious yet humble citizen of the cosmos. In this unique state the seedlike forces of life liberated at the change of teeth can be directly experienced as analogs or signposts giving reliable directions for the journey of the human soul through the various stages of life. Through the waking dream, the researcher begins to see the forces in nature not as dead abstractions, but as morphologically creative beings. They become capable of sustaining an ongoing dialogue with these beings, which live on the other side of the threshold between this world and the next. Awakening in the dream is another way of describing the onset of imaginative cognition.

In imaginative cognition, the conflict between mystical abstractionism and analytical reductionism can be resolved. Entering into the life forces consciously reveals a world of numinous and cosmic beings intent on interacting with other conscious beings. This intent to interact is at the very heart of the mystical yearning in modern physics. The step that needs to be taken is to transform an abstract universal void filled with impersonal forces by entering the beingness of beings exponentially mightier in degree in their world-creative Imaginations than the human being. The humility that this transformation can engender in the soul can bestow great powers of spiritual perception upon the seedlike life forces that presently animate the sense organs of human beings in all stages of development. Creative beings would then once again flow into our eyes through the inpouring sunlight, just as they did when our souls were engulfed in the world of fantasy before the change of teeth. The difference would be that then, when the life forces have been consciously purified in the waking dream practice, our seeing would be as exact as when an analytical reductionist describes a chemistry experiment or a theoretical physicist documents a particle track in a cloud chamber.

But the insights of imaginative cognition are not composed of linearly arranged bits of data. They have a morphological, organic wholeness. Examples of this kind of thinking can be found in the thought experiments of projective geometry and in the intimate laws of the development of the embryo and the morphological development of flowering plants. Awakening in the dreaming of the life forces is a way of reconciling the split in the sciences, the even greater split between the sciences and art, and the greater yet split between the human being and the cosmos.

2

SACRED SLEEPING
THE TRANSFORMATION OF DREAM LIFE

IN THE CULTIVATION OF THE INNER LIFE one of the most useful capacities to develop is the transformation of dream life. Esoteric development requires the student to make a clear distinction between personal fantasy and true objective imaginative experience. Developing this ability is the very essence of the struggle to enter the spirit, as the whole dialogue between the soul and the higher world revolves around the ability to distinguish fantasy from fact. And although it may seem strange, the dream space is the place where the greatest part of this dialogue must take place. Dreams are revelations of how the soul is reacting to its experiences in the spiritual world.

Unfortunately, for human beings the spiritual world lies hidden either deep in their own psyche or deep within the disguise of the world available to the senses. Dreams can be responses to either of these two worlds, so they must not be taken too literally, which can be tempting to do since they are usually clothed in images of the physical world. But the laws governing the physical world do not apply to dream experiences. The laws of dreams are the laws of the psyche, but the images are the images of sense experience. Dream, then, live in two worlds, or, to be more accurate, in a space between two worlds. Dreams having more of a footing in the body response to anxiety and stress in daily life are the most common.

Rudolf Steiner calls these organ dreams. They are a kind of safety valve for the soul, allowing it to digest and assimilate difficult or stressful sense experiences from daily life. On one side of the psyche, organ dreams inform the soul of how things are going on in the day-to-day unfolding of biography. On the other side they express a fundamental language of relationships by which the soul can regularly integrate higher spiritual perceptions into the chaos of living. Dreams, then, can be of great use to the esoteric student wishing to plumb the depths of the biography to find the answer to the question, "Who am I?"

However, to be serviceable in esoteric practice, dreams must be accurately perceived. Projecting physical or even symbolic meanings on dreams makes them caricatures of their true function as a space in which this world and the next can meet in fruitful dialogue. At the level in which they exist, dreams already are symbols and projections. The real task in transforming dreams is to distinguish between the objective level of dreams that convey true imaginations to the soul for the purpose of inner development and organ dreams, which are by far the most common. Organ dreams apply simply to impulses related to the human dreamer's maintenance of the physical organs. Organ dreams could be seen as manuals for the maintenance of the physical body; they are like a desktop shortcut that points to a computer application but is not the application itself. Organ dreams are usually triggered by some sort of anxiety state and contain very little in the way of creative dialogue. They are indicators of the need for the soul to instigate a deeper level of involvement in the life processes. Basing esoteric protocols upon observing and recording organ dreams will at best yield only conflicting patterns until the dreamer develops a heart eye that can see with clarity through the dark boundary between this world and the next.

Developing the heart eye requires that the feeling mood of dreams be distinguished without paying too much attention to organizing the details into meaning gestalts. Correct perception of details will come to the practitioner as a kind of grace. It is given to students as a gift of the higher worlds once they have worked to free themselves from the inflation leading them to believe that almost everything they imagine is objective or that everything they dream is valid grist for inner transformation.

To provide protection against such inflation, a useful technique for transforming dreaming is to saturate the going-into-sleep and the waking-up times with as much attention and devotion as possible. Rudolf Steiner gave a number of very safe and effective exercises and indications, but the fundamental idea in self-transformation is the realization that each student must find the most appropriate exercise to do the work; no particular exercise from a teacher is most appropriate. Zen practice teaches that the goal and the way are one. Finding the appropriate exercise that will make it possible to enter the spiritual world is the healing that the soul seeks through guidance and submission to the influence of a particular teacher. It is the beginning of the path to self-knowledge, but to progress the student needs to realize that the ultimate goal of self-transformation is to be your own teacher. If the goal and the way are one, then the beginning student should strive to find the way into the spiritual worlds as a daily exercise. If through inner working we find an exercise to be effective, then we can be sure we are becoming our own teacher. The esoteric task of finding an effective exercise is an analog or microcosm of the sources of anxiety that give rise to organ dreams in the first place. To find an effective exercise, we must dive into the very roots of our anxieties and try to see what life would be like if we were not anxious about the things that threaten our equilibrium.

Anxiety states stimulate the production of endocrine secretions, which produce dreamlike stimulus-response conditions in our organism. The reactive patterns held in our organ systems are the source of the organ dreams that are the common stuff of dreaming. The patterns themselves are objective (such as fight-or-flight responses) and can be found in many biological systems. In animals these automatic responses to stimuli provide the organism with instructional patterning; they serve an objective purpose. At the biological level in human beings, these patterned behaviors also serve the organism as instructional. However, human beings have the potential to act creatively against these patterned responses, but to do so we need to remove the associative links that are the very roots of successful biological strategies. Individuation is not really as simple as a collective-unconscious model would have it. The true esoteric task is not to dream collective dreams but to wake up objectively in the place where dreams originate.

To do this, we must face the subjective links each of us has as personal stimulus keys to patterned responses and choose not to allow a subjective associative link to serve as a trigger for the objective biological response. We need to learn to see the dream state as it arises and unfolds in us, and then choose not to react in the programmed way. As esotericists we strive to become aware of which subjective trigger releases the biologically objective instinctual reaction. In nature, assimilating and healing the various experiences that lead to stress and anxiety states during the day are taken care of in dream states, either during the day or more completely during the night. The common dream is like a summary of the work done by the soul during the night. The sense stimuli cease to create stimulus patterns, and the soul is free to work on assimilating the previous day's sensory/endocrine events.

The assimilation of these events occurs in the context of the biological imperative on one side, while on the other side the free associative triggers unique to the particular soul do not really operate in a collective context, as evidenced by the new psychological pathologies now appearing in abundance as psychology tries to keep up with them by giving birth to what amounts to opposing schools and theories. The problem of having a subjective trigger for a biologically objective pattern puts the focus of dream work squarely in the realm of the individual human soul. Even though the patterns are collectively shared, the triggers and associations connected to the collective patterns are purely subjective to the individual dreamer. As a result, the details in organ dreams are collectively objective endocrine impulses of individually subjective anxiety associations encountered by the soul in the preceding days. They come into the soul in dream states to provide automatic or unconscious healing and balancing so that once the stimulus is removed the physical organs do not have to work continually under the pressure of the anxiety state. The anxiety state can be looked at as a kind of wound we receive daily from our interaction with the sense world, sending us to our beds every night seeking healing. When we begin to tread the path of self-development, this wound becomes our most constant and effective teacher. But as esotericists we need to separate the objective nature of the wound from our subjective response to it.

Children have such abundant energy because the intensity of the daily wounding produced by the awake consciousness is not as severe in them as it is in an adult. They are already living in a dream state most of the time, so the daily attack on the life organs is not as taxing. However, since they are living in a dream most of the time, the wounding can imprint itself on the soul more easily than is the case for the more awake consciousness of an adult. Psychology proves that these childhood wounds are precisely what form subjective anxiety patterns in the adult. The wounds are in such dire need of healing that our dream life must intervene to give us warnings that something is not working well in our waking life. It is here that the daily practice of sacred sleeping can be most effective. An esoteric student who wishes to heal soul anxiety must face the wounds within the soul in a direct way. The encounter between the soul and the wound takes place on the border between this world and the next, the boundary area between the awake consciousness and the sleep consciousness, the realm of the dream.

The work on dreaming is divided into two distinct phases: the entrance into sleep and the time just after awakening. Each phase brings into play very different aspects of the problem of transforming the wounds in the soul. In the evening, when the day's experiences are fresh, it is useful to begin the approach to sleep life starting with the evening meal. Avoiding heavy protein and eating instead more digestible or enzymatic foods like salads and vegetables allow the liver to disengage from the enormous task of digestion and shift to the task of assimilation. Digestion is a catabolic, or breaking down, process, and assimilation is an anabolic, or building up, process. In digestion, each part of the nutritious substance is rendered into its most fundamental form. The liver begins this process at 4 a.m. every day. In assimilation, all of the parts broken down in digestion are transformed into a unified soup in which the component parts of the nutrition lose their separate identity. The liver begins this process at 4 p.m. every day. These liver imaginations are exact analogs of the processes we want to develop around waking up and going to sleep. At night we want to disengage from the process of digesting the enormous amounts of experiences we have encountered during the day and focus instead on the process of dissolving them in order to better assimilate their lessons. Working with the liver is a good approach to dream transformation. We could say, with Rudolf Steiner, that the sensory contents of daily life are a kind of cosmic nutrition for the soul. That this sensory cosmic nutrition can be transformed and assimilated is the secret of inner work.

Going to bed at the same time every night is a good way to help the liver. It is also a wonderful way to get some power into the process of assimilating sensation in the dream state. Every hour of sleep before midnight is equal to two hours of sleep after midnight. Once in bed, the real work of processing impressions of our day begins. The various types of sleep anxiety point to the importance of establishing some form of protocol for going to sleep. It sounds odd, but practicing going to sleep is of great benefit for the health of the soul.

Rudolf Steiner has given the daily review as an ideal practice for going into sleep. The goal is to form images of specific events of the day, but to see them in reverse order. Trying to see too much detail in the memory pictures is a common frustration for those just beginning this practice. The goal is to feel the day as a kind of backward gliding through the events. See yourself doing something and then see yourself doing the thing you did immediately before that, and so forth. This exercise is most effective when we can imagine our way backward through the day to the place where we were when we just awoke. We have then successfully imagined ourselves to stand at the threshold between this world and the next. When the practice is done regularly, the capacity to remember details gradually unfolds in the soul, but gliding through without editorializing or commenting is a most useful capacity to develop. Gliding without blaming or commenting about our failures and successes eventually transforms by itself into the ability to see oneself in a more objective way.

A useful aid to maintaining a good gliding technique is to prac-tice the art of Goethean observation of nature. The accurate inner depiction of the form of a plant, animal, or cloud pattern builds a rich reservoir of gliding pictures in the soul. These images of nature are actually coded lessons on how anxiety states manifest in our dream life. Flowers are images of the trials we are overcoming. Ani-mals teach us about how our soul moves when under the influence of particular desires. Weather is full of pictures of inner states such as depression and mania or the fury of a tempestuous temperament. When we practice forming accurate inner pictures of nature, we strengthen our capacity to bring the daily review into a gradually increasing power of perception. We can even go so far as to do re-search by taking particular images from the natural world into sleep as a conscious question-and-answer process between the True Self and the soul.

Phenomenology and the picture-forming processes of the daily review give us access to a place where we can ask our dreaming self to go into the next world and search for significant images there which can be useful in our work of self-transformation. The images will come to us out of the spirit and clothe themselves in a dream as usual, but we will be able to access them at a level of day-awake con-sciousness that is embedded in the dream state we have consciously formed into the boundary between the worlds. "And so to sleep, perchance to dream."

The daily review and the memory processes arising out of the practice of phenomenology are only the first half of the alchemical art of transforming dreaming. The second half of this most interest-ing art is the cultivation of a particular state of awakening in which the soul learns to hover just on the edge of a complete awakening in the physical body so that the dew of the night can be gathered into the soul to offset the drying effects of a too bright day-awake con-sciousness. The period of awakening provides an enlivening spring of creative image-forming forces to instill the mood of the thresh-old into daily life. The problem with images is that they tend to die into meaningless husks when they are produced out of personal forces of imagination. The personally imbued forces of imagination are actually only programmed responses to external stimuli, which arise in the body as daydreams. Daydreams produced in this way are the basis for the instinctual life in animals and produce childhood fantasies in human beings. Childhood fantasy has its place during childhood, but an adult prone to acting out fantasies is often heading toward pathology. At the change of teeth the human being must transcend fantasy into an active and living imagination, and this transcendence will not be accomplished by producing ever more elaborate memory pictures. Memory pictures or abstractions provide the basis for building intellect, which is the necessary stage in human development after fantasy, but it is not the last nor the highest stage of understanding humans can aspire to. Educating the memory to remember specific pictures of earthly phenomena is not sufficient preparation for the struggle with the beasts of anxiety the esoteric student must face on the path to self-knowledge. For this work, the soul must be shaped by pictures that it can access only in the realms of the spirit.

Rudolf Steiner's work continually returns to a fundamental picture that can be used to establish a morning practice for catching the dew of the night. It is an image of what we could call psychic breathing and is best described through example. In the course for doctors, Steiner gives an exercise in which they are told to imagine they are in the center of two concentric circular bands of color. One band is close to the body and the other farther away, but they are concentric. For the doctors, blue is on the outside and yellow within. These two colors are Goethe's primary colors, out of which the whole spectrum can be made. The doctors are then asked to imagine the blue circle shrinking and the yellow circle expanding until they meet in a common green color. The blue continues to shrink until it is around the body, and the yellow continues to expand until it is on the outside. Now the outer circle is yellow and the inner circle is blue. Once this image has settled, the whole process is reversed, and the colors once again resume their original configuration. This exercise can be successfully directed at the area of the throat and it establishes a wonderful, peaceful mood that can be easily transformed into a mood of the threshold.

Performing this exercise before any activities or even any thoughts of the day have occurred provides a safe and devotional space perfect for listening in silence into the space of the dream, which can happen when the Earth is breathing out in the early morning. Different complementary colors can be worked with to approach different areas of the soul. Magenta and green bands are effective with the area around the heart. Violet and indigo are effective in the area of the head. As the colors breathe in and out of the soul, the student learns how the language of the soul can be integrated in an objective way into the processes of imagination. Ten minutes of color breathing, followed by ten minutes of prayerful remembering of those who have passed on and then a few minutes of prayerful remembering of those who are undergoing trials in this life provide a good place to meet the onslaught of the day.

These day and night rhythms can be called sacred sleeping. In sacred sleeping we daily renew our vows as mystery pupils to reveal the great mystery of life in the small mystery of our daily life.

3
HEARTFELT THINKING

IN ALCHEMICAL PRACTICE, the heart is the organ or crucible that contains the materia prima, or first substance, that needs to be transformed so that the soul, as Virgin, can be married to Christ, the archetypal spirit of the eternal human being. The materia prima is the dark matter present at the beginning of the work. It contains everything the finished work will contain except that in the finished work every last part of the original substance will be purified and exalted by the conscious work of the adept. To do this transformation has been the goal of alchemists since the Middle Ages, although by the 1800s it had become confused with the development of modern chemistry. The original alchemical worldview understood that once adepts have transformed their own soul forces, any physical substance will yield to their intensified and purified will. This understanding is symbolized in the transformation of lead into gold.

The materia prima contains the lead, the gold, and every other metal, as well as the substances necessary for their transformation. These substances are the Salt, or universal salt, the precipitation of a manifestation out of a potential condition, and its polar condition, the Sulf, or universal sulfur, the dissolution and combustion of a manifest substance into a condition of potential. The third principle of transformation is the universal mercury, or Mercury, that is the rhythmic interplay of the primal yearning of the two polar forces of Salt and Sulf to interact with each other.

Every thing is considered to have these forces in its makeup, with particular conditions and substances having more of one than another. The differing constituents make up the manifold world with its incredible diversity of appearances and its simultaneous unity of relationships – what alchemists call its intelligence. The alchemists' task is to find the proper constituents in a given substance, identify the proper state of consciousness the constituents represent, practice to attain that state in their own soul to the exclusion of all others, and then dialogue with its energetic archetypal intelligence to find out how the substance can best be used for healing.

As the images of myth and legend and the accounts of meditators the world over show, the content of the soul is composed of images – in our inner life we live literally in a world of pictures. Some of these inner pictures relate to reality and some unfortunately do not. In soul alchemy, the heart is considered to be the bodily organ in which transformation is most effectively initiated, because alchemists understand that the heart has the capacity to think by pondering pictures over a long period of time. "Ponder" originally meant to weigh carefully, exemplified in the biblical statement that Mary "pondered these things in her heart." For alchemists, carefully weighing means considering relationships. In chemistry it became the weighing of substances and eventually the abstraction of the periodic table of atomic weights, but for alchemists the qualities of relationships are what is pondered in the heart, not the quantitative weight of the substance.

This understanding is linked to the heart's physiology in a direct way. Organs in the heart constantly monitor the blood coursing through the circulatory system. The velocity, pressure, and fluidity of the circulation are key elements in the sensory tasks of this organ. Any unusual movements in the circulation are immediately noted and balanced. We could say that the heart is a movement specialist. It is sensitively aware of qualities of motion. Heart specialists go so far as to say that a study of the heart when it is not in motion is not actually a study of the heart.

Every sensory experience stimulates fluctuations in these subtle motions. The heart experiences sensory experience as qualities of motion in the blood. Esoterically, images that stimulate sense experience are considered to produce different qualities of motion in the blood. The door to the heart, then, can be worked effectively by giving particular sensory inputs to the senses so that the heart can experience particular qualities of motion.

In general, alchemists believe that images that give only information do not develop higher capacities in the heart. These types of images are called signs or ciphers. A sign like a stop sign gives us information that is very useful for our safety, but it must be pondered differently if the heart is to understand the meaning of the sign rather than its information. We could ask why a stop sign is the only highway sign that is octagonal. What does an octagon have to do with stopping? In the alchemy of numbers, the octagon is linked to the forces of the Moon. This can be seen, for example, in the octagonal compass used by feng shui geomancers working with the lunar calendar. The forces of the Moon are the forces of salt or manifestation. The Moon governs the reproductive cycles of women and dictates the egg laying of many lower animals. It is a force for the manifestation of bodies. Alchemically, it is salt. The Moon likewise governs the brain, as well as the genitals. The brain is the salt organ par excellence of the human. With it we manifest thoughts out of potential states of consciousness. Magicians used the Moon to explore signs and omens. All of these are salt, the manifest falling out of the potential. To go back to the stop sign, its form is telling us to salt our motion; in other words, STOP. In this way the very form of the sign represents a hidden movement language.

Alchemists understand that this motion language of form has great potential for healing. The problem is to keep the sign from salting out too quickly in the consciousness before the mercury forces have a time to fully ripen the rhythmic healing forces of the image. For this reason alchemists of the past regularly included mistakes in diagrams to catch the unwary or the lazy minds of those most likely to betray the sacred forces of the diagram by wanting only to get the information, without transforming themselves morally. As a result, ambiguous, hermetically obscure images were used so that only serious hearts and minds would take up the work of entering the workshop of the hierarchies that made the world. Ambiguous, complex, and occult images have more potential to feed the heart the correct forces of motion that will lead to prudence, responsibility, and industriousness in the student.

Once an alchemist finds an image that serves as a potent sign, the next task is to represent that image in the inner eye as a kind of movie of relationships, or what we could call a symbolic map. In the mind's eye the image is reproduced and shifted to allow the heart to circulate "around" it. This pondering enables the heart to glean more and more insight into the archetypal intelligence of the image. An image treated in this way can then transform from being a sign into being a symbol. A symbol is a sign that has been infused with a tincture of willed attention from an alchemist. As a further step it is possible to so intensify this symbolic relationship that the symbol can serve as an icon or door to the domain of the intelligence of the archetype itself, which will then serve to bring even more insights into consciousness. This process is short-circuited by images that serve only to give information or to produce answers. Much that comes to us today by way of alchemical imagery seems strange and remote because the obscurity has a purpose other than giving information. Its purpose is to energize the will to stay in an open question indefinitely in order to enhance the soul's flexibility.

In summary, images used in alchemical transformation of the soul serve the following purposes:

1. Pictures that are ambiguous allow the heart to ponder the problem in a rhythmic way, returning again and again to the same image to savor its gradual unfolding.

2. The technique of asking unanswerable questions is a positive step toward greater flexibility of imagination.

3. Gradual symbolic insight into the problem will yield a sense of resonant harmonics and a flowing of consciousness among the particular aspects rather than focusing on a final solution based upon one fixed relationship between a series of aspects.

4. Tolerance for ambiguity cultivated by pictorial meditation on ambiguous images is considered to be a primary and potent key to self-transformation.

The basis of these meditative techniques is known as the method of analogy; metaphor and analogy are employed as the key to entering symbolic space. Symbolic spaces are much more poetic and flexible than analytical spaces and allow for a much more dynamic force of soul transformation than analysis. Symbolic thinking helps the soul forces build bridges between the sense world and the inner world of the soul that are not available to analytical processes. Through this work it is possible to transform the life of desire in the soul into a more dynamic force known as *manas*. Manas is the sense that unites all of the other senses. Rudolf Steiner calls it the sense of the senses.

When soul alchemists produce manas during meditation, a very small part of their everyday sense experience is redeemed. Everyday sense experience needs to be redeemed because it represents the fall of humanity. In the Bible, the fall is described as the opening of the eyes of Adam and Eve. Seen in this light, every sense experience is a recapitulation of the fall. This may seem strange to contemporary thinking, but esoterically it is an idea of great importance. In modern physiological terminology, everyday sense experience is found in the dynamic relationship between the autonomic nervous system and the endocrine system. Sense experiences result in a manifestation of hormones that regulate the soul life of the individual. In alchemical terms, the sensation is sulfur and the endocrine reaction is salt. There is very little conscious control over these patterns. The lack of consciousness in this realm is a deep symbolic image of the separation of the human being from the Godhead: in other words, the fall.

The work to transform the relationship between sense experience and bodily response is focused on consciously purifying and strengthening what is known esoterically as the body of sensation, or, in the old terminology, the sentient body. There are various symbolic terms for this process: constructing the New Jerusalem, forming the Spirit Embryo, recasting the Molten Sea, redeeming the senses, the School of Michael, or building the New Temple. The reference to the Temple comes from the Temple Legend, which describe the building of Solomon's Temple. Perhaps the images of the Temple and the Molten Sea can be helpful in understanding this subtle and vital contemporary mystery task.

Solomon himself was in the lineage of Abel, who was a child of the God of Living Form. The activity of Solomon's God was to create forms out of transcendent living cosmic forces. In physical terms this activity can be imagined in the process by which a sandbar is formed out of the dynamic forces of a moving river: the form arises out of forces already given in the environment. Since the God of Living Form was Solomon's God, he had no knowledge of how to construct a new Temple other than by using what was given by forces already in existence. Solomon had already received the plan of the Temple from his God but could not imagine how it could be constructed. To come up with a different way of building, a new type of formal principle was needed, one in which the form would be created by charming life out of what was lifeless. A person in the lineage of Cain was needed, for the descendants of Cain were the children of Fire, who could conjure life from the lifeless. For an analog we can think of a sculptor creating a living form out of a dead piece of stone or wood. Cain was the first technologist, and his creation of new forms of agriculture and smelting metals out of the earth was not understood by the God of Solomon. This conflict led to the death of Abel and Cain's banishment. So Solomon had to summon the architect Hiram-Abiff to build the Temple.

Solomon was in love with the Queen of Sheba, who recognized in him the highest perfection that the God of Form could produce. He was the zenith of the forces of the past. When the new Temple needed to be built and Solomon could not do it using his wisdom, she met Hiram and recognized in him the forces of the future. Here was a person who had the potential to become like a god himself. He could think in a different way and imagine forms and processes that had not been seen previously. She turned her heart toward Hiram, and when Solomon saw this he plotted to have Hiram's trusted apprentice builders destroy his masterwork, the Molten Sea. The apprentices plotted to throw water on the Molten Sea just as it was being cast, and when they did the Molten Sea burst into many pieces. We could say that the sense activity of human beings was split into many different senses, each one separate from the other, yet having a common link in being patterns of sensation.

Hiram despaired when his masterwork, the Molten Sea (the integrated flowing life of sensation), was destroyed; he was about to cast himself into the flames when he heard the voice of his ancestor Cain speaking to him from the center of the Earth. Cain gave him a magical hammer and told him to forge the pieces of the exploded Molten into a new form that was not part of the forces and forms already in creation. The children of Cain are themselves to take on the building of a new world by transforming the old shattered life of sense experiences and forging it into a new form capable of creating new worlds.

Alchemically, the Molten Sea, or, as it is sometimes called, the sea of metals, is the term for the body of sensation, also known to esotericists as the sentient body. In physiology every sense impression is accompanied by stimulus/response patterns existing between the nerves and the glands. Nervous activity stimulated by the senses results in a depletion of vital forces as the glandular responses stimulate the metabolizing of substances in the blood. The patterns for these interactions are imbedded in the unconscious life forces of the human being and are not considered to be accessible to conscious control. If we could peel out all of this flowing stimulus and response patterning and focus it into one level of consciousness, we would have the finest of ghosts. Dynamic, patterned, and almost bearing its own personality, the consciousness of this body of the forces of sensation exists far below the level of the discursive consciousness. The forces and patterns in this area of the human soul are linked to the deeper forces of life throughout the entire cosmos. Esotericists connect the forces in the sentient body to the most distant forces in the cosmos. The great alchemical adept and physician Paracelsus called this body the Star Body. Rudolf Steiner calls it the etheric body and links it to the human capacity for free thinking. Paradoxically, in undeveloped human beings it is not free at all.

In discursive, day-awake consciousness we can focus on the motives for doing deeds or having responses. In contrast, the consciousness of the body of sensation is reactive and automatic; initially there is no freedom in this process for humans. In essence our sense experience preys upon our life forces. In this view, we are preyed upon by our sensory appetites and habits that destroy our vitality. Rudolf Steiner describes our experience of this destruction as becoming one with the mist of worlds (anxiety at feeling our conscious self dissolving into the world ether). The mist of worlds refers to the patterns of life forces that lie completely out of our control and keep life processes and systems forever coagulating and dissolving. In alchemical thought, the body of sensation is the source of forces that threaten the integrity of the human being. It is symbolized as a chaotic sea of molten metals, full of potential but devoid of form.

When we work alchemically to transform the senses, the soul is often immersed in a deep mood of impending chaos and destruction as we consciously enter during meditation the stimulus/response patterns linked to sensation. In this state of consciousness, we experience ourselves as a dissolving cloud of hot desires flowing into a whole galaxy of shifting forms, none of which is clearly ourselves. Symbolically, this is like melting into a sea of molten metal. It is actually a conscious experience of how the forces of desire in the body of sensation are reacting to sensory input. Energies are seeking cognition and meaning. Light is seeking to become sight.

When we meditate, we pass through the turbulence of the sea of metals. That is, we confront consciously the pushing and pulling of the life of desires linked to sensory experience. We experience this mostly as the inability to still the mind and concentrate on the theme of the meditation. In this turbulent state, we are actually living in the body of sensation, experiencing how the sea of metals shatters into pieces as our consciousness is pulled this way and that, flickering from sensation to sensation. First there is an itch, then we have to cough, then a sound disturbs us, then our legs fall asleep, and on and on. This sensory turbulence actually covers a deep fear of not having anything happening in the consciousness. We are afraid that if we finally penetrate through the sea of metals, the pushing and pulling that allows us to feel ourselves as a living being will stop. We have the deep feeling that if that were to happen there would be no one home in our soul. We are afraid that we will dissolve into the mist from which the worlds are made and to which they always return.

All of us have this experience when we begin to walk the path of self-development. We place the exploded sea of metals in our consciousness as a remedy for the anxiety of the potential for being dissolved. The anxiety keeps our conscious entrance into the life forces at arm's length so that we do not have to experience non-being. However, when we take our hammer and consciously try to forge the pieces of the exploded sense life into a new kind of sensing, we can heal the anxiety of the mist of worlds and simultaneously begin to build the New Temple in the New Jerusalem.

But these activities are not easily accomplished. There are beings living in our own soul that have a vested interest in keeping themselves hidden – imagine termites that eat the inside of a piece of wood, leaving only the shell of the outer part intact. As a person undertakes this type of inner work, these beings dwelling in our soul become perceptible. Therefore, forging the Molten Sea could also be called dealing with the voices from the abyss. In the abyss we meet beings living in our own soul that create turbulent feelings surrounding the sense impressions coursing through the body of sensation. In the beginning of the work, we are simply dealing with sense impressions. As we go further, using the methods of working with images given earlier in this chapter, we gradually realize that our soul is populated by beings that have infiltrated our sense life and created patterns our spiritual being cannot at present overcome. When this happens, it is up to us to take up Hiram's hammer and consciously forge relationships between the senses based upon heartfelt thinking.

The term "heartfelt thinking" is specific to this work since a seed is hidden in the sea of metals. It is the seed of our future apotheosis, our path back toward God. Rudolf Steiner called this seed hidden in the body of sensation the human Gemut. Gemut loosely translates as warmth of heart. The heart needs to be taught how to think precisely if the senses are not to destroy the human being. However, the heart does not think with abstract thoughts, the heart thinks in pictures that move. It is the task of the alchemist who wishes to develop heartfelt thinking to transform the sea of metals by consciously forming representations of sense images and consciously dissolving them again, in a rhythmic way, as the foundation of a modern meditative path. In this work, the metals of the senses become purified and less prone to stimulating pathological reactions in the organism.

It should be added that the sense experiences themselves are completely lawful. Light and dark, color, and the laws of optics and sound are not part of the pathology of the soul. They are still in the hands of the hierarchies. The sensations themselves are part of the world, and the forces that animate the senses are lawful and coherent. They are from the work of the God of Solomon. When, in sense experience, human beings induce the forces animating the senses and make them personal to their own biographical needs, the forces lose their purity and become compromised. To help understand what happens, an explanation of the idea of metals as it was understood in alchemy might be useful.

Alchemically, all of the metals we can see in the body of the Earth were considered to have an extraterrestrial origin. Certain mysteries of metallurgy and mineralogy point to the validity of this idea. One of the greatest is the metal mercury, which is fluid at room temperature. Another is the mineral sulfur, which is actually a kind of congealed vaporous fire. Another is the incandescence of phosphorus at room temperature. There are others, but these will serve to illustrate the idea that metals are really congealed flowings of forces. For alchemists the congealing of a more refined and rarified state was one of the three fundamental forces in the life of substance. It was called the salt process. Salt was the manifestation of what once existed in rarified potential. The second force was the rarefaction of a congealed manifest substance, which was called the sulfur process. Sulfur kept the refining processes active, always creating more potential, the ultimate potential state being non-manifestation. The third fundamental process was known as mercury. Mercury kept the other two processes in constant interaction; it was the totality of flowing forces present in all transformation in the natural world. All metals were considered to have a common origin in mercury.

If the forces of mercury met with a strong sulfur process in an underground cavern, the mercury would be constantly energized by the sulfur to realize more and more potential. It would be more and more refined until it met the nobility and potential of its archetypal existence. The physical substance formed under these rarified and noble circumstances would be gold. If the forces of mercury met sulfur forces in an underground cavern and a salt atmosphere was present that would impede their constant refining so they did not progress as far toward the ultimate potential, then the result would be silver. If the forces of mercury met mostly salt conditions with very little of the sulfur forces to keep the process transforming toward greater potential, then lead would be the result. According to the alchemists, all of the metals have the same fundamental patterning of forces and the same origin in mercury; they differ in the combinations of the forces. Therefore any metal could be transformed into any other metal by arranging to have the forces meet in an energetic sequence.

Returning to the Molten Sea, we could say that the senses all have the same energetic source in the relationship between the nervous system and the endocrine system. Higher senses like the senses of sight and hearing can be more easily penetrated by our consciousness than the more bodily oriented senses such as the sense of touch or the sensory integration patterns such as proprioception. More noble sense impressions link us to others when we are in moods of surrender and admiration; less noble sense impressions link us to others when we are in possessive and jealous moods. More noble expressions of sense experience have an element of compassion and sacrifice; less noble sense impressions stimulate judgmental and lustful or consuming elements in the soul. More noble sense impressions allow us to maintain a sense of self in the context of the object of sensation, whether it is a chocolate cake or an attractive person. This state of consciousness is the alchemical equivalent of gold or silver. Less noble sense experiences do not allow us to maintain a discriminating consciousness under the influence of the sense experience, and we are driven to enact imbedded patterns of sensory impression and physiological response. In this case our consciousness is the equivalent of lead. Taken together, all of the possible responses to sensory experience could be experienced as a flowing sea of intense, surging antipathy and sympathy toward the sensory object. This totality of sensory input and reaction is the Molten Sea, the sea of metals.

Persons who are working to develop themselves often find that the sensory metals are mixed and polluted in myriad ways. Inner communications and insights often come toward us as if we are hearing distant voices rising out of an abyss. The voices speak in a symbolic language about fear and doubt and a fundamental tendency of the human being to judge everyone else as inferior to oneself. At this stage we are actually entering into our own body of sensations and experiencing how most of our inner life is spent doing the bidding of sensory stimulus/response patterns. We awaken in our body of sensations like swimmers caught in the churning Molten Sea of sensory unconsciousness.

All of us have this experience when we begin to walk the path of self-development. Some get to the anxiety of the mist of worlds by facing a life-threatening illness. Others experience the pain of complete dissolution due to a loss, others awaken in the surging swells of the Molten Sea as a result of meditative exercises that loosen their bodily sheaths to such an extent that they begin to live in two worlds simultaneously. The experience of the mist of worlds is truly a universal experience at the onset of higher consciousness.

One of the most effective ways to begin healing the anxiety of the mist of worlds is to consciously experience gratitude for the life of sensation that allows the soul to say, "I live." Gratitude for sensation is a gift from the hierarchies to the striving human being, but, like grace, it is only given in relation to the effort made by erring humans to undertake self-transformation. Gratitude for sensation is most effectively developed by paying attention to small things in life in a concentrated and devoted way. For instance, paying attention to the biography of a flower is a way of disenchanting our sleeping relationship to the flower. We sleep into the flower when we have no interest in it. Inwardly imagining the plant growing and then producing a flower goes a step deeper in the possibility of

awakening into the flower. Inwardly forming the flowering process
of a plant in a meditatively rhythmic way goes a step further. When
our relationship to the flower is disenchanted, the elementals can go
back into the world ether, and our consciousness can follow them
there without experiencing fright at dissolving the physical body.
We can steady our attention through inwardly picturing the flower's
processes of incarnation. The inner picture we form in the meditation connects us to the elemental beings and hierarchical beings that
stand behind the patterns of the flower's becoming. Our attention is
gradually made resonant to the lawful patterns in the manifestation
of the flower out of the archetypal realm into the sense world. Since
we are consciously and devotedly practicing visualizing the flower,
our own consciousness forms an analog to the flower that provides
insight into our own biographical pattern of becoming. The insights
gathered in such a practice then fructify the imaginative forces in
the eye of the soul, and we begin to understand the patterns of destiny in the forces of our own life. Feelings of devotion accompany
such insights as our own life forces participate consciously in the
transformation of the senses from being simply reactive to being the
doors to perception of creative patterns in the cosmos.

Through this practice we begin to experience the sense world as
a world in which images are given to us as teachings about our own
incarnation process. We find analogs for our own patterns of destiny
in the life found in the world and develop a deep devotion to the
small things of the sense world as a laboratory for the production of
analogs. When the practice of devotion to small things is intensified
by the practice of thinking lawful becomings of beings in nature in
precise ways, a further step of potentiating the inner images is available to the alchemist. This next step is the practice of thinking the
images backward into silence. Through these techniques the soul of
the alchemist is transformed and becomes capable of living outside
the physical body as a spiritual being among spiritual beings. The
stages of initiation presented in this work are meant to act as aids in
the alchemical transformation of the soul. The images taken from
artworks that were made so long ago can provide a contemporary
person with a link to the past and a doorway to the future.

4

THE PRAYERFUL WARRIOR

THE DEVELOPMENTAL SIGNS in an alchemical soul practice usually involve some sort of healing crisis brought on by a discharge in the soul of accumulated assumptions and belief structures. Often these assumptions are not perceived by the student in a conscious way. They arise like dream fragments in daily life and invade the serenity of the soul with impulses that are not aligned with progressive development. Usually, only after an event or situation has wreaked havoc in our lives can we dimly divine the deeper meanings and assumptions behind our moments of suffering. We could even say that esoteric development is really the cultivation of the capacity to consciously experience the arising of dysfunctional patterns based on faulty assumptions before they fret and strut across the stages of our lives. The capacity to recognize these patterns is what is known as *metanoia,* or changing the thinking.

Normally, when we are under stress our will comes forward and we use an instinctual force to fight the intrusion. We act aggressively as warriors toward the stress. In each of the following situations the solution to the dilemma will be approached as if we were warriors who use prayer instead of threats and aggression. The idea is that the will force in prayer is what is important, just as will is the most important force for the conventional warrior. The difference is that the prayerful warrior has gone through some degree of metanoia, which allows the will to be employed in a more holistic and creative way.

The alchemical approach to metanoia is known as "turning the soul." Turning the soul is the initiating process for any attempt at developing the inner life. A few different stages of inner development can be seen as good signposts for determining how much capacity we have to turn our souls. These signposts are indicators of the direction and intensity of blaming that goes on in our inner dialogue when we are under stressful or threatening situations.

In the first stage, the roots of blaming lie in the firm belief that another person is the source of our misfortune or dissatisfaction. This stage is known technically in psychology as projection: we project our dissatisfaction onto another, and that becomes the only way we can see the situation. In projection we leave ourselves with no options. The belief structures and the inner dialogues in the projection stage of blaming completely fill the soul with pictures of anger and resentment, while the thinking processes flow into thoughts of justification and retaliation. Some personalities spend whole lifetimes in the first stage of projection. Newspapers are full of stories based upon the belief that someone else is to blame. The whole culture is devoted to finding blame.

As a healing for this first level of soul work, attention can be given to addressing the Creator in a mood of thanks. Imagine you have given others something that has helped them to advance in their lives, which they took and then went away without thanking you in some way. How would you feel? Then imagine that you are the Creator of the World and the beings to whom you have given life and livelihood do not thank you for their gifts, but instead spend their days moaning that their needs have not been met. Imagine how you would feel. Then give thanks and send prayers of sincere thanks that the Creator is not a vindictive god. The prayer does not have to be longwinded, but the mood must be sincere. Genuine affection for the benevolence of the Creator heals the tendency to project blame on others. The returning prodigal has little time for resentment or casting blame on others.

Rudolf Steiner suggested that we imagine that the others we are blaming were denied an opportunity that instead was given to us. That denied opportunity was the source of their downfall into the state for which we are blaming them. Imagine this, and then give a prayer of thanks to the Creator for the blessings that have been given to you in your life. Then send a prayer of humility to the angel of the other people for judging them, in your ignorance, to be so bad. By using prayers like this over time, our soul may come to realize that others are not really to blame for our misfortunes. We see that there are patterns in our lives that have to do with our own inabilities. This realization is a healing, but it often leads to the second stage of blaming.

In the second level of blaming we have a sudden realization that we are to blame for most of our dysfunctional experiences. This realization is hard to take, since it can make us doubly mortified: once for truly being to blame, and once for having, up to the present moment, blamed everyone else. This level of blaming is a burning process with very intense flames of shame and blame, and working in this stage for extended periods can be a dangerous and unbalancing activity for the soul. Sooner or later, however, the self-blaming will become bothersome and boring, even to ourselves. When any form of blaming is no longer a reasonable option, that is the sign that the capacity of Moral Imagination is unfolding in the soul. Then we are truly on the threshold of turning the soul toward Inspiration.

The life of prayer in this stage can be focused on the use of what could be called creative suffering. We cannot develop soul forces without owning our own projections; this process involves fierce suffering, often self-inflicted. In alchemical language, this stage is called "cooking and eating the shadow." It can lead to deep characterological problems such as depression. In our suffering we can no longer blame others; that is clear. But someone must be to blame; so around and around we go, getting ever more tightly wound.

In these dark hours, it is useful to dedicate our suffering to someone we deem to be suffering a bit more than we are. It could be a sick person or a more severely depressed person. We picture that person and ask our angel or the Christ Being to please take the will forces we are learning to develop in our trials and apply them to the account of the other, more needy person. By the incredible action of the spirit, every force so designated for another has a healing force on both the giver and the recipient. It is like a two-for-one bargain with the Christ. Of course we cannot pray in this way with the idea that we will also be the recipient. And do not be tempted into imagining that the other person will be made well by your prayers. That is called petitionary prayer, which is an inflation and will nullify any will force you can contribute to the other. Simply imagine that your prayers are like a good home-cooked meal that, through your angel, you place before the other. Just paying attention to the other person in his or her suffering is a good prayer. Dedicating your own suffering as a help toward the other is a doubly effective prayer. While immersed in this type of prayer activity, we do not sit and suffer and get tempted back into blaming. The other person benefits with help received in the spirit through your purified will. In this type of prayer your imagination is made into a moral force. Your inner picturing can then be called Moral Imagination.

In Moral Imagination we work with the force of the realization that blaming is a useless waste of human life. No one wins in a blaming situation, neither the blamer nor the one who is blamed. We see blame as the work of adversarial spiritual beings who deceive humans into inflation and projection, activities that always result in blaming. These adversaries use deceptions to hide their own roles in the ongoing fantasy lives of humans.

We usually fully realize that there is actually no blame simultaneously with the realization that there must be an accounting of our actions. We begin to see the cosmic nature of karma, a deep conundrum for a soul habitually used to blaming. The conundrum of accounting with no blame brings the forces of Moral Imagination to the fore in the human soul. These are the forces human beings use to develop the capacity and will to atone for being willing yet unconscious accomplices to transgressions against the progressive will of the Creator; we hunger and thirst after righteousness without a thought of revenge. At the level of Moral Imagination the soul comes into contact with the higher spiritual members of its own being. This process is a foundation for metanoia, which is brought about by the actual willed deed of turning the soul. While turning the soul, the student must encounter the laws of karma.

There can be no conceptual teaching about turning the soul, since each of us must find our own way, out of the unique qualities of our own soul constitution, into the threshold between the worlds. In practice, all a teacher can and must do is to point to certain problem-solving techniques that, if practiced, allow a student to stand the experiences at the threshold without losing a grip on reality. Keeping a grip on reality is most important, since the membrane between the worlds becomes very thin just where Imagination begins to yield to Inspiration.

We are receiving Inspiration from beyond the threshold all of the time. However, only esotericists take the time to develop a practice through which Inspirations can be experienced cognitively and objectively. The essential problem for the esoteric student is that Inspiration cannot be cognized during the experience of living into the silence: Inspiration can be recognized and understood only *after* the inspiring experience. Further, postrecognition is possible only if the mind is prepared in a particular way. The foundation of this method of preparation is found in the whole nexus of qualities involved in the process of metanoia. When the level of Inspiration has been attained, the will to turn the soul away from its habitual instinctual emotions is the door to higher wisdom.

At this turn in the road, the prayerful warrior usually finds what in other traditions is called the petty tyrant, a person in control of a situation in which the student is engaged. The student who is crossing into Inspiration needs to find a way to enter gracefully into the petty tyrant so that the karma binding them to each other can be understood. This can only be done in an Inspirational consciousness since any attempt to do this work in Imagination is sure to lead to further difficulties. The higher level of Moral Imagination is called Moral Technique in the language of Rudolf Steiner. Moral Technique cannot be simply imagined; it must be worked out between two people, usually two people who have some karma that needs to be adjusted.

Often a student meeting a petty tyrant will imagine that the person is a petty tyrant for everyone, which is not actually the case. The petty tyrant is petty because he or she is actually just another human, who is surrounded by blame and shame patterns that work a strange alchemy on the forces of the student so that old unconscious memories arise in the student's soul when in the presence of the petty tyrant. It is here that the Moral Technique of turning the soul is necessary. It is very effective when the student decides to pray in a hygienic way for the petty tyrant.

PRAYERS FOR THE DEAD

In the training for Inspiration, the concentration exercises that have led to the state of Imagination must be systematically purged of thought content and the focus of the work placed on the quality and purity of the intent in the will. In some ways this task is made easier by the unfolding of vision in Moral Imagination. We see what we are working on very clearly and learn to form accurate inner pictures of the problems we encounter in our souls. However, this very capacity is also the biggest stumbling block to developing Inspiration. In the state of Inspiration any imaginative image, color, or sound arising in the mind must be taken to be merely the shadow of a true experience. Only into a soul that is silent can the spirit speak in an inspiring language composed of soundless sounds.

These wordlike or tonelike silences carry deeper meanings into the soul that awaken movements and currents beyond our understanding. However, through practice these movements can later be cognized as feelings. The later task is to constellate the feelings experienced in Inspiration into a soul language that is objective and subjective at the same time. It is objective because it is a language of universal meaning spoken by all souls when in the presence of the spirit. It is subjective in that it comes into each soul in ways only that particular soul can divine. The objective nature of the spirit in the soundless tones helps the soul to overcome long-held feelings of resentment and denial. The subjective nature of how the soundless tones flow into each soul becomes a transcendent life element that fructifies the individual and reciprocally fructifies the spiritual worlds from the realm of the human soul. In this way the cosmos is redeemed by humans acting in the imitation of Christ, who, as a member of the Trinity, came to the fallen Earth and united his destiny and body with the very substance of the Earth so that it could eventually arise in the old cosmos as a new star, the seed of a new cosmos of Love.

As the subjective and the objective begin to interpenetrate each other in the soul realm, a keen sense of needing to make amends arises in the soul. Here a great danger makes it necessary to balance the activity of meditation with prayer, for actually realizing the extent and weight of our errors in a cosmic time frame can create a profound feeling of suffocation and despair in the striving soul. The closer we move to the Divine Light, the more we appear to ourselves in our daily life to be simply apparitions made of shadows. This can be very disheartening. The temptation here is either to completely give up on striving to develop ourselves or to become enamored of magical practices that promise to give the student occult power and knowledge.

Since in this condition we are already on the other side of the threshold, little in the way of physical or palpable support is available to assist a soul encountering the spirit to maintain its equilibrium. This situation is pictured in the Bible in the image of Jacob wrestling through the night with the angel. Meditation in such circumstances is almost impossible since such a frenzied and overwhelming force of failure and alienation is experienced in this dark night of the soul. The soul is being asked to willingly transcend the very foundation of its conscious existence. It does not calm easily into exercises of concentration and meditation. The only thing that helps is direct experience within the transcendent, so that the soul can once again have a feeling of participating creatively in its life. In effect, in the realm of Inspiration we must consciously and willingly face our own dying processes. Through Inspiration we must learn to die to self. This is the inspired way of the new warrior in the modern mystery schools.

Without Inspiration, the soul is bound to wander in the past, in the chaos of conflicting impulses and soul eddies based upon instinctual patterning found in the realm of Imagination. The great challenge is that, to begin with, any dynamic is completely absent in the realm of Inspiration. The new warrior stance is to endure with one's own soul forces the ultimate feeling of rejection at the foot of the throne of a silent God. God is silent in the modern mysteries because the next cosmic deed of new creation calls for human beings to turn their souls toward God out of their own free will. This is exactly what always happens in Inspiration, but a soul schooled in having the right answers and knowing what to do in life is particularly uncomfortable with sitting in the presence of a silent, all-knowing God Consciousness. We all know the inner dialogue. What are they waiting for? Did I do something wrong so that they are angry with me? They must think I am not worth the effort to communicate. Silent deities make us nervous. Waiting in silence without playing old blame and shame tapes in our heads and hearts is the singular task of the prayerful warrior.

Part Two

The Path
to
Seeing

1

How to Begin
Basic Exercises

ALL HUMAN BEINGS, NO MATTER how old they are or what their situation, have a part of themselves that remembers how life used to be before they lost control of things. No amount of misunderstandings, mistakes, ridicule, taunts, humiliations, or abuse can erase the memories stored in this part of every single human. We could say that there is an inner being in every person who is doing this remembering of the essential or True Human at all times. This inner being is the very kernel and core of our humanness and lives in an inner, timeless world among memories of how it was when someone was running things in our universe besides crazy people. Our inner being lives constantly in this timeless world where there is some peace of mind at all times, even though things in the regular time-driven world often seem to be getting more and more insane.

The true nature of time is freedom. In their inner being all human beings are given time as a free gift of the Creator. We have a fundamental resentment about our time (freedom) being taken away or being controlled by others. This fundamental resentment is at the root of our feelings about things like slave labor, working below the minimum wage, or even having a boss or coworker who is driving us against the wall. The key to surviving this chronic resentment about freedom and time requires that the angry resentful part of ourselves get in touch with the free inner part of ourselves.

Somewhere deep within is a free being who is continually living in a timeless world. Remembering this helps the better person in us ask the reactive person in us some basic questions such as, "How did it become like this in my life?" or, "What would I wish to do better?"

A big task is to find out how to contact the timeless inner being who remembers how it was before life got unpredictable and then to forget the crazy parts so that the True Human can emerge. Of course, this is easier said than done. Usually, all of the resentment stored in our soul rises to the surface of the mind as soon as any kind of remembering is done. Then the whole process starts over again. A useful technique to break this chain is to regularly ask significant, tough questions of ourselves as if we really didn't expect answers, as if we were talking to a tree. Ask the hard questions regularly. But do not expect any answers, because these questions do not really have any answers. Their secret and profound value lies not in asking them just once, but in asking them on a regular, rhythmic basis. Asking ourselves questions rhythmically, in time, actually forms a spiritual practice. We can develop a practice of asking the same questions at the same time every day. Asking questions in this way is like doing stretching exercises before and after a vigorous exercise.

The most important thing we can do for our development is to learn to control our mind. We must build mental strength to be able to withstand the craziness and resentment that can make life a mental and emotional chaos. Unless we work on ourselves in a rhythmic way, going inside ourselves can be like descending into the deepest darkness imaginable. Without regular work on ourselves, our souls can go flat from the intense burden of time in our lives. Through working on ourselves, we can actually form a different, more conscious relationship to time. It is very useful in the pursuit of seership to develop another relationship to time itself. We try to remember that our True Human is always living in a timeless realm. If we can get access to that being, then time begins to change in our lives. Actually, time remains as it is, but our perception of time changes to our benefit.

Some fundamental things keep our inner being of freedom buried under resentment. The first and foremost is our inability to pay attention and concentrate the mind. A simple exercise to strengthen the attention is to practice watching the second hand of a clock tick off thirty seconds without thinking of any other thing except watching the second hand tick off the seconds. If no clock is available, then counting backward from thirty at one-second intervals will work. For people who either have a lot of time on their hands or are slaves to a time clock, this is a precise and very beneficial mental exercise. A number of important things can be learned. The first is that in the beginning it is almost impossible to do. It is so deceptively simple and yet so difficult to accomplish. The beauty of it is that it is so short and does not cost anything, and when we fail there is an infinite supply of minutes available to continue the work.

Well, we could ask, why do an exercise that is almost impossible to do? Won't it just lead to frustration and then more resentment? The secret of this and any other mental exercise is that the outcome of the exercise is essentially unimportant. Whether we succeed or not is truly irrelevant. No one is giving us a reward for doing the exercise or watching over our shoulder to see that we do it right. No food pellet drops into a great cosmic food trough if we press the lever when the light goes on. The truly liberating part of concentration exercises is that you are the only one who knows what you are doing. The best attitude for concentrating the mind is that no matter what happens, whether I succeed or fail, I will just do the same thirty-second exercise at the same time the next day or the next hour or whenever I am feeling bored. If I manage to get one thirty-second exercise done, then I am free to try another repetition in the soul gym.

After a few repetitions of the exercise, as a cool-down I can ask myself, "Is there anything today for which I can be grateful?" We should ask this without really expecting an answer. If I think of something to be grateful for, then the gratitude will eventually help me to overcome slight periods of depression. If I cannot think of anything to be grateful for, then just asking the question is steadying and cooling for the mind. This is the gratitude exercise. After asking the question, spend a few minutes listening into the silence of timelessness as the question disappears in the silent darkness beyond.

Find a time when it will be easy to do these things at the same time every day. Each day do a few repetitions of the thirty-second concentration exercise and then ask the question and listen a little bit into the silence. The whole thing should take about five to ten minutes total. But it is time well spent. During the whole exercise period, no one except yourself is dictating how you should be using your time. It is time spent in complete freedom, whether the exercise works or not. This is the great secret of training the mind – the time spent doing any mental exercise, successful or not, is time spent in complete freedom. This freedom is born out of an impulse in our own soul to take back control of our own mind. The real benefit in this exercise is in remembering daily to ask the question and do the exercise. The forces built up by making many repetitions of this exercise can someday be available to us when our inner peace is threatened by some circumstance that is out of our control. This exercise can make us free not to have to react. With this freedom, we become aware that we are aware.

Once this idea begins to take root in the soul, it is usually followed by a wish to search actively for our inner being. No other person or memory or system of power can pollute this quality time we spend with ourselves in these exercises. This is true even if the exercise we are trying to do is a complete disaster. The exercise is working in us even if we only *remember* to do it without actually doing it. The goal is to try anew each day to form the impulse to develop concentration, whether or not the exercise works or whether we missed it yesterday, or even whether or not we can actually ever do it. This type of unattached acting makes us aware of our awareness.

After a month or so, a subtle mood comes over the time spent doing the exercise. When the mood develops we feel during the exercise as if we are having a talk with someone we trust. This feeling does not come as a big revelation with light shows and voices speaking to us out of clouds; it is just a subtle feeling of being in a regular conversation with someone who we know will never lie to us. This feeling tells us that the inner being who remembers how life was before things got out of control is beginning to talk to us once again. Some cultures call this approaching the guardian.

When this feeling emerges, we can begin to do another very effective exercise to develop a new way of seeing the world. We can practice looking at the common everyday things around us in a new way. We could call this exercise new seeing. We might choose to practice looking at the bed or the sink or our clothes and trying each day to notice something we had not seen before about that particular thing. It helps to keep a list of what we have noticed to make sure that every day something different is observed. When we can no longer notice anything new about the thing we are observing, we can pick another thing to observe. This exercise has a curious effect on time. We can become so absorbed in thinking about and observing common, boring things that time seems to melt away. If this exercise is added to the thirty-second exercise and the gratitude exercise, followed by listening to the silence of timelessness, then a very absorbing practice can result.

An exercise like new seeing can open whole worlds to a mind locked shut with anger, blaming, and fatigue. This exercise is fundamentally the kind of activity that grew into the study of birds that saved the sanity and the humanity of the Birdman of Alcatraz. Through an exercise like new seeing the soul is led back into having an interest in life and in developing itself through a living, active thinking. We are training ourselves to see in a more fluid and process-oriented way. After this exercise, a good question to ask yourself is, "How has my life become like it is now?" Like the gratitude question in the first exercise, this question is followed with listening into the silence of timelessness.

Alchemically, this work on concentration is the earth stage. Asking myself a hard question such as how my life became as it is now, or what I would wish to do better in my life, brings an earthlike sobriety to my work on myself. To go to the next alchemical level, we need to take the question into the water mode of consciousness. We do this by visualizing ourselves doing what we wish we could do. The visualized movements we make add a liquid dynamic dimension to our inner work. I should spend three minutes each day asking myself questions, then three minutes visualizing myself doing what I would wish to do "as if" I were actually doing it. Then I can follow up the visualization with a question like, "Is there anything today for which I can be grateful?" The question is the earth, the visualization of the movements is the water, the silence is the air, the enthusiasm and the will to do this exercise are the fire.

With these simple things I have a practical, alchemical meditative practice that takes a few minutes every day. These are a few minutes out of my day in which I am not worrying. If I can ask a question to myself every day, I develop concentration. If I can visualize myself doing something, I develop powers of contemplation. If I can think these questions into silence and be comfortable without getting an answer, I develop patience in living in the open question with the spirit. If I think of something to be grateful for, then the gratitude will eventually help me to overcome periods of depression so that I can see my destiny working in my life.

The ideal would be to set aside fifteen minutes in the morning, before starting any of the day's activities, for this practice in developing the mind. The sense of mental freedom these exercises produce when practiced regularly can offset years of hectic living. Once again, it is not the success of a particular practice that is of value. It is the doing of the practice, even when we are failing dismally at it, that moves the mind slowly toward the timeless state of the inner being who remembers.

A final simple exercise that makes the others blend into a seamless whole and gives them much more power is to add a practice of reviewing the day backward at the end of each day. It is most effective if no judgments are made of anything that happened during the day. To begin with, simply remembering in reverse order what you ate for each meal will provide a good start. Visualize dinner, then lunch, then breakfast. Do not try to remember too much detail, but simply glide over each event as if you were watching a movie in reverse. When you encounter something negative, try to see it as if you were watching someone else's life and not your own. If dinner was not really enjoyable, try to visualize it as if someone else were eating it. Try to make no judgments; simply visualize the facts of what happened in reverse order. Some persistence is required to do this exercise successfully, but since we are trying not to let success be the determining factor here, once again it is the rhythmical effort that allows for the most effective practice. This exercise may take ten or fifteen minutes to do in the evening. It is most enlivening and powerful if it is done just as you are going to sleep.

The total time spent each day doing the morning and evening exercises might equal half an hour. These are thirty minutes in which you yourself are the shaper of your own destiny and of your experience of time.

Esoteric teachers throughout the ages have always been aware that most people are imprisoned within the walls of their own minds. The great philosopher Rousseau said, "Man is born free, but everywhere he is in chains." However, in the realm of the spirit a person's mind has an inherent freedom. The freedom of the one who remembers how it was before everything became chaotic is available to anyone willing to control his or her own thoughts. Gaining this freedom does not require a successful practice, but it does require a regular practice to discipline the mind and strengthen the spirit. Time spent in disciplining the mind every morning can give the soul a sense of purpose even in a seemingly purposeless environment. The fruits of a morning practice are a gradual feeling of hope for the coming day. Hope appears magically where there was nothing but despair and pain. The fruits of a practice continued every evening are that the soul eventually develops an inner strength and repose in the face of life's many trying circumstances. The soul is given poise and resolve that can help us overcome many difficulties.

Eventually the morning and evening rhythms of these practices meet in an experience the Rosicrucians called sacred sleep. Sacred sleep brings to birth in human beings the consciousness that can remember how life was before free time was taken from us and everything became chaotic. Sacred sleep helps us learn without resentment or blaming the tough lessons life must teach us. In sacred sleep the practices done upon awaking and just before going off into sleep begin to awaken in the soul a sense of belonging to something much larger than our present condition. We awaken in the morning with thoughts of how it could be if we had control over our reactions, and we go to sleep remembering the events of the day in a mood of serenity. Through inner work and sacred sleep, our soul begins to participate in ever higher dimensions of freedom.

We could call this sequence "seership lite." These simple exercises run from basic elemental mandala exercises of concentration, through the metamorphosing images of contemplation, to reversed thinking and the silent spaces of meditation. In the forming of inner images and the eventual meeting with the Doorkeeper, this sequence shows a simple yet coherent path of development for those interested in renewal or guarding against burnout. For those who wish to deepen the capacity for seeing, the more complicated path is presented in the following chapters, beginning with the elemental mandala exercises, then the development of the chakras, and finally the dialogue with the Doorkeeper.

THE LEARNING JOURNAL

The following learning journal form is offered as an aid in making the exercises more effective. Make some copies of the form, leaving room for your responses, and use it if a particular exercise starts to initiate an inner process of transformation. The purpose of this journal is to document the images, feelings, and concepts that arise as insights during the course of an exercise and seem particularly significant at the time. Over the months, these insights, like seeds, will grow and change. The danger is that the seed insights of today are often forgotten, like a dream. Unconscious forgetting tends to obscure the progress the soul is making toward wholeness and self-reliance. The questions in the learning journal are designed to provide a short-term evaluation of progress in a given exercise, a possible plan for future learning strategies, and a long-term ready reference for review.

Name of exercise:
- *Name some new concepts the exercise allowed me to understand.*
- *Were there any turning points in which I received a cognitive insight/ question?*
- *Did the insight/question come through another person? Who?*

- *Did it come to me alone? If so, what was the circumstance?*
- *Were there any significant feelings accompanying an insight/question?*
- *If negative feelings arose, how did I deal with them?*
- *Were there any images in the exercise that precisely expressed a feeling I was having?*
- *Did anything in this exercise help me to see myself more clearly?*
- *What am I grateful for in my life? What is changing? What could be done better?*
- *What was my level of involvement or commitment in this exercise? What would I wish to do better? What plan or protocol can I form to do this?*

2

THE ELEMENTAL MANDALA

ALCHEMY IS THE STUDY of how to dialogue with the beings that stand behind nature as archetypes of substances found in the manifest world. When an alchemist is successful in harmonizing his or her mental state with a particular archetypal being, the lesson of the being is given as an insight into how to transform a particular substance. The substance is considered to be the sign of a process in nature that has some significance for the alchemist emotionally. The sign has a specific relationship to a specific challenge or dilemma hidden in the alchemist's soul. When the soul has been sufficiently prepared through inner thought purification, the being of the spiritual archetype standing behind the substance can approach it with an insight. These activities of transforming the lower impulses by realizing the nature of the True Human constitute the work against nature, or, for short, the work. An alchemist understands that any work on oneself is also a work on nature and that an adept can transform nature in more efficient or, we could say, magical ways than are available to persons not undertaking the work of the alchemical marriage.

The archetypal beings that are guardians of the secrets of nature provide visual images for educating striving esoteric students. The images are primarily dream images that come to the student, or artist, when the proper stage of inner development has been reached. To be effective, the dream images need to be transformed into the language of the awake state. The purpose of this book is to present techniques for this transformation.

In the past, the artist/student in the alchemical tradition was charged with the vow of secrecy so that the sublime secrets given by the archetypes did not fall too early into the unpurified consciousness of the general populace. It was felt that if the secrets were given to unprepared minds, insanity accompanied by a lust for power could be the result. The alchemist might then become a sorcerer or dark magician and stray from the narrow path of humble dialogue with, and service to, the doorkeepers and archetypes standing behind the forces found in substances. Over time, the techniques of these masters were passed on through symbolic maps and charts that enabled student alchemists to journey through the dangerous places and achieve the work without the danger of revealing the secrets too early. This precaution explains why so many manuscripts were arcane and seemingly written by unbalanced persons. The thought was that if you wished to get into the secret places you had to do it slowly and thoroughly and with a mood of reverence for the mystery beings standing behind the phenomena in the laboratory. An old alchemical mantra states that you must be able to "work and pray" without expecting any results. The alchemists sought to reveal the mystery, while modern science seeks to solve the mystery. Thinking you have solved the mystery can easily become a dangerous Faustian conceit.

The charts for the alchemical journey most often take the form of a mandala or sacred wheel, because the sacred journey never ends and usually brings you back to where you started. However, when you come back you have changed; you now know where you have been. The mandala is a dynamic map of the stages of development necessary for the transformation of the soul.

The most basic mandala form is the four-step diagram known to adepts as the rotation of the elements (figure 1). There are four stages, one for each of the classical elements. Earth is followed by water, followed by air, followed by fire, which returns us to earth. This pattern follows the laws of nature where earth is on the bottom with water next, then air, and then fire. This is the normal sequence.

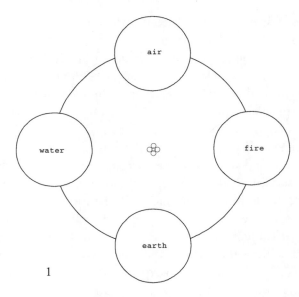

1

Beginning to work on oneself is seen as the act of putting fire under earth – a work against nature. When putting fire under earth, the alchemist is working against the natural order of things. Cooking a meal is working against nature, according to these ideas. From this viewpoint, we can see that for an alchemist not much that human beings do technically follows natural law. The legacy of this work against nature can be seen today in such things as pollution and the overtaxing of natural resources. Remember that in the past the alchemist was expected to purify the self at each stage of the work, which meant saying a sacred mantra while cooking dinner, saying grace before meals, and praying before doing a scientific experiment. These common safeguards were employed by alchemists so that their work against nature would not result in personal inflation or the actual destruction of nature, a sobering consideration for modern scientific researchers. To guard against such hubris, safeguards are necessary at each step of the way, sequences of questions the alchemist should ask.

Earth/physical thinking is the fundamental stage in problem solving. Facts and data are gathered by asking, What is different? The answers to this question result in abstract categories.

In water/living thinking, the facts are arranged into sequences of typical movement or flow patterns by asking, What is changing? The answers to this question result in morphological systemic thinking.

In air/simultaneous or reciprocal thinking, the patterns are considered from the point of view of how they were likely to have evolved to where they are today by asking, What is reversing? The answers to this question result in an inner experience of the reciprocal nature of all solutions. At this stage it is understood that all systems go through the process of reversal.

In fire/pure thinking, the rhythm of the problem-solving process is considered from the point of view of what the problem is likely to look like in many years by asking, What is the whole? There are no "answers" to this question since it is asked by being completely silent inside. What is revealed from a fire question is a better question.

These four stages are an archetypal pattern underlying most interactions between humans as well as most patterns of change in the natural world. Practice in recognizing and implementing knowledge about these patterns is an invaluable aid to group process and personal growth. These questions can be arranged in the form of a mandala that is useful when undertaking alchemical transformative work on the lower self in order to perceive the True Human.

SALT, SULFUR, AND MERCURY

In figure 2 we can see a further modification of the elemental mandala. A diagonal line through the center separates earth and water from air and fire. Earth and water are elements related to the physical process of precipitation in which salts settle out of solution. Air and fire are related to the physical process in which a physical element is incinerated, or, as alchemists called it, "calcined." They used that term because if anything organic is burned to ash, the ash usually contains a great deal of calcium or calx, which is chalk.

The alchemical forces of salt and sulfur are also known as *coagula* and *solve*. The salt coagulates or precipitates from the solution, and

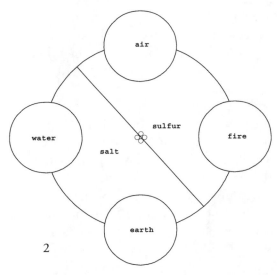

2

the sulfur is a solvent form of a mineral. Alchemists called sulfur "rock grease." The two forces of salt and sulfur, or *coagula* and *solve*, are also considered to be forces in the human soul. Salt is the *coagula* quality in the thinking process, and sulfur is the solve aspect of the will. Thinking comes into being like a salt crystal falling to the bottom of a jar of brine. The unknown suddenly appears to solidify in the mind and then can be grasped. The will, on the other hand, is constantly slipping away from the grasp of the human being, even as it is being employed to do something. The esoteric trick is to unite the salt and the sulfur. Then the crystallized thinking can be softened by the sulfurous will and take on more of the dynamic nature of the will. When this happens, the newly transformed thinking can dissolve the crystals of what is known and find a new solution to the problem. At higher levels of the work, the will becomes thoughtlike and precise in its effectiveness, while the thinking becomes creative and fluid. The union of these two soul forces is described as the alchemical marriage.

For the alchemical marriage to take place, however, another soul force needs to be brought into the mixture. Alchemists know this soul force as mercury. Figure 3 describes the relationship of the other two forces and the four elements to mercury.

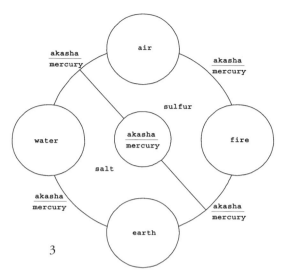

3

We see that the center area is designated mercury/akasha. The force of mercury is seen as the quality of consciousness needed to get salt to marry sulfur. Mercury is the great healer that, through rhythm, influences all polar opposites to integrate into new and higher orders of being. We also see in the diagram that mercury/akasha is likewise present at all other levels of transformation. It is the agent of transformation from earth to water, which is achieved through the process of putting fire under earth. Only a being endowed with the capacity for recognizing consciousness, or, we could say, a being who could be self-conscious or self-aware, can bring fire under earth and transform nature. Mercury is rhythm, akasha is consciousness; together they make rhythmic consciousness or consciousness of rhythm. This quality accurately describes the necessary force needed to get salt to marry sulfur. A rhythmic consciousness is one in which a daily practice of stilling the mind creates a dynamic wave in the spiritual world. Time is telescoped and concentrated by such a rhythmic consciousness, and the will becomes an organ for thinking.

The four elements are transformed through the rhythmic interplay of the three forces. When this happens the center of the mandala is filled with akasha, or consciousness. The artist/student then rises to the level of adept and the fertilization of the Spirit Embryo by the activity of the True Human can begin. Establishing a practice to work with these ideas is of paramount importance to the soul life of a human being and was the content of the mystery schools from the most ancient times. The practice is the most fundamental tool of the adept. The other tool in the tool bag of the aspiring adept is the development of living picture imagination, otherwise known as "seeing." To understand "seeing" we can refer to the mandala of the last figure as we go through the process.

In earth consciousness we ask the question, What is different? The answer we get is always part of an abstract system of relationships. Analysis yields data, and data is always part of a larger system of knowledge. An alchemist would call the data surrounding the experiment the "dust of the work." Gathering dust is necessary for the work to begin, but no life, no insight, can emerge out of the dust. The dust must be taken to the next level of the work and put into the water of fluid consciousness. Here the akasha/mercury forces require that we rhythmically work over the dust again and again until some pattern makes itself apparent. When we begin to see patterns in what was previously only a collection of data, the second stage of the work is at hand. The water level of the work is what contemporary thinkers call the systems approach. In the water level of the mandala, the morphological realities flowing between the particles of data become accessible to consciousness through the experiment, which is simply a repetition of something we have already understood. We keep inwardly visualizing what we already understand until our understanding of the patterns in what we are doing more closely resembles the abstraction we are exploring. If this is done as a meditative practice, the soul is drawn rhythmically closer to the archetype and begins to be inspired to perceive what the poet Goethe called the "becomings" of nature. The becomings are spiritual activities of archetypal beings. To perceive becomings and not simply patterns of abstract forces in interaction, a significant shift in consciousness is required.

Many systems analysts stop at the perception of abstract patterns once the system reveals them, because most science experiments are concerned with the complexities of physical systems in movement. To stop when the experiment has revealed its complexities is sufficient for science, but if the alchemist stops here there is no chance for the soul forces to begin the process of marrying the salt and the sulfur completely into higher sight. The empirical scientist cannot work to form the Spirit Embryo because to do so the researcher needs to transcend the experimental data, and even the systems approach, in order to move into the higher element of air. Good researchers can have access to the air level of alchemical thought if they are also involved in a meditative discipline that underlies their work in the lab. To rhythmically meditate images of becomings is representative of the air level of consciousness. The Witness must be willfully active in the consciousness doing this work. It is here that a strong line must be drawn.

It is possible to work through the earth and water levels of the mandala and still remain only in the nuts and bolts of the physical complexities of the systems we are researching. When we get an insight, the mind will drop back from the encounter with the inspiring force of the archetypal idea into the lower level of the experiment without any cognition of an encounter with a higher force arising in the soul. This curtailing happens for a number of reasons. One is that there is absolutely no requirement for a researcher to worry about where the insight came from. No peer review committee will ask who the inspiring being was for the idea. For a scientist, such a question seems stupid, but from an alchemical view, the question is not a little thing. A second reason is that in science and systems analysis, the experiment is not done to develop moral forces in the experimenter. To suggest that the experimenter be questioned about his or her moral fiber would today be considered highly politically incorrect. Yet in the past this was the most important question because it was understood that the forces of the Spirit Embryo latent within the moral dimensions of the pharmacist or doctor actually entered into the healing force of the diagnosis, pharmacology, and treatment, and could have repercussions on the effectiveness of the healing. Today, we do not ask these questions, and usually we have to settle for treatments rather than healings. If the experimental protocol includes only questions from the earth and water levels of thinking, then the outcomes can be completely outside the realm of the moral force of the True Human. As was noted earlier, this is not a small thing. It has great implications for science.

In the modern practice that allows no spiritual parameters for the experiment, systemic analysis is as good as it gets. In science, the next higher level of the mandala, air – in which all systems go against the pattern of their own development – is given over to the drama of the peer review or journal referees working as devil's advocates for the religion of science. However, even if the theory or experiment manages to get published, the question of morals, which is so important for the development of the Spirit Embryo, is never broached. This omission has implications in the contemporary debate about human cloning. The problem is that the scientific questions being discussed by scientists are still at the level of systems analysis, yet they are masquerading as spiritual or moral concerns – and when religion or morals are actually involved, these Spirit Embryo concerns are conveniently labeled as being outside the realm of science.

To return to the world of the alchemist, the level of air requires the researcher to hold two opposing views in the mind simultaneously. The capacity to do this is the precise quality of higher consciousness that can fertilize the Spirit Embryo. An alchemist might say that angels have simultaneous consciousness that allows them to see into the record of the akasha when dealing with human karma. It is from the akasha that new ideas come to humans. The level of air is what would be called creative thinking in the language of psychology. To properly approach the air level, thinking has to be divested of abstract systems based upon information brought into the soul through the forces of memory. Abstract memory of physical phenomena will not allow two opposing systems of thought to live in the consciousness simultaneously. Try it and see. They immediately cancel each other out, and we are left in the most characteristic quality of air consciousness: silence.

Alchemists know that the development of moral insight into the proper uses of substances, which can then serve as a blueprint for work on the soul, involves the transformation of information into pictures. This understanding explains why their works are so filled with strange and evocative images and why seeing is so important. In the process of consciously forming inner images, the true imagination arises that allows the soul of the alchemist to sustain itself actively in simultaneous consciousness. To form inner images consciously, the Witness must "find" itself. A good technique to enable the Witness to find itself is to translate abstract data into accurate images of a process and then visually think the pictures of the process backward into silence. Normally only the forward process is considered worthy of our attention. However, both the forward process and the backward process are true at the air level of thinking. The polarity of anything exists on the air level of consciousness. This level is above logical abstraction. The soul intent on finding only physical results will find only the physical results that were expected, which is why peer review and refereed journals are so important. Without them there is no moral parameter to the pursuit of physical results. Think of the image of the sorcerer's apprentice.

Opposed to this, the alchemical mandala process requires that researchers submit their own results to the highest authority, which is their own True Human. The use of pictures, especially images taken from nature, allows the soul to develop and then open the inner eye of the soul. With the inner eye open, the Witness of the researcher will be drawn to the essential spiritual nature of other beings as a source of creative imaginations. Working in this way can allow researchers to ground their work in moral impulses.

The realm of the pictorial is the concern of the alchemist seeking to move into the air stage of the mandala. Once there, the opened inner eye can see more clearly into the dream space that exists behind the phenomena of the world. Exploring the dream space while one is still wide awake is known as the transformation of dream life. It represents the fire level of the mandala, where the adept is free temporarily of earthly concerns and is capable of seeing behind the mirror of appearances. This stage of the work involves conscious interaction with beings that live on the other side of the abyss between this world and the next.

At the abyss the Witness, residing within the student, is met by the Confidant Doorkeeper, who has been following the student's progress for a long time. In alchemical language, this being is called the Confidant Doorkeeper because in the beginning, the higher being acts like a stern doorkeeper, not allowing us to enter the higher worlds of understanding. Instead the doorkeeper points out our own failings and shortcomings – which initially is a less-than-wonderful experience.

The shortcomings are also beings in the realm of the spirit. Our own projections, shortcomings, and fantasies take on the form of what psychology calls shadows. Shadows are personality fragments within our own soul that have a desperate need to be linked to a personality. In alchemical language they would be called demons; in psychology, syndromes; in casual language, hang-ups. They are fragments of a whole personality that link haphazardly to the inner pictures in human souls resulting from sensory experiences that have not been integrated emotionally into the general soul life. However, through time the tough questions are experienced as a guide to higher worlds. This stern and foreboding doorkeeper then becomes like a confidant to us in our pursuit of higher knowledge. Through this process the doorkeeper, who first appears so fierce and formidable, gradually becomes a counselor for the long journey to the self. The fierce guardian becomes the Confidant Doorkeeper when the soul finds its way to the spirit, where the soul says "I" to itself.

The questions asked by the Confidant Doorkeeper are questions with a peculiarly familiar ring, like a piece of music we heard as a child and have not heard since. They seem to strike at the very heart of our existence. Actually, these questions would immolate us if they were asked before we were prepared, but through the systematic divestment and purification process of the elemental mandala, the True Human residing in the soul can stand the heat of the fierce questions of the doorkeeper standing by the abyss between worlds.

The mandala has done its work, and we are burned into ash by its/our ardent questions. The ash is once again put into the water of life as a new earth, purified, but earth nonetheless. Out of the ashes of the new earth come questions – not answers, but new questions

– and the development of the Spirit Embryo becomes a distinct, if distant, possibility for the moral gaze of the True Human. There are four stages or lights along the path whereby the doorkeeper becomes a confidant. These stages, discussed in the following chapters, are reflections of the four levels of the elemental mandala. The concept of four lights is a useful way to broadly grasp the dialogues with the Confidant Doorkeeper so that a rudimentary roadmap of the territory within and beyond the doorway to other worlds can be made for the True Human, which has come from the spirit into matter and is on the way back to the spirit.

3
EARTH/BROW/AWARENESS

EARTH/BROW/AWARENESS refers to the relationships between the first elemental stage in the alchemical mandala, the given activity of the brow chakra, and the first light of awareness in the teachings of the Confidant Doorkeeper. These three aspects of the inner work are octaves of each other. It should be noted here that the "given activity of the brow chakra" refers to the lower capacity of the chakra as it was designed by the hierarchies that look after and maintain the miraculous instrument of the human body. The task of the soul alchemist is to transform each chakra into other capacities. That transformation will be addressed later in the chapter on the chakras. In this early portion of the work, all references to the chakras will be addressing the function of the chakra that has not been modified by esoteric work and is still functioning according to the original plan of the hierarchies. The original plan can be inferred from the functioning of the nerves and glands in descriptions of the physiology and psychology of perception.

The common thread in the following exercises is that they require the student to work with an unusual polarity. In the soul, sensation is present in which there is no cognition, meaning that the sense impression stimulates a response in us that has no connection to our awake consciousness. Polar to this is cognition in which there is understanding of concepts related to sense experience but no experience of the sensation itself. The intention to bring these two polar soul forces together is the root of the question of the earth mode, What is different? At the higher level in the etheric body, the polarity of sensation and cognition is the special task of the brow chakra, existing as it does in the tension between the pituitary gland and the pineal gland.

The drama of the fall of the human being out of a spiritual existence in Paradise and into life on Earth is the realm of the brow chakra. The drama is carried further when the Confidant Door-keeper challenges us to remember that all we are and were has been given to us by the creative sacrifices of the hierarchical beings that made the world. Our fall into matter has forced this cosmic world-creative deed out of our day consciousness into a state of simple awareness. This awareness is the gift of the hierarchies to the human being on one side and a debtors' prison on the other. The human prison arises when the hierarchies are not recognized as the source of the incredible genius behind the forms and forces of nature. When that happens their forces are shattered into matter and the human being becomes simply aware rather than being aware of being or aware of self. The four-stage elemental mandala is the place where these relationships begin the process toward higher awareness. Other mandalas can be given for the higher work on the soul, but we will begin here by using the four-stage mandala form to confront the sleeping level of awareness that is our biological inheritance.

In this set of exercises the four elements of earth, water, air, and fire are presented in a mandalic form as a protocol for observing nature. Since we are trying to develop the capacity to form accurate inner pictures, the focus of these exercises will be on the creation of those pictures. Later, in the work on the chakras and in the dialogue with the Confidant Doorkeeper, these protocols will be applied to problem-solving strategies in the realm of the soul.

EARTH/WATER/AIR/FIRE EXERCISES

For the first exercise we will observe bones from an animal skeleton. The bones of a limb show sequential growth: one form follows an-other. Therefore, they can be easily worked with mandalically. It is best to do this exercise with bones from a complete limb of an animal. That way the intelligent ordering of the forming principle behind the manifest form can yield accurate inner pictures. We will go through the mandalic sequence by asking questions and then recording answers in a journal.

Earth Mode

Select any bone out of a complete limb. Draw the bone and ask, What is different? Record as many differences as you can and arrange them in pairs, i.e., this part is different from that. Record the differences by labeling them on your drawing. Draw another bone of the limb and repeat the exercise, including the labeling process. Then compare the results gathered from the first subject with the second. Record any insights in the learning journal.

If you are working with others, form conversation groups of two or three persons. In the groups, center on the differences between what was actually seen and what was thought about what was seen. Make a list of things that were actually seen. This might include bumps, hollows, holes, and ridges or serrations. What are not seen on the bone are things like tendon attachments or holes for nerves – these are thoughts about what was seen. It is very useful and difficult to do this work of distinguishing sense data from thoughts about sense data, and it is easier to make these differentiations in a group setting than when working alone. Record any results that may come up in conversation that are different from yours.

Water Mode

Try to model a bone out of clay. Try to accurately depict a bone you might expect to find between two bones you have studied. Record your reasoning process in the learning journal. Form conversation groups and present your process of thinking about the sequence of forms to the others. Focus on any changes in your understanding that arise from the comments of another person. The focus here is on how one bone went through some sort of metamorphosis as the sequence of forms that made up the limb evolved. Our question in the water mode is, What is changing?

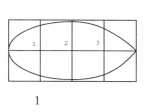

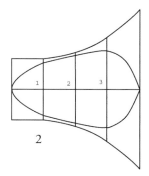

1   2

Air Mode

Construct a morphological grid (figure 1) and draw the outline of a bone on it. The morphological grid we will use has eight rectangles oriented horizontally. Increase the gradients in the grid on one end and allow the bone to metamorphose into a polar condition (figure 2). This is done in a simple way by curving the upper and lower lines of the grid but keeping the vertical lines connected to them as in the figure. Draw the second bone by transferring the information from the first block of the grid in figure 1 to the first block in figure 2, then the contents of the second block in figure 1 to the second block in figure 2, and so on. By the third block the curved lines of the upper and lower sections of the grid will start to distort the image of the bone. Try to retain the proportions of where the outline of the bone crosses the verticals. In figure 1 the outlines of the bone in block three cross the left-hand vertical line of the block about nine-tenths of the way to the top. The outline of the bone crosses the right-hand vertical of block 3 about one-fourth of the way to the top. These crossing positions of figure 1 have been retained in figure 2, but since the grid is transformed the outline of the bone, which is very regular in figure 1, is quite transformed and distorted in figure 2, though comparable in details. The grid has just given the coordinates a completely different formal look.

This type of exercise strengthens the capacity to imagine forms inwardly in precise ways. Record your results in a learning journal. You may also go into small groups for conversation about your reversals of the bone. The work is strengthened into awareness when we try to explain our linking of idea and sensation to another person or in a learning journal. The exercises begin to work on the brow chakra, where we bring into awareness just how our sensations link to our ideas.

Fire Mode

The fire mode requires that the other three questions be worked with in a rhythm. The rhythmic forming and dissolving of images in a particular sequence develops a protocol or sequence for seeing the sequences inwardly in exact pictures. Thinking the sequence of pictures in reverse develops the inner mood of asking the question. Repeating the sequences again and again allows the soul to lift the question into the fire realm, where the rhythm of the inner picturing pulls away from the expectation of an answer and simply becomes an exercise for the will. Through such repetition, we make the inner eye much more flexible. This flexibility of soul is the basis for the capacity for intuition. Take the images and protocols from the previous day and work with them inwardly, focusing on the rhythm of the inner picturing. Record results in the learning journal. Be sure to notice any feelings that arise in the exercises and include them in your journal.

Even though these exercises move through the four elements, they are considered here in the chapter on earth consciousness to show how the elemental mandala itself brings forces into play as we begin to consider problem-solving techniques. Throughout this book most exercises will be taken through the four stages, even though they may be presented in a chapter on a single element. In reality all things are transforming, even if we think that we are only repeating something.

The linking of sense percepts and ideational concepts is the realm of the brow chakra. Other exercises will be given for this chakra later, but these types of activities can be considered to be fundamental to the brow. In reality, working with the four-stage elemental mandala includes more than the brow chakra work. In the brow chakra we are aware either of the sensation or the concept.

There is very little awareness of how we become aware until the chakra is developed consciously. In an undeveloped consciousness, the focus of attention in the brow is usually directed either to the sense object or to the concept that arises after the sensation fades from focus.

WORKING WITH THE GAZE

In the throat chakra the intent is to gradually become aware of awareness itself, by which we either have a sensation or form a concept independent of a sensation. The next set of exercises will go through the alchemical mandala once again, but this time the intent is to become aware of the activity of the throat chakra with regard to how we find lawful images in the world. We can accomplish this by paying attention to the quality of our gaze.

There are three modes we can become aware of in the way we look at things: the open gaze, alchemically known as *solve*; the fixed gaze, alchemically known as *coagula*; and the fluid gaze, which is the rhythmic interplay of the two polar gazes. We will work with something as simple as a pen so that we don't become interested in the object, but instead concentrate on the activity of the seeing.

Fixed Gaze Exercise

Observe a common pen and notice a detail. Write the detail down to start a list. Return to the observation and notice another detail. Record that detail and return to your observing. Continue in this manner, and as each detail arises in your consciousness record it in writing, then go back to observing the pen. Do not record seeing something twice. We are looking for new details we have not seen before. When you stop seeing new things about the pen, the exercise is over. This is the earth level of observation. When we have made a list of the things we have seen, an alchemist would say that we have made "dust" out of the thing. An image that stays with us after we see something in the sense world could be called the dust of the world. The dust is very useful, but it is only the beginning of the work on oneself.

In the next session, before you begin observing, modify the fixed gaze exercise by first thinking of the sequence of details you have observed. Try to picture to yourself the sequence of the details as you found them. Start with the first detail of the image of the pen, which you try to clearly reproduce in your mind's eye. Then add the next observed feature, and the next, until you have a pile of dust. The first image should start to fade and each detail will start to blend with the next, but that is fine; just continue adding and visualizing each detail in turn. When your list of details is finished, once again return to actually observing the pen. See if there is a new detail you had not observed before and add it to the list. With this level we are still in *coagula*.

Fluid Gaze Exercise

If you cannot see any new details of the pen, then relax, go back to the beginning, and start to remember the sequence of details as you discovered them. Remembering the sequence in which you became aware of the details is very strengthening to the inner eye, even if the remembered details fade as soon as the next one is remembered and visualized. Seeing the detail was awareness. The strict remembering of the sequence of the details as we saw them is being aware of our awareness. This inner picturing of the sequences is the fluid gaze. In the fluid gaze we are taking elements from the fixed gaze and linking them inwardly into sequences.

We can deepen the fluid gaze when we modify the pen exercise by trying to imagine the precise manufacturing stages that produced the pen. Try to get a feeling of evidence that what you are imagining is true. That is, do not allow any detail to link to another detail unless you can see a good reason that the two should be placed together in the sequence. To do this, it is useful when observing the pen to notice a particular detail of the design for which you have no explanation. In other words, you have no idea how this particular detail fits into a manufacturing sequence. Ask yourself, How did this detail get this way? Using the fluid gaze, visualize a possible manufacturing process that might explain the detail. In forming your idea of the process, use details from the observations of the past exercises as support for the feeling of evidence. Once you think you have a good feeling about how a particular detail on the pen was manufactured, write a few sentences about this process, and then share this with a partner. This moves the dust into a movement process and into the water level of the mandala, where the question is, What is changing? Be sure to notice any feelings that arose in the exercise. The inner forming of sequences of pictures that have a relationship that can be linked to reality is the fluid gaze.

For another modification of the fluid gaze, ask yourself, What did this pen look like just before it got to the stage in which I see it now? Record any answers and then share your insight with a partner. We are moving further away from the sensation and more toward the cognition of the idea of the object, activating the throat chakra as well as the brow chakra. In the throat chakra we find objective or lawful patterns in the creations of nature. This is not possible simply by experiencing sensations. There must be recognition in order for pattern to be analyzed.

In another modification of the fluid gaze, imagine as many different types of pens as you can. Make a list of them. Then imagine as many different objects as you can that you could use as a pen. Make a list of these, and share the last list with others. Note which objects are common to at least three people's lists. Note which objects are unique in being used as a pen. With this exercise, we are moving completely into the realm of the idea and away from the need to have a sense object in front of us for the exercise. In working with the mandala, as we become more aware of awareness there is often a natural movement of the mind away from the sense object and toward the idea. We are also moving into the throat chakra.

Fixed and Fluid Gaze Exercises with a Natural Object
Doing these exercises with a pen allows the consciousness to be completely imbedded in the pen as a manufactured object. A natural object cannot be penetrated by our consciousness as much as manufactured objects are. Things formed in nature hold us at a greater distance initially than manufactured objects. Nevertheless, this sequence of exercises moving from the fixed gaze of the dust

of the sense world into the union of the sense object with the idea and then to a more ideational experience can be attempted with natural objects like leaves and shells. In the places where we would try to visualize the manufacturing process, it is useful to use clay or a modeling substance to form small models of how we think a leaf or shell grew. A sample of this type of exercise is given in the following short sketch so that the pattern can be seen. It is interesting to do this with shells, flowers, bones, crystals, dried insects, or small skulls. Each presents its own challenge to the imagination, and they all strengthen the capacity of visualization.

Fixed Gaze: Observe a leaf and make a list of the physical elements seen in the form of the leaf. Record the details as before.

Fluid Gaze: Modify the leaf "dust" of the fixed gaze by making a model of the development stages you think the leaf went through as it grew. Next, sketch a rough diagram of at least four stages of development in the growth of the leaf. Then imagine that sequence inwardly in the fluid gaze. Share these drawings and any insights with a partner. The partner should ask you questions about what you did but is not allowed to make statements. Be sure to notice any feelings that arise in the exercise, and mark them so you can find them later.

Modify the fluid gaze of the leaf by observing a leaf that is part of a fresh shoot from a plant. Try to imagine the exact sequence of leaves on the shoot in your mind's eye. Then build a shoot from your memory. When you feel that you have duplicated the sequence adequately, share your model with your partner, who should ask you a few questions about what you did. Then write a few sentences about the experience. Be sure to notice any feelings that arose in the exercise and mark them in your journal.

The Open Gaze

The fixed gaze is linked almost exclusively to the earth mode in the elemental mandala. In the more developed cognitive modes of the fixed gaze, the mind just begins to enter the water mode. In order to develop the type of consciousness seers need for exploring the abyss and beyond, they should also have the capacity to use what is known as the open gaze, or *solve*. Alchemists knew the open gaze and the fixed gaze as the fundamental states of matter they called *solve* and *coagula*. One of the most useful capacities in soul alchemy is the rhythmic practice of *solve et coagula,* dissolving and coagulating. Undertaking the exercises in a rhythmic way opens the door to the ability to see with the heart.

The heart is the only organ that can see across the divide separating this world from the next. This ability does not come easily to a human being because there are many beings, both benevolent and malevolent, that await the human soul at the threshold between the worlds. These beings may not appear to be what they truly are. A being malevolent in appearance may in actuality be a benefactor; likewise, an adversary may appear to be radiant and warm. This situation is really not so different from daily life, but at the threshold the problem of knowing who is who is amplified because on the other side we have no experience of separateness. We become the one we are addressing, and it becomes us. We could say that we breathe into it and it breathes into us, until there is no sense of having a separate existence. Since this intermingling is a distinct impossibility for our bodies of flesh, we have a safeguard here in our everyday world that we lack on the other side of the threshold. On this side we simply believe with our utmost attention that we are a separate being from all other beings. This belief is both a gift and a challenge to our soul. It is a gift because it allows us to have the experience of being an ego-endowed entity; it is a challenge because it alienates us from all other beings in creation.

The fundamental struggle of the human being is to maintain a sense of our own ego presence while simultaneously entering the lives of other beings in acts of surrender. To do this effectively, it is useful to practice *solve et coagula.* We will begin by doing soul breathing exercises gazing at objects and work up to human beings who have done things to us that we resent. These are large steps, but the practice of soul breathing can be useful in all of them.

We have worked with the fixed gaze in the first set of exercises; now we will work with the open gaze and move into the practice of soul breathing.

Observe a pen, but focus your attention on the space around the pen. Do not allow any thought or image or insight to arise while you are looking at the pen. If a thought or image arises, acknowledge it and let it slowly dissolve or drift away, or even push it off to the side and put it in a box if that fits your temperament. The important thing is not to let the encounter with the random thought start to occupy front and center in the consciousness. The exercise is about maintaining an open gaze that is focused on the object but is aware of the ground *around* the object.

This gaze is much harder than it sounds at first, so an exercise to find the place where this seeing is found will be useful. In the formation of the eye, the optic nerves emerge from the brain and cross each other in an area known as the optic chiasm, depicted in the figure. The nerves emerge from the optic chiasm and then go into the back of the eyeball. If the eye saw straight out from the optic nerve we would never have binocular vision – our eyes would be turned out at a twenty-three- degree angle from where they have to point in order for us to blend the two images into one. A muscle (gray curve) pulls each eye inward against the socket so that the two eyes can be trained to see straight ahead. If left up to nature, each eye would drift out to the side at about a twenty-three-degree angle from the center. In the open gaze, the eyes are left relaxed so that they can focus at this "natural" twenty-three-degree angle. The open gaze is softer and more intuitive than the fixed gaze so intimately connected to conceptualizing. The soft gaze is useful for seeing the subtle changes in situations required for entrance into the throat, heart, and spleen chakras. By alternating the fixed gaze and the open gaze at will, a seer can flow into or separate from any visualization. This is of great

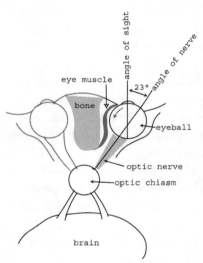

help when working on the other side of the threshold trying to determine the intent of a being or situation. The question is usually
whether you can breathe out into this being or situation, or whether
you need to experience being separate. Breathing into the other is
sympathetic, and separating is antipathetic. These two motions
must be balanced in the soul in order for it to wait patiently at the
threshold while the Confidant Doorkeeper gives instructions. The
process of training the soul to be flexible yet strong can be called
soul breathing. Through soul breathing, the soul of the researcher
moves in and out of the body in a rhythmical way. It moves out in
sensation and in in cognitive thinking. Psychologically, every chakra
helps the soul to breathe in a different way, and the alchemist who
cannot determine the correct type of soul breath for the situation is
at a distinct disadvantage when trying to establish equanimity.

Choosing the Gaze for Soul Breathing
These initial exercises will form a foundation for deeper aspects of
soul breathing. In our daily life we often are not aware of the quality
of attention we put into looking at something. It is well understood
that in certain situations if someone glares at you it is best not to return the glare unless you can handle the trouble it will bring. What
is it in a gaze or a glare that is so powerful? In the situation in which
we get a glare from someone, we realize something that usually remains well below the threshold of consciousness: that our entire life
is spent adapting the intensity of our gaze to situations around us.

We will begin this sequence with the fixed gaze. Choose a manufactured object like a button or pencil for the subject of the exercise. Place the object in your field of vision and, similar to what you
did in earlier exercises in the earth mode, try to notice three details
that are new to you. Write down the details and then try to find
three more details new to you. Once you have six details, look at
the object and mentally list the details. After you have remembered
the last detail, bring into your mind the phrase "I am looking at
this." Repeat this phrase three times and then listen into your soul
in silence. See if there is a mood connected to the experience "I am
looking at this." Write a few sentences about this mood and how

it feels to you. Then relax a bit and let the experience sink in. The mood of antipathy in this phrase characterizes the fixed gaze. Be sure to notice any feelings that arose in the exercise; mark them with an infinity sign and include them in your journal.

Once more place the object in front of you. Once more focus your attention on picking out details on the object. See if you can find three more details you had not noticed the first time. When you have gotten two or three more details, do the following. Imagine that you and the object are trading places. Leave your "looking at" consciousness and go to the object and look back at yourself looking at the object. Try to imagine seeing your own eyes probing for details. Imagine how it feels to be looked "at" this way and then write a few sentences about it. This mode of looking often gives us the feeling that we are fixing a glare on the object. Relax a bit and let this feeling sink in.

Once more place the object in front of you. This time do not try to see details but open the gaze and try to see the object as a whole. That is, do not mentally make a list of details, but simply look at the object as if you had never seen it before. Use the open gaze to do this. With the open gaze established, place your attention on the space around the object rather than on seeing the object. Go so far as to let the image of the object disappear in your open gaze. When you can make the object fade in and out even though you are looking directly at it, that is the open gaze. When observing in this way, see if any thoughts come into your consciousness while you are paying attention to the space around the object. Record any thoughts. After observing in this way for a minute, imagine once again that you are trading places with the object. Look back at yourself looking at the object in an open way. Write a few sentences about your feelings and then relax and let the experience sink in. It would be appropriate to speak of seeing this way as looking *with* an object rather than looking *at* it.

The fixed gaze yields information. The open gaze creates a mind clear of any perception or idea. Between these two states of consciousness the fluid gaze can become a link to transformative inner representations. A technique that can be a big help in establishing the fluid gaze is called ABC/CBA. Every idea that you can think has behind it a hidden process: first there is a movement of the will, then a feeling of knowing arises, and then a particular thought appears. The movement of the will and the arising of the feeling of knowing are usually far below the capacity to grasp them in the awake state. In the ABC/CBA exercise we can think ideas about something in a slightly more structured way than was originally given for the fluid gaze. Suppose that we think of the manufacturing process for making a pin. We try to see in the pin itself if there are any marks or indicators of how it was made. We could ask if the point was cast or filed, for instance. Or, was the head soldered on or was it forged? If, for instance, the point was filed and not cast, then the pin existed as a piece of wire that was not pointed and then became pointed after it was filed. In this visualization of the manufacturing process for the pin, we can now think a two-step sequence. This is our A and B in the ABC/CBA exercise. If we keep visualizing the AB sequence, we may see another piece of evidence, which escaped our attention initially. This is what we could call making ourselves ripe for an insight. If by thinking the AB steps we can find some evidence for a manufacturing step C, then we have a good question in our minds about the idea of the pin. We have interest in a small thing. This exercise is wonderful for our mind. Practice thinking the ABC sequence and visualizing the steps of the manufacturing process of the pin. Even if we are not correct in our thinking we will be corrected if we persist in the exercise. When we can clearly think ABC then the next step is to think CBA as a series of inwardly perceived images.

Think the ABC/CBA pattern a number of times and then, when you can clearly think CBA, take the sequence into a silent space within and listen to the idea as it fades from your consciousness. Hidden in the echoing of the movement of the idea is the answer to the question you are asking by visualizing the process ABC/CBA. This technique of thinking something forward and then backward into silence has infinite applications and will serve as the basis for the higher visualization work in the air and fire levels of the mandala. It is introduced here as a first step in that direction. This work with fluid visualization can eventually allow a person to see into karma and to surrender to spiritual beings or even to awaken within other human beings. These tools are extremely useful for contemporary humans when they are faced with the challenge of transforming the senses. The transformation of the senses by controlling the production of spontaneous inner representations is the fundamental task of contemporary mystery training.

Touch and Go Exercises

The next set of exercises can be used to develop the capacity to witness the arising of an inner representation. Each of the three gazes has a particular feeling connected to it. We have been journaling feelings; now we can also journal insights. If you get an insight into anything during an exercise, write it in your journal. Later we will sift through the journal and collate different experiences as a way of assessing our path through our own soul.

A researcher can use the three gazes to explore the outer world or the inner world. We have called this process soul breathing. In a sensation the soul breathes out to the object that is stimulating the sensation. When the soul breathes out to the object, that is a *solve* experience. We sleep into the creative will impulse present behind the becoming of the object. If, for instance, we look at a button, our soul must leave its experience of being in itself or being in its body and move out of the body to have a perception that in its general proximity is a thing that is not itself. The soul then must contact that thing visually or through some other sense. Then the soul comes back to the body with a perception, and a sensation arises in the body that is an echo of the experience of the sense object we had during the perception. The sensation then gives rise to a sense/response pattern in which various glands and organs are stimulated and an inner picturing process is instigated. Normally this process from stimulation to the formation of an inner picture is completely unconscious in the soul. The motion out and in of the soul is not perceptible because the soul is usually focused on the object of the sensation and not on the response pattern within the soul. As we work with exercises in which we try to determine whether the soul is in the fixed gaze or the open gaze, we can gradually become aware of this subtle and hidden image-making process and the soul movements associated with it. The soul movements are really feelings we have about the qualities of the images arising within us as a result of sensory stimulation. The feelings linked to the fixed gaze are most often polar to the feelings linked to the open gaze in a particular person. It is useful to practice paying attention to the feeling qualities that arise from the two gazes. A way to develop this capacity for observing the feelings in sensation and the formation of mental images is the touch and go exercise.

Take a button or some other manufactured object devoid of interesting details. Place it in front of you on a white sheet of paper. Do not touch the button during the observation exercises. Start the fixed gaze exercise, but as soon as you feel that you are noticing a detail on the button, stop using the fixed gaze and switch to the open gaze. Let the detail you were focusing on slide away from your consciousness, and pay attention to the space around the button. As soon as you realize you are focused on the space around the button, shift back again to the fixed gaze until you notice something. The purpose of this exercise is to place an element of the witnessing consciousness into the habitual and subconscious oscillation between the fixed and the open gaze. A kind of breathing process occurs between these two modes of seeing, but it happens unconsciously. This exercise is aimed at eventually making this shift more conscious.

When you can feel that you have some bit of control over the awareness of whether you are in the fixed or open mode, try the following exercise as a development of the touch and go. Place a button on a white sheet of paper. Work with the touch and go exercise until a subtle awareness of the shifting of the modes is available to you without having to focus so much on telling the difference between the modes. The next level is to try to shift the touch and go away from the object and into the soul. Start the exercise in the usual way, but this time after you look at the object in a fixed way and then shift into looking at it in an open way, take the next fixed-gaze oscillation into your soul and try to see the fixed image of the button clearly in your mind's eye. Try to apply the same will forces to the perception of the inner image as you did to the perception of the outer image. When you feel that the inner image of the button is fixed in your mind's eye, wake up to this feeling and consciously dissolve the inner image by bringing into the soul the intent to use the inner gaze in an open way. When you have dissolved the image from the inside, remember to go outside the soul and move to the fixed gaze of the actual button. From there, go to the open gaze done while looking at the button, then go inward to the fixed gaze perceived inwardly. This is not an easy exercise, but it is of great benefit for later work when we try to awaken in another person. Moving from the object to the representation, then dissolving the representation, then moving out again to the object is the soul equivalent of the process of breathing in and out with our lungs. This is soul breathing.

Seeing into Works of Art
To try out this new way of looking with things and compare it to the more familiar looking at things, it is useful to work with artworks in a mandalic way. For the purposes of this work it is best to use an artwork that has socially redeeming qualities and feeds the soul imaginations that are morally significant and healing. We will use "The 100 Guilder Print" by Rembrandt sometimes known as *Christ Healing the Sick.* It was made by an artist with a deep social consciousness who was reputedly a student of Christian Rosencreutz himself. With such a work the higher levels of soul transformation requiring soul surrender can be exercised in safety.

Take tracing paper and trace three main lines around a figure of your choice. Do them slowly and try to make them exact. This is the earth mode. On another piece of paper, repeat the traced lines but do them freehand. Accent the motion of the lines and not so much the exactness. Can you feel that now we are moving into the water mode? The throat chakra will keep you informed of whether you are looking with the lines or at them. If you are looking with them, you will be able to enter into the flow of the lines rather than being worried that they are not so exact to the tracing. Try to listen to the inner dialogue during the process. If a persistent message emerges in your inner planes, write it down and then go back to retracing the

Rembrandt's "The 100 Guilder Print" (also known as *The Little Children Being Brought to Jesus* and *Christ Healing the Sick*), 1647–9, etching and dry point, 1st state, Rijks Museum, Amsterdam.

line. Continue retracing in a freehand way until you feel inwardly that you can remember the motion of the lines of the figure in a fairly exact way without looking at it. Stop drawing and try to still your mind. When you are reasonably still inwardly, form an inner picture of the figure made of the motion of the lines. Don't worry about seeing anything like a figure or a drawing. Just try to "see" the movements. When you can feel you are somewhere near the mood of the Rembrandt lines, look back at the original figure. How is your seeing working? Are you looking at the figure or looking with it? Write a few sentences about your experience and share them with a friend. Once you can do this, try to see all of the lines being drawn simultaneously instead of one after another. This would put the throat chakra in line with the function of the heart chakra.

Let's take the idea of looking with something a step further. Pick one of the figures in the print and imagine you are looking out of your eyes at it with a fixed gaze. Then consciously shift to the open gaze and look around the figure rather than focusing on it. Rather than trying to see something, try to just see. Soften the gaze until you are just seeing the print as patterns of light and dark. From this open place softly focus back on the figure you have been working with. Still keeping a kind of middle gaze not too soft and not too fixed, make a conscious decision to slip out of yourself and enter the figure in the print. Breathe your soul out of your eyes and try to feel that a stream of attention from your eyes is reaching out to touch the paper. Then feel your soul enter that stream and go into the figure. Inwardly, feel your body take on the position of the figure as it is depicted. You are now surrendering in your imagination to the inner vision of Rembrandt. How is this different from the earlier exercise when you put your body in the position of the figure? Now it is all happening in your imagination. Try not to linger in the figure or start to fantasize. Be sober and awake, just not in your own body. Practice that as soon as you can experience being with the figure you awaken in the figure and then immediately decide to come back to yourself as the observer. The purpose of this kind of visualization is to see if you can determine when you have surrendered to the figure and when you are the observer. Write about how it feels to shift between participant and observer, subject and object. Share it with a partner. This exercise moves between the throat chakra and the heart chakra.

Now we will take the Rembrandt print into the heart chakra directly. Turn the print upside down, then take tracing paper and trace the *main* motions of the whole composition. You might want to use a soft vine charcoal or conte crayon to record simply the large dark and light spaces in the composition. Or you might want to go freely over lines with flowing movements, creating a web of lines instead of blocks of dark and light. See if you can form an inner picture that is faithful to the feeling of the composition. The feeling of the whole composition arises by what we could call feel-seeing. Imagine that there are small arms coming out of your heart and feel-see the web of lines with those small arms. Run along the lines of the picture or feel the qualities of the light and dark blocks with these arms coming from your heart. Write a sentence or two about this experience.

In this process we have moved through the artistic context of a figure in the print. We have concentrated on the lawfulness of the movements that make up the visual image as a way of entering an imaginal process about the life of the figures. We have looked at the way a line is used by this master and tried to enter into its lawfulness of movement. In this way we are working with the forces of the throat chakra by trying to perceive the lawfulness of the motion of Rembrandt's line. Through the throat we have made an approach to the heart.

In order to move to the next level in the mandala, we can do another exercise in visualization, but this time we will try to enter imaginatively into the "biography" of a figure in the print. Look at the Rembrandt print. Observe a figure and make a list of the elements of its costume. This is the earth mode and fixed vision. Then describe the figure's posture. Can you feel that we have gone into the water mode and are describing a process rather than making a list of objects? Then describe the figures who are interacting with the figure you have been describing. Can you feel that this places us in the air mode, since we are moving out of the figure itself into the context? Then place your own body in the position of the figure in the etching. Write two sentences about this process. How has your viewpoint on the figure changed, or has it? Share this result with a partner. Be sure to notice any insights or feelings that arose in the exercise and mark them with an infinity sign, an exclamation point, or a star.

Through soul breathing, inwardly become the same figure you have been working with imaginatively. When you are surrendered to this figure, look out through its eyes and try to see how the other figures in the group look from this perspective. Now, as the figure, look back at yourself looking at the figure. Then slowly return to yourself and look out of your eyes at the figure in the picture. Write a few sentences about what you felt and share them with a partner.

For a variation in the water mode, in which the question is what is changing, try to ask yourself why the figure in the picture is part of this group. What does he or she expect to change by being here, or what is actually changing in her as she hears the words of

Christ? For the third level, air, try to image that, point for point, what you have just determined that she wishes to change is changed suddenly into the reverse. What would the others she is interacting with do when the figure you are exploring goes through a reversal? When you have found the earth, water, and air levels of the figure in your imagination, write a few sentences. Share your findings with a partner, who can only ask questions. Record any shifts in your understanding that may arise in telling the story or in the questions from your partner.

Many other exercises could be given for the elemental mandala, but these show the gesture of this level of working. The work on the elemental mandala is influencing the brow chakra, in which sense impressions and cognitive insights come together. It is an example of the questions the Confidant Doorkeeper asks about the patterns of awareness already imbedded in habits and physiological syndromes that escape our higher awareness. The exercises given in this chapter are aimed at this exploration of the ways the outer world and the inner world interface with each other in our soul life.

4
WATER/THROAT/
AWARENESS OF AWARENESS

IN THIS CHAPTER WE WILL FOCUS on exercises that utilize the elemental question What is changing? This question points to the problem the alchemist faces in trying to keep a pointed awareness focused on something that is constantly changing from one thing to another. In alchemy a reaction sometimes took months to complete, and the researcher needed to keep one eye continually on what was changing while the other eye was continually trained on what was staying the same. This juggling act exactly describes the requirements of the water level of the alchemical mandala. In the language of Goethe, this is the mood of metamorphosis or morphology. Morphology, the study of metamorphosis, is the science of how form alters as organisms grow and transform.

Morphology is the particular realm of the throat chakra. With this organ of cognition we can distinguish between patterns in the world that are closely connected to their archetypes and those that have lost touch with their archetypes, or animating principles. An organism loses health and resilience when it loses contact with its animating principle or soul force. The throat chakra, the center for the language capacity in human beings, has the task of expressing the ways in which the archetype of a form in nature is manifest in the form. The expressions of a particular language give meaning to the forms found in the soul's environment.

In the second light of the Confidant Doorkeeper, these throat perceptions are brought together in teachings about how it is when we rise from simply being aware to becoming aware of our awareness. This shift brings with it implications of morality not present in the forms of nature. As we develop the second chakra through exercises in the lawfulness of patterns, we gradually come to see that we ourselves produced our flaws and our gifts in a past life, but until now were only aware of the effects of these qualities and did not feel responsible for them. In other words, we were simply aware, and now we become aware that we can become aware.

Since the awareness of awareness hinges upon the cognition of meaning in our perceptions, geometry in its various forms is a very useful training for enhancing these capacities. In the following exercises, we will explore the levels of geometric thinking that approximate the elemental mandala process, the activities of the second chakra itself, and finally some projective geometry exercises that can develop a sense of how a geometric cosmology can be formed.

EXERCISES WITH GEOMETRIC FORMS

Triangle Exercise

The first exercise is a simple one in which we try to hold the image of a triangle in our mind's eye. Write a sentence about what happens when the image begins to fade away or transform. Focus especially on the things you say to yourself when the image fails to perform to your will. A sense of limitation is inherent in this exercise; we realize that we are powerless to hold onto an inner image. This sense of limitation is the very root of the shadow forces in the soul. We could call it the work of the serpent in Paradise. We want to know what we are seeing, that is, we want our eyes to be opened (to control the image). The image is changing and flowing, and we want it to stay the same. This control issue is a narrowing down on the forces of life that wish to flow away so that life can go on. As we concentrate and narrow down on life, anxiety arises. We become anxious that we cannot control things inside our own soul. The etymological root of "anxiety" means "to narrow." It is a fundamental and remarkable thing that when we narrow down on life we become anxious. When we are aware that we are aware, we are inclined to narrow the flow of awareness into "our knowing" instead of just knowing, which is the temptation of Adam and Eve in the Garden. In this exercise we encounter it while just trying to stabilize the inner picture of a triangle. So let's see if there is something we can do about this inner anxiety.

Visualize an equilateral triangle. Try to hold onto the inner image. If you cannot, try to first draw the triangle in the air with your fingertip. After drawing, try to inwardly see your finger drawing the form. Write a sentence about the experience.

If it is still impossible to see the triangle, then imagine a triangle on the ground and walk along the lines of the triangle. If that does not work, try to imagine you are seeing yourself from above with a light on your head and that as you walk the triangle on the ground you are also drawing a triangle in light.

Breathing an Image

If you still can see no inner image, you can try to breathe the image. Try to place the image of the triangle on your forehead and to either see it there or feel it there. Then try to imagine the same thing, but try to find the image as if it were forming slightly behind your eyes, as if it were inscribed on the front of your brain. The imagination is that we are trying to breathe the image more deeply into our organism. Then try to see it in the center of your head. Then try to see it in the back of your head, then on your Adam's apple, then at the base of your throat, then on your lungs where they join in the center of your breastbone, then on your heart. If at any time you get the feeling of being more in contact with the triangle, the feeling that you are seeing it without really seeing it, that is a good place in your body to look for images when you want to visualize something. This exercise could be called finding your "feel-see" spot. When people visualize something, they usually have a habitual place where they go to look for it. There are systems for retrieving images by moving your eyes into particular quadrants, and they do enable you to find mental images, but they are not useful for our purposes because they focus the mind on the technique, which will need to be overcome later when the image needs to be dissolved. It is more hygienic to try to find the place where you experience images out of your own awareness rather than using a retrieval technique. We are after the awareness and not the image or the technique.

After a bit of work with this exercise, plus some drawing or modeling exercises, it is usually possible to find the visualization place after a few weeks. Once you can visualize, the anxiety about narrowing down the life forces gives way to a profound sense of freedom on the inner planes whenever we are visualizing. It may be that we feel the lawfulness of the inner image rather than actually seeing it, which is the reason I call this mood feel-seeing. It is the equivalent of what Rudolf Steiner, in his early work on the senses, called the sense of visualization. He points out that it has nothing to do with the sense of vision other than that we first see sense images through vision. Eventually we must visualize things no one has ever seen, and we must do it exactly. Therefore we do not use techniques but try to find the visualization or feel-seeing place in our organism. In doing this, the old rule holds: practice makes perfect.

Moving an Image

Once we can feel-see or visualize, a more advanced exercise is to visualize two triangles in the form shown in figure 1. Then visualize what would happen if you pushed the top triangle into the bottom triangle so that their tips penetrated each other as in figure 2. Then go on pushing the triangles further into each other (figures 3 and 4) until they push completely through each other and end up looking like figure 5. This exercise strengthens the forces in us that can see lawful patterns in movement. The arising of new forms as a result of the motion of the two triangles is alchemically linked to water consciousness and the question, What is changing?

As a way of stretching the capacity of the inner eye to visual-ize, try doing the initial visualization sequences with a circle. Most people find that the circle is much more difficult to hold in the in-ner eye than the triangle. Work with your fingers and body until the

circle can be held without changing color or dissolving. After a few seconds, any inwardly perceived image, whatever it is, will start to either dissolve or transform into something else. When it happens, it is a sign that the seer has left the realm in which physical forces dominate the inner life and has entered the realm in which life forces dominate the ways inner images arise in the consciousness.

A circle is more difficult to hold in the imagination because it is always shifting in the inner eye. It is round and, as a result, is slippery to hold as an image. A triangle can be seen as a thing, whereas a circle asks us to participate with it even when we are just looking at it. We could say that the form of the triangle is more akin to the way we process sensations in the brow chakra. One side plus one side and one side equals this triangle. This thing that we see is defined completely by its measurements. By contrast, the form of the circle is more like the way we process things in the throat chakra. The circle can never really be completely and thoroughly measured since part of its inherent mystery is the measurement of pi, an irrational or inconceivable number. It cannot be measured; it can only be inferred ideationally. This transcendent quality of the circle makes it difficult to hold inwardly. There is something irrational about a circle. We find it difficult to work with the circle in the brow chakra, but it comes into its own in the throat chakra. In general, geometric visualizations that metamorphose lawfully from one stage to another help the throat chakra to develop. The following circle exercises can be used to limber up the throat chakra for more involved geometric exercises.

The Intent to See

The ability to see inward pictures has a lot to do with the intent to see them. Before trying to visualize a circle, sit quietly for a few moments and intend that you are going to see the circle. Bring to mind the feeling that you know or feel that the circle will appear in your consciousness. We most often see the intent before we see the circle, just as weight lifters or Olympic divers see themselves lifting the weight or doing a particular move before they actually try it. Intending to see makes the organism aware that something is about to happen. Continue intending the circle until you sense it somewhere in your sphere of awareness.

As we did with the triangle, imagine a circle, and if it starts to move or dissolve, reestablish it by drawing it in the air in front of you. If you can imagine the circle but it keeps fading away, try to visualize the following. First intend the circle. Then, imagine that when you are drawing the circle you see your hand drawing. Then try to hold the inner image. When the image starts to fade, imagine that the inner hand that drew it is now erasing it. See the circle being erased in the opposite direction to which it was drawn. After it is completely erased, intend to see the circle and then redraw it.

After the imaginative exercise, get a large sheet of drawing paper and, drawing with a pencil, cover it with circles of all sizes. After drawing, intend to see the circle and then visualize a circle. With this technique you should sooner or later be able to stay in the circle for a minute or two. This means fading with it and reestablishing it as it pulsates. The inner image is oscillating with the pulsation of your cerebrospinal fluid. If you hold your breath, you will most often find that the inner image stabilizes. When you breathe, your spinal fluid circulates and the inner images flow away with the current. In this exercise we learn to anticipate this flowing away of the image and try to work consciously into the rhythm of the fading and reestablishing of the image. An exercise like this, preceded by a conscious period of intent, strengthens our capacity to visualize.

Practice intending the circle and then breathing the image deeper and placing it at various places within your body. Focus your attention on where the image is stabilized. Pay attention to the forehead area, the back of the head, and the throat. Somewhere in this region you should find that the image will be stabilized. Being stabilized means that you feel you are in contact with or can feel the image even though you may not necessarily be able to see a clear image inwardly. This experience can be illustrated by recalling a time when you and a friend were trying to bring to mind a mutual acquaintance but neither of you could remember the name. Both of you might say a number of names that sound like the person's name, but none of them would be right. You knew you would know the correct name when someone said it, but neither of you could recall the name itself. Recalling the name itself would be equivalent to actually seeing an inner picture. The recognition that the other names were incorrect is equivalent to the experience of feeling an image without seeing it. We could call this capacity feel-seeing. In feel-seeing you might not actually see the image inwardly but you are in contact with it enough to select it from a series of similar images. If you practice feel-seeing often enough, the actual seeing of an inner image can be developed.

A simple word game illustrates this unusual condition in which we both know and do not know simultaneously. Look at the following sequences of letters and see if you can make sense out of them.

MRSNAKES
OARNUT
OSAR2
UCMEDBDIZ
LIB
MRSNAKES

A rebus like this is completely obscure to our inner sense of meaning. It appears to be a nonsense pattern since we cannot use the normal verbal clues to understand the wordlike nature of the text. The letters are recognizable but the meaning is not. It is similar to a text written in a Romance language we do not speak; we recognize the letters but not the words. When we are trying to visualize an inner picture, we may even be able to recite a whole list of remembered details about the object but still be unable to form an inner picture. The movements we have to make to understand the nonsense words above require us to drop any associative patterns we have concerning these letters and allow a soft-focus capacity for synthesis and judgment to come forward to help draw out the meaning. The letters above are a dialogue in colloquial English between two country boys about snakes, and they are best recognized when read out loud. The dialogue sounds like this when it is written out in colloquial English:

'Em are snakes.

Oh 'ey are not.

Oh 'es 'ey are too. You see 'em eddy beedy eyes?

'El ah be. 'Em are snakes.

When the context and the sounds are available, the images gel into meaning structures. We have a similar experience when a list of remembered qualities of an observed object suddenly form inwardly into a picture of the object.

The inner reproduction of an exact image is equivalent to the earth level in the elemental mandala. The exercise of transforming one image into another image, as we did above in forming the Star of David by moving two triangles, is equivalent to the water level. The brow chakra, being connected to the element of earth, is active when we form an inner image of a triangle or circle that we just saw in the world. The sense impression of the geometric form is linked through the willful creation of an exact inner image to the concept of the geometric form. This activity is moved to the throat chakra when some sort of meaning or structure is present for the soul to move within. The motion of the soul moving through an idea or the sequence of an inner image is the special realm of the throat chakra. In general, the throat chakra is most benefited by practicing the visualization of geometric sequences of forms, because geometrical transformations must proceed according to prescribed or "mean-ingful" sequences. The imaginative force of the idea unfolding in a lawful way is very healing to the throat chakra and gives the soul the experience that the world is lawful and that it can learn to trust the images living within it. This point is very important in the unfold-ing of seership.

The throat chakra is, in effect, a gate for what is known in eso-teric language as the descent of the Holy Spirit. The brow chakra has the potential for the seer to realize ultimately, "I Am That." This realization is attained by the seer's penetrating into the deepest level of existence. Paradoxically, the brow chakra is involved in the redemption of the sense life, a great Rosicrucian mystery that will be addressed more fully later. When the student/alchemist becomes a seer, the brow chakra awakens to the idea that "everything that was made, was made." This awakening allows the seeker to begin to be a seer. The Holy Spirit first reveals what was made but not the making nor the Maker. It is for the aspirant to strive to work first toward the making and then to identify and subsequently become one with the Maker.

Therefore, in the brow chakra the Holy Spirit simply helps the seeker see the field of activity of cosmic creative beings. In the throat chakra, the Holy Spirit helps the seeker see the lawfulness of the coming into being of the imaginations of those beings. The Holy Spirit must then descend into the heart chakra, where the seeker/seer learns to form inner pictures that are in harmony with the lawfulness of the archetypal movements of the cosmic creative beings.

VISUALIZING GEOMETRIC TRANSFORMATION

Our study of geometry can be taken to a higher level where the meaning of a geometric transformation sets the stage for entering the heart chakra. To do this work, it is necessary to form exact inner pictures of geometric forms that go through metamorphoses resulting in the forms turning into the opposite conditions. The union of opposites and the condition of simultaneity is the particular domain of the heart chakra.

The set of geometric solids known as the Platonic forms can be used to visualize systems in reciprocation. In the first exercise, we will work with a relationship known as the cube/octahedron. Imagine a sphere that is inside a cube. Then imagine these two forms inside a larger sphere. The result is figure 6.

The outer sphere touches the points of the cube in eight places. The inner sphere touches the cube in the very center of each side. If we shrink the outer sphere so that the places where the cube touches it pass through each of the eight points, four triangles will be formed just below each point, as illustrated in figure 7. If we continue to shrink the outer sphere, these triangles will grow larger, as illustrated

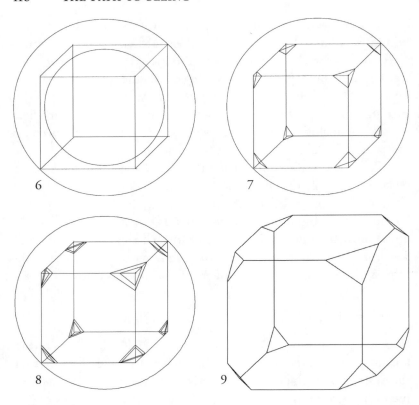

in figure 8. In this figure a larger triangle is seen inside the original smaller one. These are formed as the outer sphere continues to shrink around the cube. When the shrinking continues, the cube begins to alter in its form.

In figure 9, larger triangular planes move through the points on the cube along lines equally spaced from each other, each passing through the central point of the sphere. All of the triangular planes are equidistant from each other and are moving along the lines from the center as planes perpendicular to the lines from the center.

In figure 10, we see that the movement of the planes of the triangles has radically altered the form of the cube. It now has eight triangles that have met each other at their points. Squares have formed between the triangles, and the corners of the cube are now planes in the form of triangles.

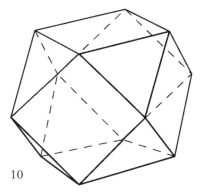

10

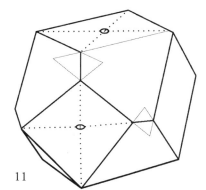

11

In figure 11, after the triangles have met at their corners
they continue to move through
each other at their points, and
a ridge forms that starts to
move toward the center of each
square. The triangles passing
through each other begin to
distort and lose their shapes as
the ridges form. In the figure,
the interpenetrating triangles
are depicted in pale lines and

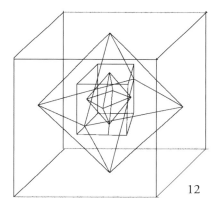

12

the ridges are depicted in dark lines. As the triangles lose their shapes,
the squares are getting smaller. The ridges from the interpenetrating
triangles eventually meet in the centers of the squares (ovals in the
centers of crossing dotted lines) as the point of a new form. In this
process the original points of the cube become the planes of the new
form, and the planes of the original cube become the points of the
new form. The new form has eight triangular surfaces and six points
where the original cube had six surfaces and eight points. The cube
has transformed into its polar form, the octahedron.

In figure 12, the cube now has an octahedron suspended inside
it. The points of the octahedron touch a sphere that fits just inside
the cube. The center of each side of the cube touches the surface of
the inner sphere. Inside that octahedron is another cube. A sphere

just inside the octahedron would touch the center of each surface of the octahedron in the center of each plane. The cube and the octahedron are reciprocals of each other, and to imagine this process in geometry strengthens the throat chakra to the degree that it begins to provide access to the heart chakra. The rigor of this type of inner visualization process is invaluable to the development of imaginative perception.

AWARENESS OF AWARENESS

The second light of the teachings of the Confidant Doorkeeper of the threshold is awareness of awareness. This teaching is aimed at the task of human beings in becoming aware that they are capable of becoming aware of much more than they might think. In the first light, the Confidant Doorkeeper teaches that awareness is the backdrop behind both the sense world and the inner world of the concept. In the second light, this awareness is enlarged to include the cosmological significance of awareness for the human being. The throat chakra searches the world for meaning, structures that are undergoing metamorphoses. The second light teaches us that metamorphosis, or soul awareness, is a particular state of the more general awareness conditions found in the world. We could say that the throat chakra specializes in finding objective pictures. To take the geometric work that especially influences the throat chakra into the realm of the Confidant Doorkeeper, it is useful to push the soul into a state in which core beliefs come to the fore so that we can become aware of our awareness. A good exercise for this is the field of triangleness exercise.

Take a piece of paper about three by five inches (an index card is perfect), and with a sharp utility knife cut a triangle of any proportion out of the center. On a blackboard or a piece of paper, draw an equilateral triangle. Stand about ten feet away from the blackboard and sight through the triangular hole in the index card. The object of this exercise is to exactly line up the sides of the triangular hole with the sides of the equilateral triangle on the board. The index card must be held perpendicular to your line of sight; turning the card is not allowed. It is fun to try this with a group of friends. Most people will declare that it is impossible, only to find out they have forgotten that they themselves are free to move, even if the card is not. When they move to a particular place in the room, they can experience that the angle allows the triangle on the board to line up exactly with the sides of the triangular hole in the card. The realization that something is possible which we once thought was impossible is a great lesson in awareness of awareness. But this can be taken further geometrically.

In figure 13, both A and B are triangles. At first sight this seems impossible. For the brow chakra this is the case, but for the brow chakra what we see and the concept of what we see can sometimes be deceiving. In order to see these two figures, we must shift our consciousness into the throat chakra and seek to understand the process by which each of these two figures can be thought of as a triangle.

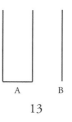

In example A, the process by which the drawing can be considered a triangle begins with an equilateral triangle, shown on the left in figure 14. Starting on the left, we see the triangle ABC. Next, point C is moved away from the base line AB. The lines CA and

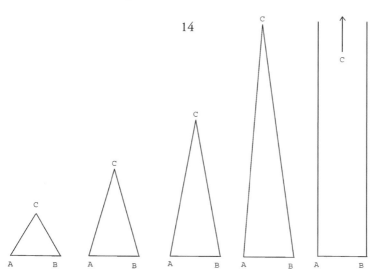

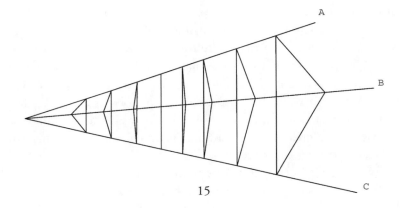

15

CB rotate, with points A and B as pivots, as point C moves away. As C gets further away, the lines rotate more until point C moves out to the infinitely distant. If we can imagine the two lines being moved to the infinite distance by point C, we see that the two lines will become parallel when the point reaches infinity. Drawing A in figure 13 is a triangle in which one point lies in the infinitely distant plane. Drawing B represents a different aspect of these thoughts about geometric shapes moving to the infinite.

In figure 15, the three lines A, B, and C meet in a common point. We begin the movement with the triangle on the left, which has a vertex on each of these lines. As we move from left to right the triangles continue to have the same configuration, but they become more distorted, until in the center of the movement the triangle ABC is seen on its "side." The triangles on the right of this central triangle still have their vertices on the three lines, but they rotate on line AC as point B moves from the left side to the right side of line AC. As a result, the central line is a triangle when seen in the context of rotational motion of the whole system of forms. The apparent vertical line (example B) in figure 13 is seen as a triangle when viewed in the context of movement of the whole.

This geometry moves us through the throat chakra into the second light of the Confidant Doorkeeper. To see these forms we must become aware of our awareness and transcend sense impression and memory pictures to enter an archetypal movement geometrically.

5

AIR/HEART/
AWARENESS OF BEING

IN THIS CHAPTER WE WILL LOOK at how the element of air gradually becomes perceptible to the seer as the heart chakra develops into an organ of cognition. The tasks of seership become more refined and much more exacting when we work within the air element. In air, the seer moves away from the lower elements and crosses the boundary into the soul/spiritual. The imaginations so carefully constructed in the lower elements are now discarded in favor of a more tenuous and ephemeral seeing. The sense/concept dualities and the perceptible images of geometry fall away in the silent and mysterious element of air as the seer seeks to enlist the capacities of the heart itself in order to see.

In the elemental mandala the air level requires that a system which has been developing in a certain direction move into the stage of reversal. Alchemically this means that a process reaches its ultimate state and goes into a reaction to the previous movement. A growing plant stops forming leaves and instead sends out flowers. The emergence of flowers represents a reversal in the growth processes of the plant and the commencement of the processes linked to reproduction. The plant is now ready for a higher stage of development. This is the analog to human beings who reach the air stage in their inner life; a flowering takes place in which the soul is preparing to meet the spirit.

On the elemental level, the preparatory study for the perception of the air stage is the study of growth and decay processes in nature. Alchemically, the growth process is linked to the idea of *solve*, or dissolving. This may seem strange, but for an organism to grow the materials that will build up the body must first go into a solution (*solve*) form so that assimilation can take place. Since we are talking about the formation of exact inner pictures leading to seership, it is useful to see these ideas not as fixed things but as processes. The growth process begins by *solve* and accelerates through more and more assimilation. Then, when growth is rampant, the opposite process of *coagula* starts, and the swelling form begins to hypertrophy. This *solve* to *coagula* process is growth. The opposite process starts with a form that is already in existence and continues to be more formed. As the forming process reaches a maximum, the *coagula* forces cause a rigor mortis to set in with its accompanying rigidifying, mortification, and then decay. The decay process is once more in the realm of *solve* as the form once again dissolves into nature. Alchemically, the growth process and the decay process are in constant reciprocation in living forms. We will look at some plant forms as a way of working on the elemental level of air. But before we do, a simple exercise of awareness can help in developing a sense of the polarity of growth and decay or *solve* and *coagula*.

Let's do an exercise we could call virtual aspirin. Some evening, take an hour or so and lie down on your back. Close your eyes and let your mind travel through your body searching for a muscle group that is under tension. A particular muscle group probably comes to mind. Allow your mind to enter the muscles and just listen quietly for a moment. Sense the tension in the muscles. This tension is *coagula*. Imagine there are two hands hovering above the tense muscles. Imagine that there are warm pulses coming from the hands and that the tension is leaving your body and going up into the warm hands. Then relax the muscles under the two hands. You may feel that the tension leaves temporarily but then returns. That is fine. Just repeat the exercise by replacing the tension with warmth and the sense that the muscles are dissolving into fluid. It may take two or three passes of the warm spiritual hands to allow the muscle to really dissolve.

Usually when it does, a big yawn or stretch, often accompanied with tears from your eyes, will let you know that *coagula* has been replaced by *solve*. Contemplate the two polarities and how they feel to you. Sense the coagulating forces in the tension. This tension is actually our sense of strength. We need it to get through the day. But we also need to balance it with the *solve* of dissolving forces in order to nourish and heal the effects of the tension.

SEEING INTO THE GROWTH OF PLANTS

In general, plants are representatives of forces of growth. They are spontaneous growers when supplied with the proper environment. The growth process in plants is balanced by the processes of form and order. Order limits growth; form damps down rampant growth. Growth comes from the forces of shadow in the plant. For a plant, the shadow force is the dissolving capacity of the minerals in the soil solution, which comes from the earth and water. The ordering or forming forces limit the growth and give it a particular form. These forces come from the light. Plants grown in dark, damp soil conditions lack form and structure. Plants grown in dry and mineralized soil grow hard and formed with many spikes; there growth is limited by the light and they form woody or resinous outer layers.

Take some modeling wax or clay and make a model of a cactus covered with spines. Try to enter into the feeling of how it is to make all of the spines. Write a few sentences about this feeling. Then take some more modeling wax and make a model of a spinach leaf or a cabbage or a frond of kelp. Try to feel the fluid dissolving forces of these plants and write a sentence about the feeling. Then write a sentence or two about the difference between these two kinds of plants. The next series of exercises is designed to develop the imaginative capacity to see into the growth of plants.

Exercise 1

This exercise helps us understand the basic forces for the forms in a plant shoot. Make three small identical cones in wax. Then make a flat plane and a small sphere. Try to balance the plane on the flat end of one of the cones. Q.: How many degrees of freedom does it have? A.: One. It can rotate in one plane.

Try to balance the plane on the tip of one cone. Q.: How many degrees of freedom does it have? A.: There are an infinite number of rotating planes in a point.

Then try to balance the plane on the tip of two cones. Q.: How many degrees of freedom does it have? A.: One degree of freedom, but an infinite number of planes can rotate in a line.

Then balance the plane on the three cones. Q.: How many degrees of freedom does it have? A.: One; it can rotate in the plane that the points of the three cones have in common.

These are analogs of the forces that can be seen in the next modeling sessions. Try to remember these exercises when you are looking at a plant and see if you can identify them in the forms.

Exercise 2

In most constructions three geometric forms appear in sequence: the point, which is usually first; then the line, which emerges from a point; and then a series of lines, which make a plane. The sequence is usually point to line to plane. Make a wax model of what you think the shoot of a plant looks like. Look for sequences of point to line to plane. Work in groups of three persons. After modeling the shoots, work in the group to arrange them into the correct order for a plant. Which shoot goes on top, which one on the bottom, and which one in the middle? Discuss the correct order with your friends, and then present your "plant" to others with your explanations. Later, observe a plant shoot in nature.

Determine in a thought experiment how many planes can be tangent to the surface of a sphere. Try to visualize a sphere of infinite dimension and recall from the work on the Platonic forms how the infinitely distant plane is present when a line goes to the infinite. If there are an infinity of lines through the center point, and each has a plane at its infinite extension in the infinitely distant, how will the infinitely distant sphere appear and how many degrees of freedom will each tangent plane have? The forces of growth come from the infinitely distant and return there when the plant "dies." In reality the plant does not die, since its genetically identical brethren are still here on Earth. The plant that appears to our senses is not the "real" plant. The real plant is an activity that leaves the sensible plant before our eyes like the wake following a passing ship or a sandbar forming in a river. The sensible body of the plant is the sandbar; the true plant is a process passing like the force of the river. The plant falls out of solution and into form under the influence of light. The light comes from the starry realm in the infinitely distant.

Exercise 3

Choose two different leaves from two different plants. Make a model of one of the leaves in wax. Work according to the model of point to line to plane. Try to duplicate not the outer form of the leaf but the actual process by which the leaf has grown. Form an inner picture of how you think the leaf grew out of the stem, and try to describe this in writing. Write a sentence or two about what you considered to be the difficult part to imagine or to duplicate in wax in this process.

Exercise 4

Based on these ideas, go out and pick a leaf from a branch, tying a piece of string to mark the branch so that you can find it easily again. Make a model of the leaf in wax. Then try to imagine what the leaf that was two below your leaf and the one that was two above it would look like. Make a wax leaf as a model of either one of these leaves. Then go back to the plant from which you took the leaf and pick the whole shoot with the rest of the leaves. Compare their forms to what you thought they would look like. Write a few sentences about any surprises and what you think you saw in the leaves when you went out to them. Before going to sleep that night, form the sequence of the leaves in your imagination and grow them forward and backward in your mind's eye.

Exercise 5

Plant growth is divided into two distinct phases, the early one governed more by *solve* and the later one more by *coagula*. Take some modeling wax and make a model of the root of an annual flowering plant. Then make a model of a leafy shoot of the same plant and then a model of the flower of the same plant. Write a sentence or two about the feelings and thoughts that came to you during the process of modeling. Then dry the parts of the plant thoroughly. When there is absolutely no moisture left in the plant tissues (be careful to fully dry the root), put the dried root on a brick and, using a propane torch, try to set the dried root on fire. Do the same with the other dried parts, then write a few sentences about the process. Which burns brighter, the root or the flower? Which produces more smoke or ash? When you are done, compare the two paragraphs. Try to determine which part was more *solve* and which more *coagula*. In your thinking try to place the plant parts on an elemental mandala of earth, water, air, and fire.

Exercise 6

Inwardly form a picture of the flowering plant germinating from a seed and growing, leaf after leaf, up to the formation of the flower. If you miss any step in your mind's eye, observe the step carefully and then imagine it. Then try to imagine the steps backward as if the plant were growing down and not up, as if it were contracting once again into its root. Work until you can reproduce the image of the plant, from seed to calyx in an exact way. Then do a similar exercise with the flower that emerges from the green shoot. Build up the sequences of the flowering parts and the growth of the stamens through to the setting of the seed and the swelling and ultimate shriveling of the ovary. Work to make the image of the flower grow in your imagination. When you can imagine the two sequences, draw a sketch of the movements of each. Don't worry about details; just make a sketch, concentrating not on details but on where there are forces of *solve* and where there are forces of *coagula*. Try to feel where the plant is dissolving and where it is forming. Label the drawings *solve* or *coagula*, and share them with another person.

These exercises are useful for developing a sense for the air level in the elemental mandala because they involve the inner perception of images of natural forms that are in the process of reversing. The

plant often reveals reversals between the forms in the lower vegeta-
tive growth cycles and the reproductive organ forms in the flowering
cycle. When we can inwardly imagine these processes as pictures,
our soul forces are being trained to withstand the processes of reversal in our own lives. These practices are in line with the ancient
mantra of Hermes Trismegistus, "As above, so below; as below, so
above." Reversals always include the opposites united in polarity,
the signature of the air stage.

Another exercise with the processes in nature can also put us in
contact with the elemental level of air. Watch a cloud on the horizon
long enough so that you can tell whether it is growing horizontally or vertically. This exercise is subtle and demanding, because we
must keep our attention focused over a longer period of time than is
usual in life. This exercise slows the mind and helps it to become ac-
customed to the timeframes of spiritual research, where a question
can be carried openly for years without any answer. Once again the
qualities of the air level of the alchemical mandala are being developed. In reversal we move into a timeless space on the other side of
the threshold, and we need organs of cognition that can function in
these immense timeless experiences without fear or anxiety.

The air level of the elemental mandala introduces the soul to the
task of crossing the threshold. We could say that students approaching this level of work are engaged in retrieval of their own souls. The
student/seer must enter this work of crossing the air threshold with
a calm heart or else the forces there will obliterate and inundate the
soul with tremendous fear and loathing for journeying further along
the path toward self-realization.

THE HEART CHAKRA

For the seer, the heart chakra is a sublime and yet difficult area on
which to work. There are so many levels to this organ of cognition
that it is not easy to tell where you are in the work. Rudolf Steiner
gave some indications about this enigmatic chakra that will serve
as the basis for the following exercises. There are three levels of development in the heart chakra: the heart eye, the soul eye, and the

spirit eye. In the heart eye and the soul eye we are working directly on the organ. In the spirit eye we are working more on the relationship between the heart chakra and the spleen chakra. The descriptions and exercises for the spirit eye will therefore be given in the next chapter, on the spleen chakra.

Green/Magenta Exercise

The heart chakra is an area rich with currents of blood that circulate throughout the body. To work consciously into these currents is the fundamental approach to transforming this chakra. Some first steps can be made by working with the two polar colors of magenta and green. The symbology of these colors can be found at the end of this chapter. Imagine that your heart area is surrounded by a sphere the color of an emerald. Then imagine this green sphere is surrounded by another, larger sphere the magenta color of a ruby. Try to see both of the spheres simultaneously. Some people can do this better by actually seeing themselves from the outside looking at the spheres as if they were looking at someone else. Others can best get this feeling when they imagine themselves in the center of the two spheres. Use whatever way works for you. Once the two spheres are established, imagine that the outer magenta sphere starts to contract and the inner green sphere starts to expand. When the two colored spheres meet they turn a cool grayish blue. Then the shrinking magenta sphere is seen around the heart area and the larger green sphere is outside. This is a very peaceful exercise that takes great concentration but yields great stability for the inner vision.

Soul Breathing: The Arms of the Heart

The magenta/green exercise is a form of soul breathing. Soul breathing is a way of developing capacities in the heart chakra. Simple exercises in soul breathing can be found in the earth/brow/awareness chapter. Once we can choose the gaze with some capacity for understanding, we can morph that capacity into the next level, the development of the arms of the heart. The heart currents are similar to the currents of vision. They are subtle, but once identified they are unmistakable. Using an imagination similar to the earlier one of hands coming out of the eyes, we can imagine that there are fine arms coming out of the heart, with which we can feel the currents of the spiritual atmosphere. With practice this imagination becomes a direct experience.

The arms and the circulation of blood in them are intimately linked to the heart. Each artery is connected to a vein through a system of capillaries. This means that in the arm the blood courses through a series of loops. Esoterically, looping motions are considered to be an image of the pattern that energetically links the motion of the planets and the fixed stars. The True Human living in the motions of the blood uses these motions to express inwardly perceived living pictures. In everyday life we can see some of this expressive activity of the arms of the heart when someone is speaking. As the heart is moved to express something of a feeling nature, the arms and hands naturally move in response to the feelings and concepts being expressed. It is the True Human living in the movements of the blood in the arms and hands that is active in depicting the forces involved in what the soul is trying to express. The arms of the heart are making movement pictures of what is being expressed.

With practice imagining the currents streaming out of the heart and into the hands, a stage is reached where it is possible to see examples of this living picture imagination when others speak. With further practice it is possible to realize that these motions make up a universal language of feelings and will impulses that are the matrix of all form. Using the arms of the heart consciously to explore this living picture language, the Witness eventually becomes capable of discerning the more intimate ideas and experiences that the True Human is constantly transmitting to the heart across the threshold between this world and the next. The True Human is verblike. It lives as a creative movement potential among other creative movement makers in the spiritual world. There are no things in the realm of the dead, only doings and doers who are identified with their doing. The True Human Being is an invisible spiritual will force that is constantly active, making movement patterns in the spirit. When this active being is absent from the physical body in sleep or later in death, we see revealed a fundamental reality about human beings.

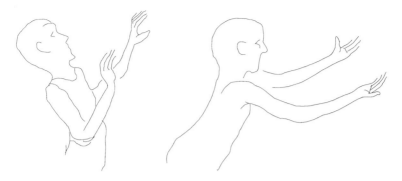

The active presence of the True Human in the blood, especially the blood of the arms and hands which has such an intimate relationship to the heart, can be developed into an organ of cognition of the activity of the spirit realm and the activities of the so-called dead. A basic form of this work can be experienced in the next exercise.

In this training the circulation of blood in the limbs is used as an organ of perception for the subtle motions the movements of the planets impress upon the formal becomings in the sensible world. That is, the patterns of blood in the limbs can be used to inform us of the lawfulness or unlawfulness of things that are part of our sense perception. Suppose that when we experience the color red our hands and arms express how the red is impacting the blood. If we were suddenly put into a searing red room, we might make a gesture that looks like the one shown in the left figure above. The impulse would be to protect ourselves, and the blood in our arms would rise up as we put our hands between us and the advancing red. The opposite gesture would occur if we were suddenly put into a radiant blue room. The blood in our hands and eyes would sympathize with our gaze following the retreating blue to the infinite distances by making a gesture of soul yearning (right figure). In this practice the motions of the blood in the organs are used as a clairvoyant tool for fine perceptions of motion. Through this type of work we can arrive at an objective experience that red advances on us and blue retreats into the background. These are archetypal movements of the colors, which the blood perceives by sympathizing with the motions the colors are enacting. To a seer these concepts and practices compose what Goethe called the attainment of the subjective/objective. That is, we use our subjective experience to discern an objective reality. In a more feeling way, we could call this capacity to use our own sense activity objectively heartfelt thinking.

Heartfelt Thinking

Heartfelt thinking is the dynamic basis for modern seership. This state needs to be cultivated in as many ways as possible, by working to make our subjective and sensory experiences objective in ourselves. This results in a new openness for life, a new enthusiasm and confidence that our life has a larger meaning. It is developed by being involved in activities in which we can experience that something progresses our work besides our own effort. When we plant a seed in the ground and later a plant emerges from the seed without our own effort, we develop a new confidence and enthusiasm for life. Similarly, when we give ourselves research questions and then watch as our thinking, over time, gradually ripens to deeper insights, we are developing the same confidence in life.

The pursuit of heartfelt thinking requires that we start new things every day and let them run on in our lives and grow into things we never could have predicted. Our instincts deny that there is hope for the future. They keep us chained to past patterns of behavior. When we start to work on the subjective patternings of instinct and transform them alchemically into objective experiences, we enter the portal of the seer and cross the threshold between the world of the senses and the world of the spirit. The organ of cognition in which this transformation reaches a peak is the heart chakra. With it we perceive the spiritual colors of the aura and the creative activity of the beings that are the origin of the forms of nature. Through work on the heart chakra, we also eventually begin to develop insights into the character of others. We not only perceive lawful motion in the forms of the world with the heart chakra, but we also can create or form objective pictures that can influence those forms. A great mystery for the future development of human beings lies in heartfelt thinking. We will look at this aspect of the heart chakra when we move to the third light of the Confidant Doorkeeper. The following is another set of exercises using the idea of the periphery and the center, which can form the basis for a rational yet imaginative path of development of heartfelt thinking.

Periphery/Center Exercises: The Circle of Being

The first exercise can help to eventually develop a sense of the continuity of consciousness across the threshold to the next world. It begins with the inner imagination that we are in our bodies looking out at a starry sky. We imagine that our soul is expanding out of our body and moving outward toward the stars. It is expanding in a circle; that is, we try to imagine that when our soul leaves our body it spreads out to the right, left, front, and back of our body in a circle. The first part of the exercise involves seeing the circle spreading out right and left, front and back from our position. This is a difficult step and brings with it some fairly unpleasant experiences, as if we were seeing ourselves diffuse into a fog or mistlike condition. The mistlike form of our consciousness threatens the habitual feelings of integrity of the body. As we expand out of this habitual mode of consciousness into a more expanded and cosmic existence, a strong element of anxiety arises in our heart. The part of the soul connected most intimately with the body will struggle to maintain the perspective in which we are the center of concentric circles of relationships. We can use this feeling as a safeguard against the anxiety of nonexistence. We can imagine ourselves occupying a place on a circle composed of many beings that have the task of maintaining the universe. Try to see the circle and feel the immensity of it. It takes strong spiritual will to maintain the imagination that we can expand our awareness around the circumference of a vast circle composed of many great and creative beings.

Once we can maintain this imagination even a little, it is possible to feel a complete sense of silence and peace while our consciousness is expanded and traveling along the circle. While waiting in silence on the circle, direct your attention to the center. Consciously place an image of your own body waiting at the center for you to come back to it. This thought usually brings us back right into our bodies, sometimes with a thud. Practice gliding or hovering back into your body while simultaneously trying to maintain the integrity of your place on the circle in your consciousness. It helps to see your body in the center as an axis or hub of the circle. In the place where we exist as a True Human, we are part of a grand circle of being.

Once the imagination of yourself extended along the periphery of the vast circle of being can be maintained, try to hold onto the sense of having a body in the center of the circle while simultaneously imagining your soul is extended along the periphery. Alternate this exercise with the imagination that you are in the center looking at yourself as you travel the circumference of the circle of being.

The Heart Eye

The imaginative exercises that influence the heart chakra are of two kinds. The first level of seeing is what Rudolf Steiner calls the heart eye. The heart eye sees the motions of the planets manifest in the sense world. Plants appear as melodies in space and skeletons are like great symphonic themes in which chords and moods akin to soul feelings appear in the soul along with the sense activity of seeing the objects. A simple exercise can illustrate this difficult concept.

Pick the leaf of a dandelion and draw it as exactly as possible. Try especially to render the details of the leaf tip. When the outline is finished, continue the lines of the curves of the leaf out into space and let the lines cross each other in the space around the leaf. The drawing might look like the one below. When it is complete, make it again, this time with your finger in space, trying to imagine the proper forms. Try to picture that the loops of the drawing you are

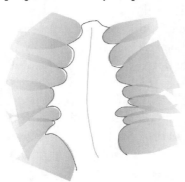 making in space could somehow be fixed, as if you were using a flashlight to draw and your markings in space were being recorded on a photographic film as light tracings. When you have completed this, try to imagine as exactly as possible the patterns of motion you have been drawing. When you can clearly see the movements, imagine that you

are drawing the leaf on the back of your tongue. When you finish doing that, see if any sensation arises. Many people can experience a distinct bitterness on their tongue after putting the imagination on it. Somehow the motions of the form seem to stimulate a particular sensation of taste even though no substance is present. As a final imaginative exercise, find a picture of the loops of the planet Jupiter in an astronomy book and compare these motions with the forms in the drawing you just made of the dandelion leaf. See if somehow a subtle feeling of relationship arises.

This type of relationship is difficult to prove scientifically but needs to be addressed in pursuing the seership of the heart. Ordinary ideas about the laws of nature or science can be understood by the intellect through the brow and throat chakras, but more intimate and subtle ideas about the realm beyond the threshold need to be understood as movements in will of the creative hierarchies. The creative ideas of will cannot be understood by causality. The rules for the coming into being of the universe include every condition and its opposite as a mutually existing reciprocating polarity. To understand mutually reciprocating polarities we must think with a simultaneous rather than an analytical consciousness. For the heart to see, it must give up the idea that there are fixed logical answers to questions here on Earth. In the spirit, all things include their opposites in a paradoxical relationship. The heart must deal with these paradoxes to see or think in a feeling way. The training of the heart focuses on the perception of patterns that are constantly changing and morphing into other patterns. The most fundamental of these is the relationship between center and periphery. This imagination will be the central theme for the following exercises of the heart.

Turning the Life Body

Work with the geometric imagination of periphery and center for a while to establish a rhythm of soul breathing. When the mind is settled, imagine that a current of warmth starts from the heart and moves upward to the shoulders, then back to the heart. Do not try to force the current into the heart; this may cause congestion. Simply bring the current back into the vicinity of the heart or, more precisely, into the center of the chest around the sternum. This is the site of the life of the heart that is focused in the cardiac plexus of the sympathetic nervous system. We will practice breathing warmth from this center out into the arms and hands. Imagine a current of warmth from the heart center going out in an arc to the shoulders and then back into the center of the sternum. Then send a current out into the upper arm and back, then to the lower arm and back, and finally to the hands and back. Then rest and let the currents take their own course. There is often a sense that the arms and hands are warmer than usual. This is the first exercise. In the second level, imagine that when the warmth gets to the arm or hand it travels from the center of the limb to the periphery of the skin. This should enhance the feeling of warmth in the organ and a sense of the circulation in the limb. Over time the experience of warmth will grow.

The next exercise uses the control of the currents of warmth and circulation in the arms and hands. Establish soul breathing and then bring consciousness into the arms of the heart. Imagine that you are exiting through the top of your head and leaving your body below by spreading out your heart's arms and rising as if you were flying. Stay in contact with your day-awake consciousness by dipping back into your physical body in a rhythm. If anxiety develops, it means that you need to work on a more fundamental soul level by strengthening your capacity for imagination, or it may mean that some study or self-reflection is necessary before you can live with the experience of not identifying so much with a physical body. The exercises given previously in this handbook may be of use in stabilizing your emotions in this regard. Undue anxiety that cannot be soothed indicates that you should not proceed with this imagination. If the anxiety can be faced and soothed, it is possible to stabilize the soul forces using the arms of the heart like rudders or joysticks.

We now want to turn our body of life forces with the arms of the heart. The body of life forces has the ideal relationship to the horizon when the physical body is facing east. In that position the life body is in line with the harmonizing and strengthening currents flowing from north to south in the life body of the Earth. It may be that the position of your physical body during the exercise is not facing east. You may, for instance, be lying down. In that case you need to imaginatively turn your life body to face east. This turning is most easily accomplished by exiting through the top of your head in your imagination and spreading out the arms of the heart. Intend that the currents in your heart's arms stabilize your life body, and then, as if you were steering a sled or skiing a turn, intend that your life body rotate counterclockwise until it is facing east. Turning clockwise usually results in a rapid snapping back of the life body into the position of the physical body, in which case you will be rudely jolted into day-awake consciousness. Turning counterclockwise allows the arms of the heart to turn the life body and stabilize it in the north/south currents of the life body of the Earth.

Allow the Earth currents to stream through your arms and heart area for a short time, then return to your physical consciousness and consciously slip back into the physical body. When fully in, feel yourself touching the chair or the floor or the bed. The touching in at the end of the exercise is very important, as is the need to always maintain a gentle "breathing" rhythm in the soul between the *solve* state outside of the body and the *coagula* state within the physical body. Any loss of contact with the physical body results either in effects of astral projection or in a sudden snapping back into the physical. Astral projection can lead to severe soul inflation and emotional disturbance. Projection of the life body into the astral realm is not what this exercise is about. We are simply trying to develop the heart so that eventually we will be able to leave our own body and wake up in another person as a means to understanding their path through life. Any joyriding or anxiety diminishes the sense of sobriety needed when crossing the threshold and meeting the Confidant Doorkeeper. In working with the heart chakra, the technique of turning the life body with the arms of the heart is extremely useful for protection and further development of the right capacities.

Further Heartfelt Exercise: The Angel of the Spiritual Sun
When the feeling for the perception of the movements is a clear experience, try the following. Stand outside when the Moon is visible along with the evening star. Work to make your arms alive with

the feelings of the last exercise. Then stand with your arms outstretched in front of you as if you were going to catch a large ball
with your arms. Look at the Moon and try to feel the space between
you and the Moon with your arms. It is more an intending than an
actual seeing, but you can actually feel the space "thicken." When
the Moon is in your grasp, then look at the evening star and do the
same. Try to feel that your arms are somehow in contact with the
evening star. When you are within the mood of these two planets,
try with your arms to feel-see the space between you, the Moon,
and the evening star. This can engender deep feelings in your heart
chakra of being deeply connected with the cosmos.

A further development of this exercise is to face east and try to
remember and to imagine where the Sun is in the heavens. This is
the first stage. Then when the Sun is setting, go outside and face
the opposite horizon. Imagine the setting Sun behind you and then
imagine that as the Sun sets another Sun is rising in the form of a
great Angel. The Angel is bringing the sweet draught of forgetful-
ness and the healing oil of mercy to humans now coming under its
influence. This Angel is the very essence of tolerance and compassion. We could imagine it as a transparent deep emerald green with
golden highlights. The arising of the Angel opposite the setting Sun
is an event that is very healing for human beings.

Once we have stabilized the life body in relation to the Earth,
our Witness can participate in this event consciously. If you are doing your exercise at dawn, imagine the physical Sun about to rise
and the Angel of the Spiritual Sun about to set. With arms of your
heart raised and your life body facing east, imagine that the vortical
forces of the movements of the planets in the solar system are lifting you into the air above where you are meditating. Imagine that
the space between your heart's arms is filled with attention. With
the arms of your heart, imagine the positions of all of the planets
relative to your geographical position. "See" the planets spread over
the Earth. This seeing is as if your heart had eyes to see the motions
of the planets. Then lift your vision to the vast population of stars
above and beyond the planets. Send gratitude and love to the far
distances, then greet the rising physical Sun and feel yourself strung

between the rising physical Sun and the setting Angel of the Spiritual Sun as if you were the axis between them. Then imagine your physical body and breathe down into it. Feel yourself touch down into your physical body and your surroundings. Sit in silence for a while and steep in the sublime atmosphere of this great event.

AWARENESS OF BEING

The heart chakra has a capacity to be developed into an organ of cognition of the character of another. This capacity, when taken to the level of conversations with the Confidant Doorkeeper, becomes the capacity to become aware of spiritual beings and enter into dialogue with them. The training of the heart chakra involves formatting lawful and objective patterns in the inner eye, which then become a kind of primer of lawful transformation for the seer working on transforming and purifying the soul. In the previous exercises we presented a method for assessing the stage the transformative process has reached and what the researcher needs to do at that level. In the third light, two systems will be given, one for the heart eye and one for the soul eye, both functions of the heart chakra.

The exercise for perceiving the Angel of the Spiritual Sun involved the heart eye and the soul eye. The heart eye sees the lawful motion of the planets with the organ of cognition that monitors the movements of the blood in the limbs. The soul eye is an evolution of the heart eye that sees the movement of the Sun in front of the fixed stars in the movements of the blood in the limbs. Once they begin to function, the Witness, working in dialogue with the Confidant Doorkeeper, begins to perceive the lawful patterns of planetary motion as symbolic aspects of self-development. This perception is often accomplished by compassionate interest in our own and others' soul pathologies. The next two systems of thought are compendiums of planetary and solar qualities that a seer might find useful when encountering the advice of the Confidant Doorkeeper in the realm of the heart. They will be given in summary form in order to fit them into the purpose of this book. In reality they can be extended into many years of work and research.

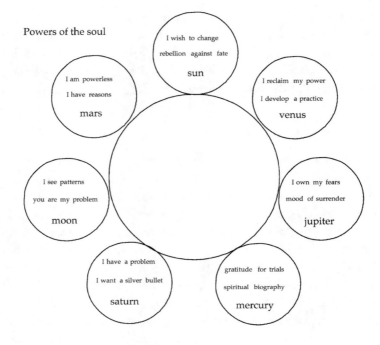

Powers of the soul

I wish to change
rebellion against fate
sun

I am powerless
I have reasons
mars

I reclaim my power
I develop a practice
venus

I see patterns
you are my problem
moon

I own my fears
mood of surrender
jupiter

I have a problem
I want a silver bullet
saturn

gratitude for trials
spiritual biography
mercury

The Powers of the Soul Mandala

The first system is the powers of the soul mandala. Instead of the now familiar four-stage mandala, we find a seven-stage mandala (figure). This form describes the planetary patterns that often arise when a person is faced with a crisis and must transform some aspect of the soul to get beyond the dilemma.

In the first stage of the work with the third light, a person is usually presented with a problem in life that threatens him or her with death, shame, pain, or alienation. These trials are specific to the heart chakra. Whatever the cause, the soul finds itself unable to integrate the lesson of the trial. The inner stage of first finding out about the trial is the stage called Saturn. In Saturn we enter the darkness, and nothing is familiar or recognizable. The mood in Saturn, which overwhelms the soul, is, "I have a problem." In itself this mood is a great aid to the soul, but it often comes as an indictment or sentence surrounded with dark import and fear. Usually a person begins the journey through this stage by looking over events in the past that may have led up to the problem. Frequently this results in the formation of a belief that some silver bullet or magic genie will be found that will instantly relieve the problem.

Since a magic genie almost never appears, the second stage on the soul mandala, the Moon stage, follows. Here the soul searching and review of sins results in the person forming beliefs about which patterns led to the problem, in the hope that by this process some form of amelioration will still emerge. Searching for patterns in the past most often results in a few wounds and grievances being brought up out of memories and projected onto the current situation. Sometimes the person is seen to be the source of the blame, but most often the source is projected onto another person or situation. The reflective mood of this stage of the process is the planetary mood of the Moon.

Projection of blame onto ourselves and others does little to move the problem toward a solution, so in the next stage, the Mars stage, the person often begins to get angry that the problem won't go away and rationalizations begin to take the place of projections. Much energy is put into forming elaborate schemas of rationalizations and motives for how the problem has come to pass, but under it all the rationalizations are a last-ditch effort to avoid the growing awareness that one is powerless to solve the problem without some level of soul transformation and integration. To reach this level takes a great deal of fretting and agitation, which is indicative of the Mars stage in the planetary mandala.

The soul is now in a tight place. Realizing the level of powerlessness often brings two simultaneous but polar reactions: total rebellion and indignation at the circumstances and a deep wish to change oneself in order to solve the problem. This emotionally complex and paradoxical attitude is really the key to the healing process since it represents simultaneously the recognition of the parameters of the problem and the possibility for a new life after the crisis. This stage is the stage of the Sun, where the problem burns off the dross from the soul. It may signal the beginning of a healing or the onset of a capacity to endure a negative prognosis with dignity and peace. The Sun represents the forces of balance among the planets.

After visiting the Sun, the soul has a different posture toward the problem. With the wish to change comes the desire to reclaim the power lost to the soul in the earlier stages. The soul becomes open to other possibilities. This is the mood of Venus. In the Venus mood, the suffering person begins to take the lessons given by the pathology and form them into a practice that can develop new capacities. A change of vocation or a religious conversion may accompany the new attitude of openness toward the problem. Venus gives the sense that everything has a purpose if we can just allow the process to develop. This attitude forms the basis for a new will, which can manifest as the first seed of the inner life.

With a practice established, the soul finds new forces to use for looking at the patterns of fear encountered in the first stages. Now, however, the purpose of looking at the fears is not to deny them or project them, but rather to own them and integrate them into the life picture. To do so, we must learn to surrender to the higher wisdom and will that stands behind the events in life. Paradoxically, this Jupiter mood of surrender empowers us to rule over our life with economy and grace instead of trying to control all of the events and people with whom we come in contact. Jupiter's role is usually depicted as that of a wise king. In the powers of the soul, Jupiter is the king who has learned to rule by serving the greatest good of the people. The mood of surrender is the true road to wisdom.

In the last level of the work on the soul, the healing process reaches a climax. Here the soul has surrendered to a higher wisdom and is listening intently to the ways the trials have developed the capacity for compassion. Our worst trials are given to us to help us face the deepest learning aspects of our pathologies. The trials give us the strength and flexibility to live an existence in the spirit. Without them our learning ceases and we become flaccid in our attempt to serve the greatest good. By being truly grateful for our trials, we begin to glimpse our own spiritual biography, our own history of spiritual work and travel, which we write in the spirit world with the light of our illumined consciousness. The last stage of the work is the Mercury stage, the attainment of healing forces from the great healing Mercury. Mercury desires communication and integration more than any goal. Mercury knows that all things shall pass but the Word of God. The Word of God is known in human terms as compassion, the ultimate level of acute reciprocation.

When Mercury touches us, all of our pettiness and irritability falls away and we exist filled with the Holy Spirit, satisfied to be in the presence of our Creator and his redeeming Son. Our life is reduced to simple terms once again, and we have the possibility of integrating our trials instead of letting them linger as festering wounds of pride and resentment. One layer of the deadened skin of self-centeredness is peeled from the light of our True Self, and another trial looms up on the now expanded horizon. The new trial will most often require that we test our newfound liberation capacity by placing a problem before the soul so that we will once again begin to tread familiar territory into the abyss of despair. The question is, can we remember the mood of gratitude for existence underlying our spiritual biography that is present in the stage of Mercury?

The mandala of the powers of the soul is an endless chance for progress through failure. Living in the consciousness of a spirit among the spiritual hierarchies present in the heart eye, we see others' struggles as our own in an endless succession of developments. The sevenfold qualities of this mandala are a reflection of the planetary experiences and insights the work with the etheric arms of the heart can instigate.

The Twelvefold Mandala

> *The heart is the key to the world and to life.*
> *One lives in this helpless state in order to*
>   *love and to be indebted to others.*
> *Through imperfection one becomes suscep-*
>   *tible to influences of others.*
> *And this alien influence is THE GOOD.*
> — Novalis

A further development of the work with the etheric arms of the heart is the process leading to what Rudolf Steiner calls the spirit eye. The spirit eye sees creation in the context of twelvefold imaginations.

The mood of the one-in-twelve exercise and the mist of worlds is the first level of this work. Later, once a capacity for staying intact in the spirit has been developed, insight into the twelvefold nature of the human being can provide invaluable lessons in how to get along with our neighbor, whom we are told to love as we love ourselves.

The real nature of the twelvefold mandala is so complex that what follows will seem quite abstract. However, an attempt will be made to describe a basic twelvefoldness in a simple diagrammatic way so that the schematic idea can be presented in the context of this book. The following diagram is a teaching wheel that is a compendium of color work, the twelve homeopathic constitutions, and various other healing schemas such as flower essences. A more detailed treatment of this work is in preparation and will be the subject of another book. Here, just a sketch of a possible understanding of the spirit eye is given.

In the diagram of the twelvefold mandala, the organizational principle is that each of the twelve positions on the wheel is occupied by a homeopathic constitutional type of personality. The organization is self-explanatory, but for this sketch only one polarity, green/magenta, will be explored to give a flavor of how the wheel can be used.

Green: In Goethe's color theory the color green results from a deintensification of the two primary colors blue and yellow. Blue represents the color of the light seen against a background of darkness, like the blue of the distant mountains or the blue of the sky. Yellow represents the color of a veil of darkness seen with the light behind it, as we see in a sunset. Between the yellow and the blue is a color paler than blue and darker than yellow. This color in the middle represents the color of the light between the two kinds of darkness. Esoterically and alchemically, the color of the light of the Sun is green. We could say that the green is the light falling into the forms of life. This is the significance of the alchemical elixir known as the green lion.

Green arises where the lightest portion of the spectrum is found. As the forming power of the light falling into manifestation, green

staphysagria
+ creative, inspired, charismatic
– indignant, incised wound, fears practical
  life, martyr, self-destructive
  (Nietzsche, Prometheus)

lycopodium
+ tactful, beneficent, tolerant, magnanimous, charming
– free mind, fixed soul habits, habitual denial, aversion to
  change, supports the underdog but undermines capable
  colleagues (Bill Clinton, the phoenix)

pulsatilla
+ devoted, peacemaker, sees beauty in things, sacrifices
  self to bring calm or do something
– needs noticing, easily crushed, fears anger, guilty
  conscience when angry, insecure
  (Cinderella, Mother Holle)

sepia
+ transcendent soul life, deep spiritual
  roots, devotion to causes, self-content,
  candid, has integrity
– feels entangled, avoids love for fear of
  need to reciprocate, complaining, soul
  sore, prideful (Fisherman's wife)

sulfur
+ thorough, prolific, learned, direct
– self-centered, caustic, overwhelming
  emotionally, inflated
  (Goethe, Samuel Johnson)

ignatia
+ highly intuitive, perseveres through
  obstacles, patient, selfless
– exaggerates drama of discontent,
  grieves unknowingly and constantly,
  feelings tend to become numb
  (Romeo and Juliet)

arsenicum
+ very enthusiastic, loyal,
  organized, perfection
– perfectionist, domineering,
  driven, nervous, excitable
  (the general, the thoroughbred)

calcium carbonate
mystical, intuitive, deep self-knowledge,
  supports causes selflessly
– stubborn, brooding over slights and
  hurts, afraid to act, fantasist
  (Thomas Aquinas, the third son)

phosphorus
+ witty, high energies, learns easily,
  many ideas
– scattered, absentminded, confused
  about identity, multiple personalities
  (Peter Pan, the grasshopper)

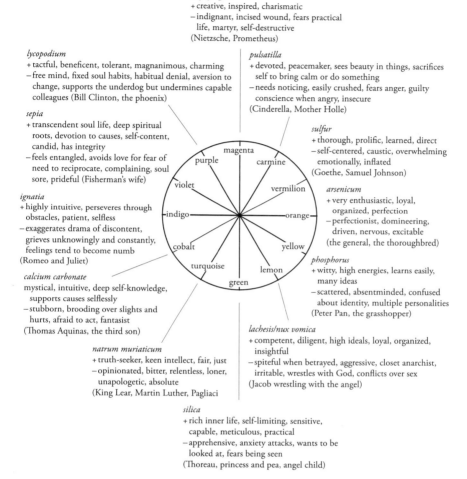

natrum muriaticum
+ truth-seeker, keen intellect, fair, just
– opinionated, bitter, relentless, loner,
  unapologetic, absolute
  (King Lear, Martin Luther, Pagliaci

lachesis/nux vomica
+ competent, diligent, high ideals, loyal, organized,
  insightful
– spiteful when betrayed, aggressive, closet anarchist,
  irritable, wrestles with God, conflicts over sex
  (Jacob wrestling with the angel)

silica
+ rich inner life, self-limiting, sensitive,
  capable, meticulous, practical
– apprehensive, anxiety attacks, wants to be
  looked at, fears being seen
  (Thoreau, princess and pea, angel child)

stands opposite to magenta, where the darkness reaches its zenith and the light bursts forth from the darkness.

Gold, long associated with the Sun, can be beaten into extremely thin sheets, which gilders can attach to windows. The gold on the glass is actually transparent enough to see through. When we look through the beaten gold the world appears to be a beautiful, clear emerald green color. The metal gold was considered by alchemists to be solidified solar light.

Among the minerals, greenstones and gems such as jade and emerald are known for their hardness. The emerald's hardness, however, is not without its paradox. When first mined, emeralds are soft and pastelike. They are gathered in this soft condition and put into lightproof boxes so that they can cure and harden. In this process, fine cracks form in the gem, making it impossible to find an emerald without some form of imperfection. Greenstones also come from a viscous or pastelike condition in the magma of the volcanic zones where they are found. The magma then hardens into the dense basaltic rock of volcanic plugs, which outlast the softer rocks around them to form the plugs and dykes so typical of volcanic extrusions.

The initial softness of these minerals, which turns into the remarkable hardness of green gemstones like jade, is an image of the forming property of the light. The light that comes out of the darkness is a forming and hardening force compared to the creative, fluid forces of the darkness out of which the magenta light springs as if from a prison. The paradox of green is that it is an image of the hardening forces that light brings to the creative, fluid nature of life. Green is present where great light is becoming form; as a result it is the most formed color in the whole color circle. A mood of loneliness and sacrifice pervades the soul yearnings of green. Green souls are extremely aware of how things that exist in potential can suddenly become limiting.

As we might expect from a color whose genesis is the light that creates the forms into which matter manifests, green contains a great paradox. Green souls are usually gifted with a practical intelligence. They are often very self-reliant and well organized. They can easily discern patterns in what needs to be done, and they can do what needs to be done in an efficient manner. Being in the light and perceiving what is wordlike in the unmanifest gives the green soul the capacity to use intellect in a clear and objective way. Being aware of how the light of the intellect manifests into forms gives green persons a keen sense of order, and they often exhibit a meticulous attention to details that pass by other less awake souls.

The green's highly developed sense of order is a great gift, but it can also be a great burden. Seeing the lawfulness of supersensible patterns in a clear way makes the green soul prone to being a little too sensitive to pathological things in the outer world. Greens are sensitive to slight disturbances in form or protocol that most others would not notice. After a time this sensitivity ends up being a reason to shut down from life as it is and retreat into a world made out of the inner light of the imagination. Usually this inner world is a lot "greener" than the one the soul is living in at the present. When this occurs, the greens' gift becomes a transparent prison in which they feel trapped by the very capacities they use to organize the world so well.

Green is the color of the pigment used by plants to capture sunlight in order to create the sugars that support all life. If the green color of the plant world were not so mundane, it would be considered miraculous. Green is the color of the Holy Grail, which by legend was carved from an emerald. The Holy Grail gave nutrition to each being exactly according to his or her needs. The sense of the appropriateness and correctness of the most mundane features of life is the mood of green souls. They serve the world in the most humble ways, usually without expectation of being recognized. This is the fundamental worldview of the green soul and at times it becomes burdensome.

On the spiritual plane, imagine the feelings of a plant that exists as a free spiritual archetype living as a being of light in the spirit world. This form of light must incarnate into the body of a plant, which will spend its life rooted in one place, unable to protect itself from the vagaries of its environment. This is a bit of the soul mood of green souls when they are faced with the prison of their own belief structures, as happens when their inner light of thinking manifests as thoughts and deeds which then surround them as the circumstances of their lives. The pure light of thinking greens itself and becomes manifest as form. In its positive mode, their gift is the religious experience of the ordering patterns of the cosmic Word. We could say that the color green is the light that is carrying the fall within itself. This is simultaneously the gift and the dilemma of the green soul. If this issue is left unaddressed it becomes a soul wound for the green soul which needs attention.

The homeopathic constitutional remedy most closely resembling the plight of the green soul is silica. The homeopathic remedy for green is a silica constitution of passive resistance.

The wound of the silica is a scarified, crystallized skin, which encloses the soul in a brittle, hard chrysalis. We could say it is the gritty skin on the top of the seething mass in the cauldron or the scar tissue on the old wound. There is no self-pity at all in a silica, but an enduring passive resistance to adversity, which can lead to long-term chronic dysfunction. The cool, conscious stubbornness of this type is usually accompanied by impaired physical capacity to lift a healing process into the acute stage. These souls often suffer from boils, cysts, and indurations. On one hand they have the capacity to be highly resistant and stubborn to outside influences, and on the other they can be extremely sensitive to small trifling irritations. The Rubicon for this soul is some bout of mental exertion that left them in a state of nervous collapse.

Never a martyr to a cause, the silica type is very aware of their limitations before they do anything. They are self-limiting and refuse, with the utmost tenacity, to do anything beyond their perceived limits. They never snap, since they fall out of the running long before they reach the point of exhaustion. "Once burned twice shy" is their motto. They are highly conscious of small and insignificant things in daily life that others pass by. They exhaust whatever energy they can muster into resisting what they are convinced they cannot achieve. Ultimately this heightened sense of self-limitation erodes their self-confidence. When this happens they suffer a psychic clogging, becoming imprisoned in their own belief structures as if they were trapped in a glass room and kept banging into the invisible walls. They have a profound consciousness of the way thinking is ordered by thoughts. This insight, the gift of an orderly consciousness, often is self-limiting and creates temerity for striving to live outside their prison.

Magenta: In magenta, both the yellow, which seeks to ray out from a center, and the blue, which seeks to ray inward from a periphery, journey through their own kind of darkness toward a climax in the deepest darkness of the color circle. In magenta, the darkness has completely engulfed the light. The creative forces are only barely revealed, as carmine, the color next to magenta on the red side, brings its power of devotion, and purple, the color next to magenta on the blue side, brings its power of authority. Authority and devotion meet in an uneasy marriage in magenta as both shift into a metamorphosis that almost defies description. From where does such a pure and vibrant pink arise out of the deepest darkness? In the sunset, magenta flashes into being just when the sky seems about to fade into the darkness of night. Long after the Sun has set, magenta descends from high above in the inky darkness, like the aura of an angel coming to resurrect the light out of the crypt of invading gloom. Magenta is a fleeting, shimmering bolt out of the dark blues and purples of the nighttime sky, coming briefly down to Earth from some high celestial place just when darkness threatens most.

In nature, magenta often appears in ephemeral phenomena. It is not often a color found in flowers that love to live in the sun. It is found on blossoms that like the shade or that only produce short-lived flowers that bloom for a day or two and then wither. This mood of magenta is indicative of the dynamic of its paradox. It is a light that appears when the darkness is greatest. It is the color in which the darkness has reached its zenith. Magenta is the most shadow-filled color, which exists paradoxically the farthest in front of the light, like a red, or the farthest behind the light, like a purple. In this paradox lies the magic of magenta. Something very mysterious is going on between the magenta and the purple and the carmine. Somewhere there is a shift of focus, a sleight of hand where the front becomes the back and vice versa. This mysterious shifting is the essence of the color experience of the magenta soul.

Since it is so filled with darkness, magenta contains a great creative energy. In magenta, the yellow yearning to ray out from a center is completed. Likewise, the blue yearning to ray inward from the periphery is at a maximum. In magenta, the green light at the center, where form is being manifested, is very far away. The assurance of clear day-awake thought is not part of the mood of magenta. It is creative in a Dionysian, chaotic, and intuitive way.

Magenta is the color of the creative forces of the Godhead. Insight comes from far above to the magenta soul. The insight is also usually accompanied by soul darkness and the inability to think in logical structures. In the movement from the yellow to magenta, we could form a temperamental sequence that may prove instructive. Yellow, the color of lovers or actors; orange, the color of diplomats and generals; vermilion, the color of philosophers and scholars; carmine, the color of priests and public servants; magenta, the color of geniuses and madmen. The moods of the colors are a result of the gradual intensification of the yearning to ray out from a center. As this tendency gradually deepens from yellow to magenta, the mood of the soul shifts from one of yellow lighthearted joy arising within the act of thinking to deep creative inwardness bordering on soul pathology. The intensifying process enhances the soul gesture of raying out and deepens it into its polar condition of delving deeply within the soul for the roots of one's own genius.

Likewise, the movements from turquoise can be instructive. The turquoise is aware of how the Word becomes flesh. The turquoise soul lives where the creative forces of the idea, which originate at the periphery, come into actual fact. In turquoise, the yearning is to live more fully in the periphery, which is the source of the truths contained in archetypal ideas. This yearning becomes more intensified in cobalt blue, where the soul yearns to become one with the memories of its existence before birth when it lived as one with the forces of the cosmic periphery in the starry heavens. This yearning is enhanced when the soul takes a step deeper into the darkness and lives in indigo. Here an abyssal experience of living between the worlds of life and death is present as a daily experience. When the experience is deepened into violet, the soul is present as a conscious witness to the activity of the archetypes living in the periphery of the cosmos. When this awareness is intensified, the soul lives in the far periphery of the darkness in contact with the power of the cosmos to create out of the authority of cosmic being. The next step into the peripheral darkness puts the soul beyond the reach of power and knowledge into the realm of creative wisdom itself, experienced as intuition.

The magenta soul, moving beyond the beyond, is, in the last resort, not concerned with ideals or philosophical truths, but is filled with the mood of the periphery of worlds where hidden truths are suddenly and mysteriously revealed to souls who wait silently in the deepening darkness. Magenta is a powerful color for bringing about changes in the soul. It bursts into a self-imposed prison of misery and doubt, flashing out of the deepest darkness, bringing with it extreme forces of dissolution and transformation. Souls living in magenta have taken steps into creative oblivion that other souls deem too dangerous to try. In a human biography, the magenta color can arise as the harbinger of a time of great change or upheaval. The transformative energy of magenta is extreme, but it is very healing. Magenta reminds us of the creative power of the Godhead and the debt we owe to the deeds of other beings greater than us who have sacrificed so much so that humans could taste the heady, magenta-colored wine of creative freedom. The ultimate color of the light of human consciousness shining out through the blood is magenta.

The trials of the magenta soul resemble in large part the homeopathic constitution of staphysagria. The homeopathic remedy for magenta is a staphysagria constitution of righteous indignation.

The wound is a seething cauldron of sorrow and self-pity due to intolerable circumstances. The sorrow builds until a violent eruption of indignation occurs, often accompanied by acute illnesses. Often the defining trial of these souls occurs following some sort of humiliating operation that stretches a body opening, an intrusion they are powerless to overcome and must submit to. After this defining event, these souls see themselves as martyrs to a cause. After their initial humiliation, they will often willingly submit to an ongoing injustice with shocking humility. Their secret fantasy is that others will recognize their superior forces of humility and dignity under pressure. They feel themselves chosen by destiny to suffer the injustice so they can rise to great things through it. When they are not recognized for their superior capacity to maintain themselves above the suffering, they snap. Their humility has become humiliation. The secret thing they dread most is being judged by others or insulted wrongfully. They are highly conscious of the personal nature or power of suffering, but when their attraction to being humbled results in their being humiliated, they seek to draw others into their experience thorough flaming indignation. This is the cauldron of suffering. They often choose creative ways like writing or artwork to express their indignation. For the staphysagria type, suffering and indignation is the only way they can find limits in their lives. Otherwise they live in creative chaos as the first light emerging out of the extreme darkness, personally striving for all of humanity.

Much more could be said about the twelvefold mandala. The third light of the guardian admonishes us to develop the capacity to become aware of the qualities of being in other humans and ultimately in other spiritual beings. These brief indications are tentative suggestions for a much more involved possibility of developing a schooling for strengthening the capacities of the heart chakra into the heart eye and the soul eye.

6

FIRE/SPLEEN/
SURRENDER TO BEING

FIRE IS THE SUBTLEST OF THE ELEMENTS in the elemental mandala and the most difficult to understand from the point of view of physical properties. It is the least physical of the elements, yet it is present in all transformations at all levels. When earth transforms into water, it is the warmth of fire that causes the transformation. Earth becomes molten in fire. An alchemist would say that the molten rock had undergone an elemental change from earth to water. In today's language, we would say a phase shift had taken place. In transforming water into air, the element of fire is again present as the catalyst for the phase shift. We could say that fire is the very spirit of transformation.

The spleen chakra is considered by Eastern adepts to be an inferior or minor chakra, sometimes linked as a minor chord to the major chakra of the navel area. In Western alchemy, where the descent of the Holy Spirit is more the focus rather than lifting the serpent power of the kundalini from the base chakra, the spleen chakra, connected with destiny and karma, is decidedly more in line with the inner work. The struggle to lift the instinctual sense-driven life into higher capacities is centered in the relationship between the spleen chakra and the heart chakra.

Elementally, any exercise that enables us to feel that transformation is happening in our lives is useful for developing the forces of fire in the soul. Projective geometry can lead the mind to these places, as can the study of naked-eye astronomy. In these disciplines the mind is led to the place of fire, where all is transformation. Earlier we used exercises in which the point of a triangle moves to the infinitely distant. In such concepts as the infinitely distant, the space in which projective protocols work is a space, or rather a counterspace, in which all things are becoming everything else. The theorems of Euclidian geometry fall apart in a space where points of necessity become planes and there are an infinity of planes in a point. To deal with such transformations, it is necessary to enter fully into the fire level of consciousness.

The fire element makes our inner work more and more subtle. Silence and patient waiting are the characteristic of the element of fire as it oscillates between its lower chaotic nature as fire and its transcendent healing quality as soul warmth. This transformation is accomplished in the soul only with the help of the transformed higher soul forces of the Witness, which is brought into contact with the True Human by dialogue with the Confidant Doorkeeper. Such contact dynamizes the Spirit Embryo, the kernel of the potential or future human being. The Witness is a fire being whose task or joy or vocation is to observe the sublime and radiant will nature of the True Human. When the Witness recognizes, identifies with, and surrenders to the eternal beingness of the True Human, the Spirit Embryo is generated, fertilized, and incubated in the lower sheaths of the soul related most closely to sense experience. This process is the great conundrum for the future of mystery wisdom in the West.

In teachings that focus on the divine nature of the True Human, the student is encouraged to uncover what is already divine within the self. In other teachings that focus on the role of the Witness to the exclusion of the body, students are encouraged to allow only a philosophical kind of transcendent thinking into the soul so that they can unite fully with the Witness outside of their bodily sheaths. Other teachings recognize the incredible miracle of the human body and encourage students to surrender their consciousness to the wisdom of the body in order to achieve realization. The irony is that all of these teachings are accurate. The problem is that each represents only a stage of development in a long series of stages. The generation and subsequent development of the Spirit Embryo includes all of these stages as necessary reference points in the development of heartfelt thinking. Students need to realize that the True Human is accessible to the consciousness of the human being living in a body of flesh. Likewise, they need to work with the Witness to be able to transcend thinking processes that are linked to remembered sensory experiences. The thinking must be rendered free of sense and bodily impulses through long dialogue with the Confidant Doorkeeper. However, once students can attain to this stage of consciousness, they must once again descend into the body and consciously enter into the activity of sense-bound impulses in order to generate and eventually bring to term the Spirit Embryo. The development of the Spirit Embryo is not given by the Creator or the work of the hierarchies who created the world; it must be developed by the free will of a human being in collaboration with divine beings. The organ for this development is heartfelt thinking. We could say that heartfelt thinking forms the life organs of the Spirit Embryo. These concerns are the focus of the level of fire.

FIRE EXERCISES

A good first exercise for the element of fire is to replicate an experiment done by the great English scientist Michael Faraday, who gave this demonstration in England at the Royal Academy of Science late in the nineteenth century. Set up a beeswax candle flame in a darkened room. Everyone in the room can see that the flame is a source of light and heat. Then move the candle near a wall and focus a strong light on the candle flame. At just the correct distance, the flame casts a faint shadow on the wall. Turn off the strong light, and the flame is once again a source of light. This interesting experiment reveals a profound spiritual law: a source of light can cast a shadow in the presence of a stronger light source. The warmth currents near the flame appear to have a different density than the bright source of light. If we were subtle enough and had an even stronger light, we could cast a shadow with the warmth currents coming from the strong light. Referring to the relationship between the Witness and the True Human, we could say that the Witness is a light of awareness in the soul but that it is a shadow of the light of the True Human. The wax that carries the potential to burst into flame is the Spirit Embryo.

In the inner work, the equivalent of this phenomenon is that when we lift our consciousness to a higher level, the more intense light of that level automatically darkens our consciousness. This is why we lose our day-awake state of awareness when we move into meditation. We could ask what the difference is between simply spacing out and losing our day-awake state when in contact with a higher consciousness. The difference is the quality of intent in the two states. Intent is will to do something. When we space out, our consciousness is usually clouded by beings that are active at lower stages of consciousness. We space out easily since our will is so weak when undeveloped. When we work ourselves into the presence of a higher being meditatively, our will is strengthened by the work. It takes a lot of will to hold onto an empty consciousness without having it fall into a sleeping or dreaming state. This higher will, or intent, is developed in the exercises we do and the rhythm of our practice. The rhythm of the practice develops the Spirit Embryo. The intent to do the exercise is developed by the Witness, who is especially effective in the work on the soul. The Witness fashions the intent so that even though we lose our day consciousness when an inspiring being approaches us in the spiritual world, we still maintain the intent to first address the being and then, when we have checked the cards of the inspirer, to remember the experience. The Witness perceives the shadowlike nature of its own being when in the presence of an inspiring being, and that shadowlike element becomes the form of the work that proceeds out of the inspiration. All of this concerns the protocols found in the element of fire and the spleen chakra.

Another image of the qualities of this paradoxical state is the Möbius strip. Cut a narrow strip of paper about four inches long by one inch wide. Put a strip of glue on one of the narrow ends. Then, taking a narrow end in each hand, twist the paper a half turn and glue the two ends together. When completed, the ring of twisted paper shows the curious quality that a line drawn along the strip will oscillate from the inside to the outside of the strip while remaining continuous. Try to visualize the line moving along this strip and experience the element of continuous transformation.

For another illustration of the mood of infinity in this level of the mandala, imagine a circle with a vertical line running through its center, as in the figure. As the center of the circle moves along the vertical line the circle gets larger. As the circle gets larger, the line defining its curve gets a larger arc. When the center of the circle reaches the infinitely distant point at the top of the vertical line, the arc described by the infinitely large circle will be flat and parallel to the horizontal line on which the original circle is sitting. Throughout the entire movement, the transformative force of the fire principle of the infinitely distant is working.

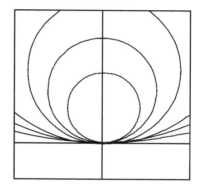

Other, more complicated, projective geometry visualizations could be done along these lines. If these are of interest to you, a wonderful book for study is *The Plant Between Earth and Sun* by Olive Whicher and George Adams. For the present work we have done enough with the elemental mood of fire because the true work in this level is recognition between beings, and that work is beyond visualization, although accurate visualizations are an excellent way to structure intent to enter other beings.

THE SPLEEN CHAKRA

The chakra below the heart is an enigmatic area. Older systems deny the value of working on this chakra since it is considered a minor mode of the more powerful second chakra below the navel. From a soul transformative perspective, the spleen chakra is the seed of an organ that will be very useful to human beings in the far distant future. The base chakra and the second chakra have been very useful in the past to human beings walking the path. Both points of view are "correct"; the difference lies in the intent. The second chakra deals with questions of power. The spleen chakra deals with questions of destiny and karmic relationships. It is for individuals to decide which is the major work and which is the minor in their life.

The spleen is a mysterious and little-understood organ. Rudolf Steiner links it to the planet Saturn. How can we understand this association? The primary function of the spleen is phagocytosis, the engulfing of foreign matter by a cell. In the body, phagocytes surround and dissolve pathogenic bacteria and other pathological debris. Often the cells surround the pathogen in an amoeboid manner and dissolve it. The mythological image of Saturn eating his children comes to mind, as well as the orbit of Saturn surrounding the orbits of all the other planets. Another major function of the spleen is to act as a container for the greater part of the blood and release into circulation just the right amount to keep the blood pressure constant. Esoterically, Saturn is the gateway from and to the stars. It is a regulator of the forces and patterns from the starry realms that need to be let in and let out of the solar system at the proper time. The spleen also serves as a destroyer of substances in the blood that would prove to be toxic if left in the circulation. Saturn, from an esoteric point of view, helps regulate human karma through the destruction of pathological patterns in the life of the soul. This destruction is accomplished when the person overcomes the instinctual reactions that dominate unrealized life and begins to act out of the forces of the purified blood in which the True Human has a basis. From these associations, we can begin to understand this mysterious organ and the esoteric functions of the spleen chakra.

The spleen chakra contributes a deep concern for how others in our life impact our destiny. The concern may be in the form of anxiety and resentment if the other person is considered an adversary, or it could be a loving interest in the pathology of the same adversary if our spleen chakra is harmonically working. If we are realized in the spleen chakra, we can see also clearly and objectively the karmic knots that keep us linked to the situation. It is also possible to perceive the gifts we are given by the presence of others in our life by having insights into their capacities and abilities. The harmonized spleen chakra gives us the capacity for having confidence in the processes that guide life on Earth. When we are anxious and resentful, the spleen chakra is upset, and we can often feel the anger or anxiety of another in that area. This feeling is commonly referred to as a nervous stomach. The solar plexus quivers and becomes cold when a person who is under stress walks into the room. Speaking becomes jittery and the digestion ceases to function, while the extremities become cold. These reactions of the spleen chakra are often instigated by stress and anxiety in another person or a situation other than our own. We take on the stress in an effort to surrender to the being of other people and resonate with them in their discomfort. When the spleen chakra is burned out or not capable of maintaining boundaries, we become sick and nervous. A fundamental healing for this chakra involves the development of an attitude in which we feel that something progresses in our work even without us. That is, we are helped by the spiritual world when we make an effort ourselves to understand what is happening in our life.

This process is pictured significantly in the fairy tale of the shoemaker and the elves. The shoemaker is not capable of making fine shoes quickly. He is working very hard, and in his fatigue he falls asleep after cutting out some shoes. In the morning the shoes are put together in the most excellent way. That evening he leaves some cutout shoes on his workbench and goes to sleep. In the morning they are once again put together in an excellent way. He continues this pattern and grows successful. Finally, he watches at night and sees elves completing the shoes. He is so overwhelmed with gratitude that the next day he cuts out some clothes for the naked spirits and puts them out instead of the cutout shoes. They arrive and put on the clothes in great glee. They leave the shop, never to return, but the shoemaker lives in peace and contentment ever after.

This story pictures how to heal the feeling that somehow destiny has given us a bad deal. We work hard on ourselves, and then at night spirits come to us and help the work along. They cannot make our work excellent if we don't do the preparation. When we finally feel strong enough to take on the work they are doing ourselves, we express our gratitude to them for helping us by clothing them. We recognize their contribution to our well-being. We are now in a better place, and they can go on to help another. This image presents an exact remedy for the spleen chakra.

We can get the feeling that we are being helped in our work by planting a garden. When we put in the seeds and cover them with earth, miraculously they sprout and grow without our influence. Of course we must have prepared the garden bed well in order for the seeds to become vital, but we have the feeling in garden work that we are not working alone. A similar mood can be realized when we are working in the arts. The unsolvable problem of yesterday somehow miraculously offers us a solution after a good night's sleep. It is the same painting or sculpture or story that we left the day before, but somehow we have the feeling that we are not working alone on the project. More examples could be given, but the mood is the same in all cases. We make an intent by creating a purposeful preparation, and then we have the feeling that we are helped along, which builds confidence in the soul that life will transform every situation.

This mood is behind the next series of exercises. In some cases the exercise might make one aware that not all transformation initially feels as if it is for the good. But when all is said and done, the spleen chakra can digest just about anything that our karma can give if we are busy preparing it with our inner work.

Becoming Another Life Form

The great task of the postmodern esotericist is to learn to awaken in another human being. A preliminary exercise that can lead up to the perception of angels is to learn to awaken in lower life forms. This exercise can be done at odd moments in your day when life starts to get boring. Observe a bird and focus on its eye. Try to enter the eye and feel as if your soul were leaving your body and flowing into the bird through its eye. The bird will in all probability begin to preen or dance on a twig or move closer to you. Somewhere in this encounter you may feel the bird is "linked" to you and is blended into your consciousness. When you feel linked, intend yourself to leave your own body and enter imaginatively into the bird. When you feel that you are in the bird, look back at yourself looking. Be the bird looking at you. If the bird moves, shift your inner picture accordingly. If the bird flies into a tree, see yourself from above. Then return to your own body and become yourself looking at the bird.

This can be done with any animal or insect, and it will respond in surprising ways. With this simple exercise, you can practice the feeling of what it would be to wake up in another being without having to spend a great deal of time setting up the practice. In general, practice coming back to yourself as soon as you find you are awakening in another being. In the beginning do not linger. The encounter with the other must be while you are in complete control of your day-awake consciousness in this exercise, but it is a good practice in developing the mood of surrender.

Angel In A Singles Bar

The angel in a singles bar exercise is an adaptation of a comment made by Rudolf Steiner that our angel is very interested in the movements we make with our hands when we write, but has absolutely no interest in what we are writing. In this exercise we try to experience another person from the point of view of his or her angel.

Begin by choosing a partner for the exercise. Each of you will make a model of the hand of the other person in wax. Each will observe the hand of the other while you both are modeling. After modeling, try to imagine that you can alter the form of your own hand to match the qualities in your partner's hand. If your hand is thin and your partner's is thick, imagine your own hand and how it would look if it were thicker, and vice versa. Write a sentence about the qualities you noticed in your partner's hand.

The next part of the exercise is to make a model of the other person's ear. You will model while your partner poses, and vice versa. Take about five minutes to make the model. Do not try to go too much into the proportion and detail of the inner ear, but concentrate on the shape of the outer ear and the earlobe. When your model is done, let your partner model your ear. After you both have finished, take the ear models and hold them up to the profile view of the other person. Look for shapes in the nose or jaw or chin or the back of the head that closely resemble the forms in the ear. Look at the other person's thumb and see if the form of the ear is harmonic to any forms there. Write a sentence or two about what you see. The next part of the exercise is to bring into your mind's eye the form of the hand and the form of the ear of the other person.

Next, draw a sketch of the curve of your partner's ear by holding the lead of the pencil close to the tip. Try to feel as if your fingers rubbing the paper are feeling around the edge of the other person's ear as you draw. This should feel almost as if you were giving the ear a massage. Then compare the drawing you made with the ear and note where you could correct it.

After noting the subtle changes, draw the ear again, but this time the task will be to draw the curve of the top of the ear and the back of the ear and the earlobe in one continuous line. First work inwardly, moving your eyes along the line of your partner's ear until you feel you have the swing of the curve inside you. When the curve is living in you, take out your pencil and draw the line in one motion. Then correct it by comparing the ear to your drawing. Pick out the drawing that you feel is closest to the ear of the person and look for the most telling or characteristic section of the curve. This should be the part of the curve that you can see repeated in the other person's ear and eye and nose and chin. There should be something you feel is characteristic of the person. Pick a section of the curve that you can see repeated many times in the face, and draw a box around that section. Then have the other person do the same process with you.

Next, have the other person tell you his or her name, address, telephone number, and birth sign. These are the things commonly traded in singles bars, and this part gives the exercise its name. As your partner tells you this information, instead of listening to the data listen to the quality of the voice. First, try to feel where the speaker's voice is resonating in your own body. Then have your partner repeat the information, and try to imagine you are entering into him or her by swimming into the sounds you are hearing. Don't concentrate on the meanings but on the quality of the sound, where it is coming from in the person, and where you are experiencing it in yourself. Write a sentence about what you experience. Then have your partner do the same exercise with you speaking.

Next have your partner write down the same information. Watch how his or her hand moves in writing. Then take the paper and move your finger along the path of the writing. Sit for a moment and try to visualize how the hand moved while writing. Try to feel how it would be to hold the pencil the way that person holds it. Inwardly move your fingers and hand in the rhythm and cadence of the movements. Then repeat the exercise for your partner.

When you are both finished, sit silently for a moment. Then compare your partner's handwriting with the section of the curve you enclosed with the little box. See if this section of the curve of the person's ear can be seen as a motif in the handwriting; people are often surprised at the close resemblance. Then sit silently again and recall inwardly the shape of your partner's ear and the shape and quality of his or her hand. Then recall the timbre and quality of the voice, the movements of the hand, and the overall look of the writing. When you finish the review of these things, look at the person and see if a deeper feeling of recognition arises. Share a few moments in conversation.

The creative movements we are recording in this exercise put us into the realm of the angels. The feeling of community that often arises during the exercise is the mood of the angels, whose task is to stand by human beings in life. It is instructive and healing for us to practice this type of seeing of another.

THE GREAT KARMA EXERCISE[g]

A final exercise, which comes from Rudolf Steiner through Jörgen Smit, is known as the Great Karma Exercise. It is included here since it is an excellent example of the type of exercise that promotes a deeper dialogue with the Confidant Doorkeeper in the context of the fourth light of surrender to being.

The roots of the karma exercise lie in the capacity to form an inner picture and hold it at will and then to dissolve it at will. Practice this form of imagining for five minutes as a prelude to the karma exercise. This practice puts the soul in touch with an inner force that an alchemist would call the aeriform metal, the ability to deepen or dissolve, a particular mood in the soul.

Then take a situation in which a particular person has been the source of inner questioning for you, and the condition has accelerated to the point that whenever the person comes into the room or whenever you think of her (or him), a particular and uncontrollable feeling arises in you. Bring to mind the person and the feeling. Then do the following exercise.

Inwardly build a sense picture of the way the person moves her body when walking or speaking or moving. How does she turn her head when she hears something? How does she move her hands when she is emphasizing a point in conversation? What is her body language when she talks to you? Does she ever touch other people? Does she meet another's gaze? These kinds of sensations are used to get a sense of the ego of the other and through that to try to see into the person's True Self, but they usually remain far below the threshold of awake consciousness. Hold these sense pictures in your mind's eye for a few moments and then erase them.

Then build up a sense picture of the way the moods of the person manifest. What are her characteristic facial expressions? How does she change her mood when encountering different circumstances? Do the moods change predictably during the day or the season? The next step is to dissolve this memory.

The next phase of the exercise is to picture to yourself how the person might form a thought. Does she form it rigidly or flexibly, tentatively or forcefully? Does this tenor of thought change with a change of subject, or is it constant? Does she follow a logical pattern when thinking, or does she jump from thought to thought? Do her thoughts come out in a rush or in a trickle? Does she think on the wing, or deeply and silently mull over a thought for a long time before expressing it? Does she offer her thoughts freely in meetings, or is she the last to speak and then speaks only when prodded? In short, how does she characteristically form and express her thoughts? This mood picture is then erased into a state of inner silence. This phase may take some time to do, so the next phase may be done at another time or done consecutively with the first exercises.

In the next phase of the exercise we inwardly picture the thoughts of the other person as if we *ourselves* are having the thoughts. We imagine that we are actually inside of the person thinking the thoughts, and that her thoughts unfold within her/us with a particular and singular inevitability. Then we dissolve this picture and its feelings into silence. This condition is known esoterically as Saturn (lead), the giveaway of the sense memory of the physical body.

We then recall the temperamental moods of the person, but this time we strive to experience the temperament as if we *ourselves* were actually in the person looking out. When this image is clear in the mind's eye we dissolve it into silence. This esoteric condition is known as Sun (gold), the giveaway of the memory of the life body.

We then build up a picture of how the person uses her arms and legs to move and walk, how she expresses herself with her limbs, but we ourselves try to be the person, moving the way she does by living into her characteristic motions. Practice walking as she walks or holding a pencil as she does or sitting in a chair as she does. Then dissolve the inner picture of how it is to move like her into an inner state of silence. This is known esoterically as Moon, the giveaway of the constant unconscious geometrizing of the astral body.

Through these exercises, the practitioner gradually distills a spiritual essence of the True Human of the other person without dwelling on all of the burdensome, alienating sheaths and habits that he or she presents to our soul, which are usually the source of personal conflicts and our resulting bad feelings about other people. These exercises render the other person transparent to the tender vision of our heart eye because they cannot be done except with the utmost feeling of attention, respect, and interest in that individual. Through these exercises we gradually can come to have an experience that we and the other person are truly one being in the Spirit, as we gradually see into the common karmic patterns that exist between ourselves and others.

This exercise is a true gem of the task of dying to self and waking in the other. The primary content of the teachings of Rudolf Steiner is found in this task. Much more could be said about the implications of these exercises for the spiritual pilgrim in surrendering to higher spiritual beings found on the path to wisdom, but these experiences go beyond the intent of this present work and move beyond the realm of exercise into the realm of experience.

7

THE CHAKRAS

ALCHEMICALLY, THE WORK ON THE SOUL always requires that some sort of conscious linking be done between the forces of the elemental body and the forces of the higher sheaths. In the soul life of human beings, the patterns of forces in these bodies regulate the relationship between the inner life of the soul and the bodily, sense-driven responses connected to it. The patterns are located in the physical body at the sites of the glands. Endocrine responses and the flowing of substances from the glands make up the majority of these patterns. From an esoteric point of view, the flowing patterns are not physical; they are representative of the forces of the life body. The soul tracks these flowing patterns of life stimulated by sense impressions and gives expression to them in the emotional life of the soul. Some of the patterns are given to humans as an inheritance from the beings that created the cosmos, which means that these forces are not under the control of the individual person. These are the patterns of codified behavior found in unconscious instincts and drives that make up the major portion of the personality. They are what the human being has in common with the animal world. These instinctual patterns of responses are known to esotericists as the forces of the elements. The patterns of the elements are unconscious in human beings; esotericists say they constitute the "given" cosmos of the human. The patterns are present to balance and heal the organism and are not in the direct control of the organism itself.

The task of the seer is to consciously develop higher relationships among the four elements within the soul in order to enter these
patterns more consciously. This work involves bringing a thought-
ful will into the places in the soul life of the personality where the
instinctual elemental patterns dominate the consciousness. The elemental or life body of a person is still governed by the hierarchies
and is subject to the laws of nature that result in instinct and drive.
The sheaths of the Spirit Embryo are octaves of the four elemental
sheaths in the elemental mandala. We could say that the elemental
sheaths are the placental sheaths of the future Spirit Embryo. The
four lights are what will eventually be the life organs of the Spirit
Embryo. They are not given to the human being as capacities, but
they are given as lessons and teachings.

In gestation processes in nature, and from the point of view of
the third light, the light of being, the hierarchies govern the unfolding of the lawful patterns of the physical organs of the physical embryo. The physical embryo leads to the first birth. In the processes
leading up to the second birth, human beings themselves must work
to consciously create the life organs of the Spirit Embryo. The plan
used by an alchemist for developing the spirit organs in the Spirit
Embryo must be in harmony with the plan used by the hierarchies
to form the life organs of the physical embryo. In esoteric language,
this process is referred to as the development of the chakras. For an
alchemist the chakras are organs of cognition used in states of clair-
voyance to see into the spiritual world for the purpose of spiritual
research. They are the organs of the future Spirit Embryo by which
it receives eternal life into itself as a form of cosmic nutrition. On
the physical side, the chakras are ganglionic plexuses of nerves and
vascular structures found in the autonomic nervous system clus-
tered around major glands of the physical body. This network is the
elemental form, the given or natural form of these organs. These
dynamic centers regulate the endocrine responses in the life organs
as the soul works to balance sensory input with cognitive responses.
In the figure the chakras and the endocrine centers are juxtaposed.

The petals of each chakra represent existing capacities of the
human being or potential capacities that can be developed. Half of

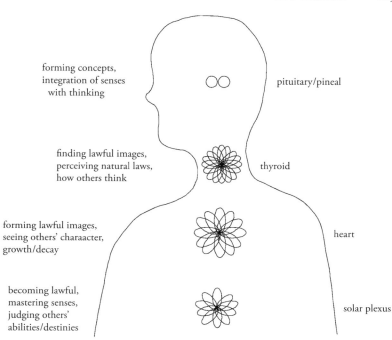

forming concepts,
integration of senses
with thinking

pituitary/pineal

finding lawful images,
perceiving natural laws,
how others think

thyroid

forming lawful images,
seeing others' charaacter,
growth/decay

heart

becoming lawful,
mastering senses,
judging others'
abilities/destinies

solar plexus

the petals of each lotus flower have already been given to the human being. It is our task to develop the other side of each chakra so that the new petals and the old petals are in harmony. Each chakra has a specific function given to it by the hierarchies, and each has a challenge the evolving human being must meet. In general, each higher chakra is harmonically linked to the functions of the corresponding lower chakra, with the higher center representing the new petals of the lotus flower. As we will see, each of the lotus flowers also has a gland or set of glands that serve as the energetic basis for the psychic functioning of the chakra.

The fundamental challenge for the whole process of working on the Spirit Embryo is that human beings need to change their thinking. Brain-based thinking is the stimulus-response type of thinking typical of memory processes arising from sensory input. We could call this thinking shadow projection. A stimulus creates a response pattern and the soul registers the experience in memory pictures. To science this is the proper realm of thinking. To an esotericist it is the type of thinking that human beings have in common with animals. This is instinct, thinking based on brain secretions and memory pictures arising from codified sensory responses. Intellectual thinking is much more than this, and higher creative thinking is much more than intellectual thinking.

In higher forms of thinking the picture-forming capacity is not based on stimulus-response patterns but is more field oriented: it includes much more than the direct response to a sense experience. The inner pictures can be composites of feelings, inspirational experiences, and actual prebirth remembrances. Physiologically, images that seem to appear in the brain are in reality linked to whole neural fields around the nerves spread throughout the whole body. Science has yet to find the exact physiological place where images arise in the inner eye. Higher picturing must also include the dimension in which the person may experience an inner image of something that has never been seen. Inventions and inspirations come out of this space, often clothed in dreamlike sequences of images. To make sense out of these inner experiences, a seer must be able to discriminate between fantastic images that are a result of a personal pathology and inner experiences that are truly the result of spiritual encounters. Much of the work on the chakras is devoted to this type of discrimination.

In the ancient world the pituitary/pineal area was known as the two-petalled lotus. This chakra is sometimes known as the brow chakra and is sometimes called the third eye. The two petals refer to the polar arrangement of the pineal and pituitary glands, the basis for this lotus flower. The two-petalled lotus is an octave of the ten-petalled spleen chakra in that it is linked to the capacity for integrating sense impressions (imaginations) with concepts (reason), which is an octave of the capacity for controlling our relationship to sense impressions that forms the task of the spleen chakra. We already have one of the two petals developed, the day-awake intellectual consciousness. The integration of sense impressions and conceptual thinking was the basis for the development of the intellect through the rise of natural science.

From the alchemical point of view, the chambers of the head are filled with a celestial dew, akasha, or fiery mist (cerebrospinal fluid), a magical elixir in which the light from the outer world of sensation mingles with the inner light of the soul, creating the day-awake consciousness. Between the first and second ventricle in the center of the brain, a wall of clear light, or septum pellucidium in standard anatomical terminology, is found. In alchemical thinking this membrane is considered to be the place where the sensation and the idea meet, providing the basis of the human capacity for forming an inner image of a sense object. In the old language the septum pellucidium was known as the speculum or mirror. On the wall of clear light the shadows of the world are cast and, as if in a mirror, rise up in human consciousness as reproductions of the outer world.

In the mandala of the four elements, this chakra, when undeveloped, represents the earth element or the salt principle, the ability to discern differences. It is the first of the four lights that the artist/student enters under the instruction of the Confidant Doorkeeper. In this chakra, the alchemist undertakes the work of distillation of consciousness in order to become aware of the difference between sense impressions that are linked to their correct ideas and sense impressions connected to personal feelings that are masquerading as valid concepts. This alchemy renders the general thinking capacity into intellect, a more potent form of consciousness. In the lower octave of the spleen chakra we work completely with the sense impression itself, with no relationship to concepts. Here we monitor the ways we link a concept to a sensory experience.

The throat chakra sits in an area thoroughly governed by the movements and impressions of speaking. We could say that this chakra is concerned with what is wordlike. In understanding language there is a peculiar paradox. We must forget the words to understand the sentence, just as we must forget the letters to understand the word. In language all is relationship and flow, and the dust must be forgotten to enter into the meaning. Take for instance the word *eros*. If I read it or hear it, the particular sequence and flow of the word puts me in mind of the meaning. If I rearrange the letters to spell rose then the same letters must be forgotten and a new meaning arises only if I forget that eros uses the same letters to give a different meaning. This fluidity of concept in language is the basis of thinking. The mother tongue first shapes the conceptual life for the adult in the young child. The structure of words and language is the particular realm of the sixteen-petalled lotus in the throat chakra.

In the throat chakra, the thyroid gland is the center of focus. The thyroid originates in the digestive layers in the embryo and is a highly vascular organ. In proportion to its size the thyroid has more blood flowing through it than any other organ of the body. The thyroid regulates the growth patterns for the whole body through its prodigious output of hormones into the blood. We could say the thyroid keeps the growth of the body within lawful limits. These are the imaginations given to it by the hierarchies.

When it is developed, the throat chakra is dedicated to the perception of how forms in nature are images of the patterns of forces that formed them. For this reason we can study geometry and its relationship to natural forms as a prelude to seeing the ideation and conceptual life of another person in terms of a particular geometric form. In the throat chakra we can move from the forms in nature to the forces in nature to the forces that animate the soul life of animals to the perception of how ideas move in another person's inner life and eventually into the perception of the movements of archetypes in the astral realm, which is a manifestation of the way planetary movements create forms in space. This is quite a sweep, but it is all potentially available to the alchemist exploring the throat chakra. We could say that the throat chakra has the capacity to help the soul forces find lawful archetypal images.

The alchemist who wishes to develop this chakra must concentrate on finding lawful patterns in the immense flow of images rushing in through the senses daily and integrate them into coherent thoughts. The task here differs from the task of the two-petalled lotus in that the concept/percept duality in the brow chakra is mostly based on differences of statically perceived relationships between a particular sense impression and its particular concept. The thinking of the brow chakra, in keeping with its elemental signature of earth, is more causal – this causes that; I think, therefore I am. In the throat chakra, it is the fluid dynamic of the sounds and sights that must be encountered and rendered into coherent and lawful themes. Here the flow of the words can alter the meaning in a very fluid way. "I am, therefore I think" uses the same words but expresses a far different thought, one that moves away from the idea of causality. When highly developed, the abilities of the throat chakra allow the adept to enter the thought processes of others more readily. Reading difficult books or listening to challenging speakers is much more fruitful when the movements of the throat chakra are enhanced.

In the elemental mandala, the throat chakra is linked to water. It perceives what is changing and how it is changing. We have called this faculty the Witness. In the teaching of the four lights, the throat chakra gives the soul the ability to become aware of awareness and to have a way to begin to control the formation of inner pictures. Through the activity of the throat chakra we are made aware of the awareness of others and can enter the stream of their ideation; we practice this daily in listening to others speak. Under the instruction of the Confidant Doorkeeper, the alchemical adept can enhance this witnessing in a radical way as an aid to transforming the senses.

An example of an exercise that would put us in contact with our throat chakra would be to listen to the tones of someone speaking a foreign language we do not understand and try to determine what that person is speaking about only from the tone. The need of sound to transform into meaning will become clear in this exercise. The soul has a yearning for meaning, and to listen to sounds that we know make a meaning structure without being able to understand the meaning is a challenge to the throat chakra. With this chakra we are able to experience the difference between what is lawful and what is not in the realm of inner transformation. In the brow chakra we can discern whether or not a concept fits a particular percept. In the throat chakra we can discern whether or not a given conceptual sequence is correct, which can lead to discernment about the quality of thought in the ideation of another person.

Exercises are beneficial for building the throat chakra through heartfelt thinking. In general, chakra exercises for heartfelt thinking need to have two qualities. First, they must work on forming an inner picture of a developmental sequence that occurs in nature. For the throat chakra, the growth patterns of a plant, the morphological sequences in the skeleton or in animals, or the metamorphic sequences in geology are good subjects, among others. The important element is that these sequences be wordlike. The second quality that benefits chakra development leading to heartfelt thinking is that the images formed inwardly should be objective. For the throat chakra, since many objective images come from the realm of geometry, such things as the sequences of the Platonic forms or the sequences of metamorphosis found in projective geometry are most useful. Exercises using these forms were presented in chapter 4 above.

The next chakra to be developed is the heart chakra. This area in a human being is a very complex system of flowing currents, both physiologically and psychologically. In the four elements mandala this level is linked to the air element. In the air level of elemental forces, the requirement is for the thinking to be capable of such great flexibility that two polar images can be held in the mind's eye simultaneously. The polar ideas or images will, of course, nullify each other, but the warming of the will needed to try to hold them is what we are after. To attain this simultaneity in thinking, it is first necessary to hold an image clearly in the mind. In a typical exercise, we hold an image of a flower in mind so that we see it inwardly. This is the earth level of the work in forming inner images. The second level is to move the image inwardly in a lawful way, unfolding the sequences of growth and change as accurately as possible. The third level of the work, the one specific to the heart chakra, is to find the polar image to the growth of the plant. We could, for instance, imagine the plant dying away. To strengthen the heart chakra, we grow the plant inwardly in the imagination and simultaneously, or nearly simultaneously, we imagine it fading away.

Often, developing simultaneity in thinking is the most difficult level of the work. An effective exercise for developing it, already presented in chapter 5 above, is to imagine that the growth sequence is a three-step process, ABC. Inwardly you picture how a flower germinates, grows, and then withers. Picture that A is changing into B, and B is changing into C. Once the image of the growth process is unfolding clearly in the mind, the ABC sequence is then reversed into a CBA protocol, and both are imagined simultaneously. It does not really matter if the visualization is completely successful. What matters is the intent in the will to feel the differences as clearly as possible even when they are dissolving into each other in a chaos of unrelated image fragments. The will to do this strengthens the capacity for heartfelt thinking.

The reversal of a previously held image that was unfolding in a logical sequence is preparation in the mind for the strenuous task of meeting with the Confidant Doorkeeper. The third light of the Confidant Doorkeeper, which resonates with the air level of the elemental mandala is the perception that "everything that was made, was made." We could add "by someone." The development of the heart chakra involves the direct perception that the universe is peopled with beings at every level of existence and that they have warm or cool relationships to us.

If an astrophysicist were doing soul work at this level, he or she would have to solve the dilemma of "dark matter" in some way other than giving this immense force a name related only to Earth existence. Perhaps the forces of dark energy and dark matter are indicating to scientists that there are mysterious and hidden beings of great power who are composed of seeming nothingness that is more powerful than all of the somethingness we can observe. Modern astrophysicists cannot, because of embarrassment, accept being as the basis for the universe. It is too retro an idea. But this lack of acceptance is precisely why the transition into the air level and the teaching of the third light by the Confidant Doorkeeper are so important for modern souls. All that we have as the basis for our current science is contained in the first two steps of the elemental mandala and the first two lights of the teachings of the Confidant Doorkeeper. The given is almost fully understood by abstract science; the great soul lesson for future humanity remains to be found in what is not given. Since no being can give this to us, we must find a way to reverse our inflated and swollen sense of self-will. Finding it is the challenge of the third light, which centers on the heart chakra and the development of hearfelt thinking.

In the heart chakra, the exercises in geometry and morphology need to be taken to a higher level in order to correctly harmonize the existing petals of the lotus flower of the heart with the new petals. The higher level consists in developing sense organs and spiritual limbs in the heart. This level of perception is approached by first finding how the creative beings who stand behind morphing geometrical sequences can be found. One approach is to once again return to the study of flowers and crystals, this trying to find out how they are constructed geometrically instead of just picturing them inwardly as they appear in nature.

We are left with the question of being, the question of the third light, unanswered if we simply see the geometry of these natural forms and cannot get to the beingness behind the geometry. To go to the next level of the third light, we must find the warmth and beingness behind world phenomena. Developing simultaneity in thinking in our inner picturing capacity at the elemental level is very useful. One effective way to meet these requirements is to study the movements of the planets in relationship to the fixed stars, as we saw in working with the throat chakra. The alchemical mantra "As above so below" refers to the developed eye of the heart chakra which sees the movements of the planets and understands them to be the macrocosmic patterning present in the spirit before a manifest form appears in the world of the senses. Teachers of the old mystery tradition understood that when the student is immersed in inwardly depicting celestial motions the soul will very likely open to experiencing Cosmic Being. It should also be noted that the heart chakra, when developed, becomes an organ for the perception of light and warmth living in other beings. The geometric and planetary movements, if consciously meditated, eventually open up the cosmos to the alchemist and reveal the activity of beings rather than abstract forces. When this shift takes place, the heart becomes an organ for the perception of warmth and light, and thinking begins to be an objective feeling in the heart chakra.

*

The final stage of development is the fire stage elementally and the fourth light in the teachings of the Confidant Doorkeeper. The chakra involved in this work is the one known to esotericists as the spleen chakra, found in the area just below the diaphragm near the solar plexus. Traditionally this chakra is the power chakra, involved in the perception of how power travels through the world. The glands linked to the spleen chakra are the adrenal glands, which are involved in the energetic functioning of the whole endocrine system. The spleen chakra is situated in the area of the pancreas, spleen, liver, and gall bladder. Rudolf Steiner links these organs to Mars (gall bladder), Jupiter (liver), spleen (Saturn), and the starry realms (the pancreas). We could say they represent the gate to the other side of the abyss.

In the brow chakra, the higher octave of the spleen chakra, there is another gate, or rather we could say a hut, perched on the other side of the abyss. The pineal gland traditionally has stood at the threshold of this hut. It is in the hut that the student first meets the lower Confidant Doorkeeper, who there begins the transmission of the teachings of the four lights. This is the commencement into the work on transforming dreams. The primary source of dream consciousness is in how we see ourselves. The solar plexus is an image of the Sun (the heart) coming down to the Earth (moving down into the belly). The parasympathetic nerves coming from the solar plexus link to the nerves of the deep cardiac plexus as they pass upward to the brain. These linkages make the solar plexus a lower heart from the point of view of the parasympathetic system. The Sun moving into the belly is an image of the descent of the Ego into the physical body, which happens at puberty when the soul is given the task of finding the maturing being's personal power and self-image. With the Sun in the belly the soul can find forces for the individuality to make a place in the events of the world. To work with this chakra requires a deep intuition of the power of others. Through others we gradually come to know our place in the whole creation and the power of our own self as a child of God and an image of Christ. Developing this knowledge is the task of the spleen chakra in the solar plexus.

This chakra is linked to the fire element and represents the ultimate evolution of the soul in the spiritual realm. The fire element renders all things into spiritual life. The fire is both a death and a birth to a new order of existence. In the teachings of the Confidant Doorkeeper the fourth light is the light of the intuition. With this teaching the artist/student learns to surrender to the being who is inspiring, which entails both death to self and waking up in the other. To accomplish this surrender, the worker must learn to assess the other being and its source of power – or we could say its esoteric name. A deep understanding and trust of the spiritual world is required. What starts out in life as the process of sexual maturation can be transformed through esoteric practice into the highest faculty known to human beings.

This chapter on the chakras is not included to promote undue concentration on these areas. There is great danger in doing unguided breathing and concentration on the ganglia and glands in these centers. However, the work on the chakras is a necessary part of esoteric training. In the alchemical path, the work on the self is accomplished by working on the ways the senses and the cognitive forces interact in the soul. The work with the mandala of the four elements and the four lights of the Confidant Doorkeeper will strengthen the four chakras without concentration being placed on them directly. The purpose of including this material on the chakras here is to help students on a path of self-development recognize the symptoms that each of the chakra manifests. In the following chapter exercises will be given that, without concentrating on a chakra directly, can nonetheless be experienced as a development of the particular mood of soul and esoteric task associated with the particular chakra. At no time is it suggested in this work that the student concentrate directly on the chakra. On the Rosicrucian path, if you wish to find yourself, look out into the world.

8

THE FOUR LIGHTS
A TEACHING OF
THE CONFIDANT DOORKEEPER

AS WE HAVE SEEN IN THE CHAPTER on the alchemical mandala, the movement from water into air is a critical stage of the work. In going from water to air, the soul is faced with the crisis of moving from antipathetic forces in the soul, which can be controlled to a degree, into the mode of sympathy, in which control over the process of surrender is not readily available to us. In the earth mode we have the facts we have garnered in our research to rely upon. We have an abiding belief in the power of facts. Armed with facts, the soul is not challenged to find sympathetic forces on its own. Any sympathy present at the earth stage is likely to be for oneself, and self-sympathy is a problem. Unconscious self-sympathy is the shadow side of sympathy for others. When self-sympathy is made conscious, it can be reversed by an act of will, and only then can it serve as a higher force in the fire mode. Until then, self-sympathy presents a sticky dilemma to the artist/student journeying from water to air. The attention of the soul is focused on self-satisfaction and cannot extend to others.

The entrance to the sympathetic, or will, side of the mandala requires that the problem of self-sympathy be faced by bringing it into our day-awake state. When seen from the other side of the threshold, the problem here is to find a way to recognize the quality of our inner state when inner images arise as a result of a sense impression. In normal life a sense impression causes an involuntary inner response pattern to arise in consciousness that obliterates our experience of ourself, of our Witness. When this obliteration happens again and again, as it does in everyday life, the self-insulating pattern builds into a dark abyss where knowledge finds its absolute limit and the things that go bump in the night hang out. At this abyss between the worlds, anxiety about losing our body prevents us from seeing our Witness living in the darkness on the other side. What we need here is a light, and it just so happens that our Witness is composed of light. Wouldn't it be convenient if we could simply turn on that light to see into the darkness of the abyss? Our doing so is such a distinct possibility that the adversaries who live in the abyss want, at all costs, to prevent human beings from discovering this miraculous capacity lying dormant in the deep heartfelt domain of the True Human.

Here the Confidant Doorkeeper has a role. The Confidant Doorkeeper has four levels of teaching – four lights. Each level is a recapitulation of the lessons learned in the lower elemental mandala. The difference is that the four lights often appear as an image of a kind of dream dialogue between the soul and spiritual beings. The images given in these dialogues are usually connected to a particular mood of soul. In fact, every stimulus-response pattern connected to a sensation creates these moods in us and is a form of dreaming. The mood images arising as a result of sensory stimuli are representations of the sense impressions experienced through unique dream imagery consistent with each individual. When we dream we are skiing down a slope toward a pond, we may really be representing to ourselves anxiety about entering our physical body waiting for us in the bed. This universal experience is clothed in the language and imagery of dreaming through the help of symbolic representations that are unique to us. Or, more significantly, in dreams that accompany significant soul transformation we may be dreaming dreams whose symbols are really spiritually active archetypes. As dreamers and seers, we need to be able to tell the difference and then form protocols of communication to engage the archetypes in symbolic dialogue. There is a hierarchy of intensity in these dream states that forms the body of teachings of the archetypal being guarding the entrance into spiritual knowledge. All cultures have such a being. In alchemy this being is the Confidant Doorkeeper.

In the teachings of the Confidant Doorkeeper the first light in the darkness of the abyss between worlds is lit by overcoming the automatic dream patterns through which we form unconscious representations of remembered sense impressions. This first light is simply having awareness. In the first light we are not really aware of representations moving through our soul; we are simply aware. This difference can be illustrated easily. Imagine that you are sitting watching a movie, and on the screen a man is shown with an ant crawling up his arm. This is the sense impression. Suddenly you are overwhelmed with the urge to scratch your arm, and you unconsciously reach over and scratch your arm. In the reaching and the scratching we are dreaming. Representations of the sense images are arising in us below the level of our awake state. We have transferred the image in the movie into ourselves and represented it there as an inner image, and now we are reacting to the inward production or echo of the representation. We become aware of the itch when we see the image outside, repeat it inside, and then somewhere in our organism form the representations that become the command to scratch. All of this is accomplished while we are engrossed in the movie. The automatic production of inner representations as a response to outer sensory stimuli is the first light of awareness. The problem is that we are totally unaware that we are forming representations. We are unaware of our awareness.

The second light of the Confidant Doorkeeper is the awareness of our awareness. In this level of teaching, we slowly become aware of the automatic production of the representations. If you wish to visualize the second light of the Doorkeeper, imagine you are sitting on a park bench and notice that a person standing some distance in front of you has some unusual physiological feature, say a large nose. Imagine that you find yourself staring at him involuntarily. Suddenly he scratches the place you are staring at and looks around directly at you staring at it. You avert your eyes and realize that you were staring. The other person is dealing with the first light of awareness; he is simply scratching an itch and turns around to find you staring at him. You are dealing with the second light, the awareness of awareness. The other person's response has awakened this heightened state in you. In your staring you were in the first light.

Even though your staring was not perceptible to the other person on a day-awake level, it was perceptible to him at the dream level in the subconscious/unconscious. He was forming very unconscious representations as a result of your staring. He simply became aware in a way similar to the way a dog becomes aware of you if you stare at it from behind. The person felt an awareness within his soul and responded automatically, below the level of day-awake consciousness. You, on the other hand, were moved by his attention toward the second light in the dark abyss. When he turned and looked at you, you suddenly became aware that you were staring. In the staring you were in the first light, a dreaming light of awareness. In the waking up in the dreaming, you entered the second light and became aware of your dreaming awareness. Your stare is the mark of your dreaming. Your shame at being caught staring is a mark of awakening in the dream. Awakening in the dream is the second light in the abyss. It is a recapitulation of the water experience in the elemental mandala, in that we become aware there is some sort of pattern or meaning in the dust of the data, or we could say in the way the unconscious representations are being formed.

Through practice aimed at penetrating the teachings of the second light, we can gradually become aware that there is some sort of pattern in the rhythm of our dreaming during the day. In a way, human beings are always dealing with this second light. Any time someone asks us to repeat something we have said or to make an appointment to be somewhere at a particular time, we are forced to be more aware than our normal dreaming state in which very unconscious representations rule the life of our soul.

However, the circumstances of this type of awakening brought on by someone else or some external circumstance are still highly self-sympathetic. In self-sympathy what awakening there is in a situation is brought to us by the flow of life, and very little of our own will is brought to bear on the response. If we make an appointment, it is usually the fear of being thought of as unreliable that makes us arrive on time. The engagement of the Witness is not really what helps us to remember to be on time. In another example, if someone asks us to repeat something we just said, we usually don't make a big deal out of it, but repeat it in the flow of the conversation. Again, in this awareness of our awareness we are not really engaging the Witness in a conscious way. The other person's request that we repeat what was not understood represents an external circumstance that is determining our response rather than an independent moral impulse from within our own soul.

However, there may be circumstances in which we respond to the outer world in a self-selected way that shows the Witness is engaged in the judgment process. For instance, if we have a speech impediment and someone asks us to repeat something, we might be very aware of our being and its impediment, and we might suddenly have an emotional response and question the intent of a person who would ask us to repeat what we just said. Are we being mocked, or did the person really not understand us? In looking at the person's intent, we would be using a level of awareness beyond that involved in simply repeating a phrase we thought had been misunderstood.

Conversely, if we are talking with someone who has a speech impediment and do not understand something he or she says, we might feel embarrassed to ask the person to repeat it. We would be aware of the person's being, not just the flow of the conversation or its content. Or we may have a hearing impediment ourselves and be embarrassed because asking the other person to repeat the phrase would reveal our dysfunction. This level of awareness is the third light in the darkness given by the Doorkeeper. At the level of the third light, we are not only aware of our awareness, but we also become aware of being and all of its manifold relationships.

The transformation from the second light to the third light involves an even deeper commitment of energy and attention to the transformative process than did the work with the elemental mandala in moving from water to air. More sympathy for the other is necessary than when we are in earth or water mode. The need for greater forces of sympathy in the approach to the third light has a great deal to do with the physiology and psychology of perception and sensation.

Esoterically, sense activity has two distinct stages within the soul. The first stage, which is primarily perception, is present in the soul without any cognition. The will forces present in perception come from a combination of soul forces. On one side of the soul, we have the sense object presented to the soul as the forces of light, color, heat, form, and so on. Actually, any perception that is part of our experience of the object is part of the will structure of the world as it is presented to our senses. When the forces flowing though perception enter the sense organ and call up a response, this response is sensation. In sensation, the formative "becomings" of the object become part of the soul content of the person having the sense impression. It is here that representations arise. The will of the person having the sensation is negligible since in sensation humans are mostly dreaming what the ruling will is creating in them. Sensation is a response in the nervous system to a perception that arises in the organism in an unconscious or automatic way. This is the awareness level of the first light.

As the human being becomes more selectively aware of particular responses to sensations, the faculty of sensing is developed gradually into a capacity for cognition, the ability to get meaning from the sensation. In sensation the sense impression is partially penetrated by the will of the person having the sense impression. We could say that in sensation the personal will of the person meets and matches the ruling will of the sense object, resulting in an unconscious representation. When an attempt is made to be aware of the sensation, the person focuses the will on the *meaning* of the sensation by trying to control the representation. In this activity the ruling will present in sensation is no longer simply pouring into the soul. Something in the person is coming to meet the sensation and give it meaning. The higher soul impulse is to match the sensation with an idea. This matching of the sensation with the idea is experienced in the soul as recognition. That is, re-*cognition,* an experience of knowing. The purely sensory nature of the sense experience is met with the heightened awareness of the person who is trying to understand the inner representations that are arising as a kind of dream. The heightened awareness requires that the person who is dreaming as a result of reacting to a sensation exert his or her own will to meet and match the patterns of becoming that are part of the manifestation of the object. This matching of sensation and idea of the becoming requires the conscious transformation of the representations that come from sense experience. This conscious transformation by using the forces of the Witness results in understanding. The will to understand the object takes the soul one step away from dreaming and one step closer to thinking. Once again, this is the experience of the second light, being aware of awareness. Abstract thinking in which we rearrange abstract relationships between sense object and concept through building and organizing unconscious representations is the level of thinking present in the teachings of the Confidant Doorkeeper.

In the third light the Confidant Doorkeeper is telling us that not only do we need to be aware of our awareness, that is, think abstractly, but we also need to be aware that where we can find meaning through control of the spontaneously arising representations we will find as well meaningful or intelligently willed (ordered) activity. And where there is ordered or willed intelligent activity there must also be beings. Beings do things with their will. Beings give meaning to inert systems of forces. For a reductionist, "will" is just a force similar to what drives the "motor" nerves in the body or causes a ball to roll down an inclined plane. For reductionists or empiricists, the forces of nature have no beingness behind them; they are just abstract forces. For this type of thinker, forces just mysteriously happen, like in "big bangs," and once the "big bang" happens, a lot of other stuff happens.

This type of reasoning, so common in astrophysics, could never be applied in a court of law. In a court of law, when things happen, someone must be held responsible for them happening. Why is it that a universe can come into existence and some humans think there is no being who is responsible, yet when we jaywalk we are held responsible? This anomaly points out in a very direct way the dilemma of the alchemist who is in dialogue with the Confidant Doorkeeper about the teaching of the third light. At this level, the alchemist must struggle with and then come to understand that "All that was made, *was made*." And some being made it.

When the lesson of the third light begins to sink in, sense objects, which used to be simply caught in systems of forces, once more become animated. Their forms once again reveal the intentions of their makers. This is happening once again because this is, after all, a *re*-cognition of something that was originally cognized. The only difference is that in the original, more subconscious sense experience of the form of the sense object, the dynamics of the becoming of the form were only dimly cognized as part of a dream. The original activity of the creative beings who make the physical aspects of human beings is present in a concentrated way in human beings as the miraculous form and function of their body of flesh. The divine activity of the creators is normally lost to human beings in sensation. The human is aware only of the sensation and the sense object, and not that what stimulates the sensation is the activity of the creative beings within the object.

When the esoteric seeker enters a dialogue with the Confidant Doorkeeper in the lesson of the third light, the task is once again seeing that all things made were made by beings. It may be that some creative beings are incarnated and some beings are not incarnated, but all things were made by beings. Our body is made by other beings just like everything else. We use our cars and computers and airplanes but we don't make them; they are made for us. Even if we work in the factory where they are made, we can at best make only a part of them. Behind every appliance and machine are beings who made them for us. Behind every facet of nature are beings who create and animate the forms used by all of life.

To a materialist or physical scientist, this idea will, of necessity, seem far-fetched. To an esotericist this idea is a manifest reality that is ignored at our peril. The Confidant Doorkeeper teaches the lesson of the third light when a human being manages not only to be aware of but actually to gain control over the ways spontaneous unconscious representations arise and mutate in his/her soul.

An example of this task would help to illustrate the work of the esotericist. Suppose that a person has a habit of looking at members of the opposite sex in ways that are less than noble. At the earth level of consciousness the image of the other person stimulates predictable behavior and a conditioned response. If a person has no inclination to esoteric working, this is simply a part of a mating ritual, and the unconscious representation stimulates a pattern in which the person of the other sex ceases to be a person and appears in the observer's consciousness as something like a commodity. The other person gets analyzed according to physical attributes in the same way we would list the contents of our office for an insurance agent.

At the water level esotericists looking at an attractive person of the opposite sex would have the same perception as an exotericist, with a similarly resulting sense impression. This is the earth level. From this encounter, an unconscious representation would arise in the soul. As the representation arose in the soul of an exoterically oriented person, awareness of the awareness would accompany the sense impression. leading automatically into a sexual fantasy. A kind of watery flowing movie would start to play in the inner eye and the person would begin moving through the water level, responding to the sense impression. Very little of one's own will is present in such an earth/water pattern, and a great deal of will is being given to us, causing us to have an unconscious representation we cannot control. Let's say for sake of the illustration that the initial interest leads to a relationship and in the relationship the air level of reversal begins to take place in which the person has to take the point of view of the other.

This type of situation requires that we become the other person since the air level is the level of simultaneous consciousness. The relationship would move automatically through the level of earth and water to the level of air. Anyone who had not practiced controlling unconscious representations would be at the mercy of the dynamic that would arise when the two souls were in contact through time. Without an esoteric practice of controlling unconscious representations there would be no way for a person to monitor how he or she was responding to the other person. The initial stimulus-response pattern that was appropriate at the level of earth and water would now somehow be inappropriate or ineffectual in solving any social dilemmas encountered when the relationship, which was initially based solely on the pleasure given by attractive sense impressions, started to move to the level of air. Marriage counselors or lawyers would eventually be needed to help the relationship get to the level of air where each partner would have to see the other person's viewpoint simultaneously with his/her own. The air level requires reversal of all things.

Let's play the same scenario, only this time we will add the capacity of being able to monitor the formation of unconscious representations developed through an esoteric practice. In this version we will say that the practice of working with unconscious representations in a mandalic way has already developed what is known in esoteric circles as the Witness. The Witness, as we saw elsewhere, is a portion of the consciousness that observes the arising of unconscious representations and transforms them into what are known as living pictures. Living pictures give the soul a clear understanding about the feeling quality of the image. The techniques for the development of the Witness and the formation of living pictures are complex and are described in other chapters.

In the pursuit of the consciousness of the Witness, each developmental level of the elemental mandala is accompanied by a parallel development in the higher mandala of the four lights. As a result of this transformation, when the sensory input from the meeting with an attractive member of the other sex is active in the earth level of the soul, an accompanying movement of the witnessing capacity integrates an element of being able to witness the arising of the unconscious representation accompanying the sensation. In the level of earth there is very little outwardly to let the soul know that this is happening. The work at this level occurs mostly in the more subconscious levels of the unconscious. However, through esoteric practices based on monitoring unconscious representations, the capacity to witness slowly moves into the higher members of the soul. Eventually, through practice in visualizing, a being is born in the soul whose task is solely to be aware of the ways unconscious representations work in the soul. We know this being as the Witness. Working according to the ancient mantra "As above so below, as below so above," the Witness is present in the unconscious as a representative of the higher worlds whose task is to accompany all sensory experience but to rise above the subconscious levels of the unconscious into the superconscious levels of the unconscious. When witnessed from the superconscious/unconscious, the arising of unconscious representations from a sensory experience is linked to a higher will nature of the beings that animate the becomings of the sense object. The Witness "sees" the inspired will patterns in the becomings in the sense experience rather than seeing the automatic unconscious representations that arise from the subconscious/unconscious. The person who has developed the Witness will have the same sense impression of the pretty girl as an exoterically oriented soul but instead of forming an abstract involvement with the sexiness of the self-feelings arising from the habitual unconscious representations, a part of the soul will witness how this particular image is arising. A more developed Witness can then see the ways the soul links the self-feelings into patterns of association. When the fantasy aspect of the water level follows quickly on the heels of the sense impression, the Witness is present watching how the images are morphing into each other to form the fantasy. The important point to remember about all this is that the fantasy is still happening in the soul, but there is also a soul component that is not involved in the energetics of investing the arising unconscious representations with power. The Witness is present, but not involved in the drama of the habit.

However, a lifetime of fantasy is usually not corrected so quickly. Many practice sessions in the conscious forming of inner pictures are usually needed to get enough will power in the Witness so that the air level of the elemental mandala can be approached with its requirement of simultaneous consciousness. Simultaneous consciousness is the lower octave of the third light. In the teaching of the Confidant Doorkeeper, the third light is the awareness of being, and this is where the Witness can make a difference. In the earth and water stages of the elemental mandala the antipathetic forces of analytical thinking create the inner feelings that what we see as sense objects are in reality separate from ourselves. This habitual experience is translated into every sensory experience, even our sensory experience of another human being. This is a fundamental error in judgment for a human. The sensory part of human beings is the least human aspect of their existence. It is the part most like nature but simultaneously the least human part. The physical body, where the senses have their root, has reached a perfection and maturation because it was designed a long time ago by hierarchical beings of great intelligence and power. It is the oldest and wisest part of the human but at the same time has the least potential for development. The least developed part of the human being is the Spirit Embryo of the True Human, which aspires to freedom and love. And the Spirit Embryo has the greatest potential simply because it is the least developed. These mysteries are the mood of the teaching of the third light. In the lower octave of the third light, the air mode, the requirement of simultaneously uniting polar opposites is the basis from which the Confidant Doorkeeper can teach the Witness.

Having looked at this from a few different points of view, we can now explore how the fantasy process can go when the Witness is present. The fantasy arises but since the psyche has been developed to witness the arising of unconscious representations, the fantasy appears inwardly with an element of caution. With an established Witness, we are aware that a fantasy is arising as opposed to simply having the fantasy arise. The witnessing capacity can already be present in a dim way in the second elemental stage of water when we are aware of our awareness. In the third light, witnessing the arising of fantasy allows the soul a bit of breathing space between the stimulus of the sense impression and the programmed response. After we watch ourselves fall into the fantasy many times, a distinct moral mood of wishing to do better arises in the soul. When it arises, we might perceive the object of our fantasy as a human being living a significant life rather than as an assemblage of sensually stimulating physical attributes. This shift in consciousness is the teaching of the third light: not only was everything made but it was all made by beings. Streaming out of this insight is the sublime realization that all life is composed of beings. Even so-called inanimate objects and the realms of the so-called dead contain the quality of being.

Through the teachings of the third light by the Confidant Doorkeeper, the Witness transforms the fantasy of habitual unconscious representation into living picture imagination. Through living picture imagination, the soul can enter fully into the inner life of another soul. We can wake up in the dream of the other person's existence and get to know him or her as a fellow pilgrim on the journey toward eventual union with the archetype of the True Human, the Christ. This is not to say that our fantasy of the person is wholly transformed in an expeditious way; fantasy serves its lawful biological and psychological function. It is simply that through the teachings of the third light the fantasy gradually becomes more exact, and with willed inner pictures the associative relationships among unconscious representations become much more accessible and controllable. These practices work to stabilize the forces of the soul. As the soul is stabilized, the abyss between this world and the next opens wider to reveal the necessity of more work on ourselves, accompanied by more sublime vistas of the spirit.

The final stage in the elemental mandala is the fire stage, where the images so carefully constructed in the first three stages must be dismantled and reduced to complete silence. The fourth light is the octave of this stage in which the Confidant Doorkeeper teaches that, once being is recognized, the urge to surrender to another is the final, furious challenge. Nothing short of self-immolation is acceptable. In the fire stage the imaginations that form the central core of the practice are reduced to nothing but "empty" silence. The emptying of the consciousness through stilling the mind is aided by the resilient will developed through the Witness by forming exact inner pictures. What is retained is the intention of the will in the witnessing; the content is discarded. The forming of the images in the air stage is merely a preparation to withstand the immense silence that confronts us when the Witness stands before the Confidant Doorkeeper completely silent and attentive. When the urge to make unconscious representations is finally satisfied, the soul can approach the spirit in dialogue.

If a hunger for unconscious representations remains, then the Confidant Doorkeeper wisely tells us to retreat from the threshold to work on ourselves. The fire of the fourth stage in the elemental mandala becomes the ardent ability to surrender to the other in the teachings of the fourth light. When we have even just the fragrance of this capacity established in the Witness, the stern reminders of the Confidant Doorkeeper become tender, guiding confidences. This intimacy with the Doorkeeper makes it possible for us to surrender our busy and attentive consciousness to The Consciousness in the plane of consciousness. The elemental fire burns while the fourth light reduces our consciousness to ash, releasing our spirit into the land of the speaking flames across the great chasm between this world and the next.

In the last resort, we all have our task on Earth that must be done, so none of us can linger too long in the land of the speaking flames listening with the heart to the intimate teachings of the Confidant. Sooner rather than later, we awake in our body of flesh, prone to fantasy, blaming others for our suffering, and in general doubting the intention of the Creator. All the while the Witness waits patiently for our next lesson from the Confidant Doorkeeper in the Art of Surrender.

9

PUTTING IT ALL TOGETHER
A SOUL BREATHING EXERCISE

THE FOLLOWING EXERCISES are an adaptation of indications given by Rudolf Steiner and are presented here in an attempt to make the series of ideas discussed in this book into one cohesive meditative practice. In them we move systematically through the lower senses of the physical body, through the life forces of the life body, and into the realm of the planets and stars as one creative movement.

1. The Sense of Touch
Focus your attention to become aware of your body touching the chair in which you are sitting. Feel your back and buttocks against the chair. Now feel the bones of your pelvis pressing into the flesh as you sit in the chair. This is the experience of touch as it happens within the physical body.

2. The Sense of Life
Scan your body with your attention and find areas that are tense or are not in your normal field of consciousness. Find such a tense or neglected area in a limb and gently shift the muscles and bones in that area until it becomes more relaxed. Now find a similar area in your abdominal region and fix your attention to relax the tension in that area. Imagine that you are bringing a warm flow of life forces into that area and try to dissolve the tension with the warmth. Try

to feel that something is softening and expanding there where it once was tense and contracted.

3. The Sense of Self-movement.

Starting with your feet, contract all of the muscles in that area and then relax them. Then move to your ankles, then your calves, then the knees, and on up until you reach the top of your head. Try to feel how it is to consciously determine the contraction and relaxation of a muscle. To help you maintain consciousness of the relationship between your will and the resulting action, say to yourself, "Now I am contracting my feet muscles, now I am relaxing my feet muscles."

4. The Sense of Balance

The ultimate organ of balance in the human body is the heart. In this exercise begin by finding your pulse rhythm in your wrist by placing your index and middle fingers on the blood vessels on the inside of your wrist. Now, try to find this pulse rhythm in your chest using only your attention. It helps to hold your breath for a moment in order to find it. Once you find it you can breathe regularly and stay in contact with the heart rhythm. Now find the heart rhythm as it flows through your ears. This is subtler, but it may sound like a little bell is ringing in your ears. Now, using only your attention, find the heart rhythm in your digestive area. It is most likely to be found around the area to the right or left of your navel. Finally, using only your attention, follow the pulse from your heart area out through your shoulders and try to feel the heart rhythm in your hands. In this way we can build a subtle feeling of how the heart rhythm permeates the physical body and brings balance to it.

5. The Sense of Warmth

Using this imagination of the rhythms flowing from the heart, try to feel the warmth that is also permeating that area. Imaginatively gather the warmth pulsing around the heart and will it to flow down the insides of your arms to your hands. Concentrate on successive, slowly moving waves of warmth gradually flowing into your hands.

A helpful rhythm is to move from the heart to the shoulder, from the heart to the upper arms, from the heart to the lower arms, from the heart to the hands. This kind of pulsing helps the imagination. The goal is to feel a tingle or a sense of fullness or actual warmth in your hands.

6. Heart Fibers: The Arms of the Heart

Once a sense of warmth is established, your arms are filled with the life forces of the heart and can be used to send warmth to other areas. These warmth-filled arms could be called the arms of the heart. Once the arms of the heart are established by feeling warmth or fullness in them, imagine you are stroking warmth from the heart toward the lower right portion of your trunk in the area of the liver. With your arms of your heart you are giving your liver a warmth bath. As you imagine the warmth flowing, it is useful to inwardly see fibers streaming from your heart toward your liver. Seeing them helps sustain the imagination so that you can remember where you have been and where you have to go.

Keep expanding the fibers by stroking the arms of your heart away from your heart toward specific places. Go to your pancreas and spleen below your heart, then down in the back to the kidneys. Then spread warmth fibers down through your intestines and the genital area all the way down to the feet, where the fibers exit through your heels. Try to imagine that the fibers are filling the inside of your body with warmth, that they go from the heart through your organs and from there spread and reach the surface of your body. It works better to establish the lower circulation of the warmth fibers first since the connection between the heart and the head is a very established one in most people. Once the lower body is filled with heart fibers, use the arms of the heart to stroke the warmth fibers from the heart up into the lungs and the circulation of the neck and into the head. Once again, imagine the body being filled up with warmth as the fibers from the heart go to specific organs and then proliferate like the root hairs of plants, spreading to eventually terminate at the surface of the body, filling the body itself with heart warmth.

7. Awareness of the Etheric Star

The previous imagination is very useful for penetrating the body with a focused attention. The next exercise takes this body awareness and lifts the attention from the physical body to the body of life forces and the space around the physical body. It is called the etheric star. Imagine that the warmth forces you have been developing throughout your body are now gathered at a point at the top of the crown of your head. Try to feel them there as a subtle warmth around the top of your head. When you can feel this warmth let it stream down the right side of your body along a line that could be drawn from your head to the outside of your right foot. Similar to the establishment of the technique for the arms of the heart, we want to start a rhythmic stream of warmth that starts at the head and through increments gradually arrives at the foot. This may take some time to develop, but it is a very useful practice. When the stream from the head to the right foot establishes itself, then the other legs of the five-pointed star usually unfold with ease.

The complete pattern starts at the head and goes to the right foot, from the right foot across the body to the left hand, from the left hand across the chest to the right hand, from the right hand down and across the body to the left foot, and finally from the left foot back again to the top of the head. This makes a five-pointed star. The pattern can also be done in reverse, with the first leg going down the left side of the body from the head to the foot. It is even possible to follow two streams starting down both sides of the body and ending up at the head as a final balancing exercise. It is useful to use the arms of the heart to stroke the warmth from place to place, especially if it is difficult to hold onto the pattern of the image of the star. It can be experienced that it is not necessary to have your physical body spread out in the form of a star in order to feel these currents. You can be sitting in a chair with your hand folded, and when your attention gets to the point in the star that approximates the folded hand in your lap, that hand will get warm even though there is no posture in the physical body to support this imagination. At the end of the exercise make sure that you feel yourself once again touch into the chair in which you are sitting. This exercise places the attention on the space around the body and serves as a good jumping-off space for the gradual withdrawal of the attention from the physical body, the focus of the next exercise.

8. Uniting with the Etheric Star

In this next exercise we will focus on building an image of the life forces in the etheric star and feeling ourselves united with the star while at the same time being aware of the link we have to the life forces in the physical body. Go through the sequence of filling the physical body with warmth forces. Then build the etheric star and feel yourself slip out the back of your body and look down on your physical body with its starlike etheric body around it. Extend your arms of your heart out to the sides of your heart and use them as a stabilizing or guiding tool to keep the bodies lined up with each other. Holding your arms of your heart outstretched, feel the streaming life forces in the star as impulses delicately impacting the outstretched arms of the heart. Practice slipping in and out of the star. You can only do this from a subtler place outside of the etheric star, in the astral body. Realizing this makes the next few exercises very interesting. At the end of the exercise make sure you consciously feel yourself touching again into the chair.

9. Rotating the Life Body

The next step is to separate the consciousness that is witnessing the star form of the life body from the life body. If you are sitting in a chair and you can slip out of the back of the physical and life bodies, pay attention to what direction in space your physical body is facing. If, for instance, your physical body is facing south, then this exercise consists in slipping out and, with the arms of your heart upraised, mentally rotating your life body counterclockwise to face east. We eventually want to have all of the subtle bodies facing east, and your astral body will follow the motions you make with the arms of your heart to turn the life body toward the east. When facing east in the subtle bodies, we are aligned with the astral and life bodies of the Earth and it is possible to bring currents through them while configured in this way. If you are facing west with your physical body, then you need to turn counterclockwise 180 degrees to face east. If you are physically facing north then the most effective motion is still counterclockwise to the east taking you through 270 degrees of a circle. Trying to turn 90 degrees clockwise from the north to face east most often results in an uncomfortable feeling of being twisted up in tangled sheets. This usually breaks concentration and we snap back into our physical body with a thud. Therefore, the easiest direction for the physical body to be facing in this exercise is the east. At the end of the exercise, always bring yourself into contact once again with your physical body by feeling yourself touch into the chair. The rotation of the life body is a very good exercise to prepare for the next imagination.

10. Placing the Astral Body among the Planets

Once a clear experience of the separation of the astral body from the life body is developed, the next step is to imagine that the geographical point on which your physical body is situated is an anchor point. From that anchor point, with your life body in its star form facing east, rise above it in your imagination and ascend to a place where you can picture the eastern horizon in your mind's eye. It is useful not to completely separate the astral body from the star form of the life body while doing this. A good imagination is that the astral body is a kite with strings attached to the points of the star of the life body. Keeping the strings attached to the life body, slowly let out the string and allow the astral body to float up above your geographical position. It is very difficult but very useful to practice keeping both the floating astral body and the tethered life body in your attention simultaneously. After some work, they are linked to each other in a way that feels very similar to a kite on a string.

Once the astral body is free, try to imagine the position of the planets at that moment. If you are working at dawn, see the Sun rising in the east and then continue east in longitude and imagine each planet in succession that you would meet going eastward. Feel how these planets and their influences are like a billowing wind for your astral kite. Periodically touch in with the tether in the life body and strive to keep a harmonious balance between the freedom of the astral experience and the nurturing nexus of forces of the life body down below. Make your imagination of the planetary positions as accurate as possible to protect against fantasy. As you complete one circuit of the Earth, slowly reel in the kite string and feel yourself sitting in your chair.

11. Moving in the Astral Body among the Planets

The next exercise develops out of the last experience of placing the astral body consciously among the planets. When this becomes a clear imagination it is possible to move even deeper into the astral realm and still maintain an awake consciousness that is in contact with the life body. Once the astral body is free and moving among the planets, the motion of your astral body can be enhanced by actually visualizing that you are moving toward the planets and through their positions instead of simply noting their positions in longitude from a fixed longitude. To do this you would imagine moving toward the Sun and then passing it to pick up a planet in a more eastward position. Try to see the Sun receding behind you and the next planet moving closer as you move eastward. When you get back to your original position once again, reel in the kite string and feel yourself sitting in the chair.

12. Experiencing the Great Circle of Being

The final exercise grows out of the last one. Once you get back to your position in longitude, imagine that you are moving backward against the rotation of the Earth, that is, you are facing east and moving west. As you move against the Earth, lift your attention to the starry realms. The human being entering this level faces a paradox of the one and the many. My limited sense of self is faced with great feelings of disintegration at this level. To deal with this it is useful to imagine the limitless expanses of space organized into twelve different realms. When I can feel myself as one in twelve, the shock of the limitlessness of space does not cause undue emotional experiences to disturb the meditation. As one position out of twelve situated on a vast circle composed of many beings, I can survive the mystery of myself as a bodiless entity and still be capable of bringing back into my body the insights that help me transform myself when I am living fully in my bodily consciousness.

Imagine that you are filled with the warmth of the forces of your heart and your astral body is in contact with it through the kite strings. Feel the forces of the starry realms coming to you as the infinite circle of being gets smaller to include your circle of being related to your life on Earth. As the infinite circle of being gets smaller imagine that you can feel the will in the beings who live in the infinite being directed to you to help you live your life. Receive this goodwill in humility by realizing that "God is in me." Let the goodwill stream into the etheric star and then mingle with the heart fibers streaming from your heart. Feel the inrush of grace and will soften the resistances to lessons involving suffering. Feel the gratitude arise from the wisdom given to you through your trials. Express this gratitude toward the creative beings living in the infinite circle of being. Devote the forces of your life toward their unceasing efforts to unfold mercy and understanding on Earth. Join your forces to theirs by realizing that your destiny counts. Express this thought by saying, "I am in God." Breathe between your own sense of self and the self that spans the cosmos. Feel yourself move once again toward the longitude of your physical body. Feel the tug on the kite string as you are attracted once more to entering your body of life forces. Feel your life forces streaming into your heart area. Feel your body touching the chair.

Part Three

The Alchemical Mountain

1

BEFORE WE BEGIN

HEARTFELT THINKING

IF WE ARE TO GO ON A JOURNEY, it might be useful to consult a map before we begin. A map will tell us not only where we are going, but also the territory we will pass through to get there. This information is useful in planning what to take and in becoming familiar with landmarks to look out for even though we may never have been to the destination before. The map gives us a kind of second sight, allowing us to make good decisions about the journey before we even leave.

The images in this part are symbolic maps of an alchemical journey through our own subtle bodies on the path toward higher consciousness. Through these images we can see that our journey through our subtle bodies is like climbing a mountain and that along the way some strange beings will be encountered. However, we can also see that there is a path through this landscape of the soul, even though it is not always apparent. To follow such a slippery path requires that we develop capacities to read the subtle clues given by the map. The exercises accompanying these images are intended to help develop these types of capacities. We could call this whole process symbolic mapping.

In symbolic mapping, the map is made of pictures that have meanings at many different levels. The pictures are made to be read like a children's picture book, that is, without words. However, this is not just like a children's book of pictures; it is more like a visual fairy tale. Like fairy tales, these pictures tell a story of great profundity and depth. To begin with, each picture is a rebus, a cipher that stands mute before us without revealing any of its meaning. We will meet a rabbit and a chicken and a stone wall, among others. None of these things are particularly meaningful symbolically by themselves; the power of the symbolic map arises in the relationships of each element to the others. As we journey through a symbolic map, the rebus, or signlike nature of each image, slowly transforms into the symbolic nature of the image. A sign or rebus simply points to something, like an exit sign or the sign on a restroom. This is the first level of meaning on a symbolic map.

However, even exit and restroom signs can be transformed into symbols by an active human imagination. In order for a sign to be transformed into a symbol, the alchemist must return to it again and again without a full understanding, while each time striving to expand the potential meanings of the image. Once the image is sufficiently permeated with the attention of the alchemist, it becomes a symbol. The image then links with others in ways that cannot be predicted. To an alchemist, a symbol has the quality of a being: it demands attention in order to be understood. Signs or ciphers simply stand for something; they do not grow until we return to them again and again as if we did not understand their sign nature. Symbols grow in the consciousness of the alchemist and deepen to encompass many levels of meaning.

Each picture in this part is symbolic on a number of different levels. A deeper understanding of who we are is the goal of this series of symbolic pictures. We propose to go step-by-step on the path up the alchemical mountain by first describing the pictures from their more common point of view, then describing them from a more symbolic, or alchemical, point of view so that the signs begin to transform imaginatively into symbols. Exercises will then be suggested that can aid in dealing with the challenges each switchback on the mountain road presents to the traveler or pilgrim.

The very structure of this work is intended to be alchemical. The image of the mountain forms the manifest or salt side of the work. As we have seen, salt is a term used alchemically to describe the result of inner work that manifests in something physical. If I am thinking of something for a while without understanding it and suddenly an answer appears in my consciousness, an alchemist would say that was the action of the great salt process. A painting gradually appearing on a previously blank paper is salt, as is the coming to term of an embryo after gestation. The opposite process is sulfur or *solve* or solution. In sulfur something that is manifest gradually dissolves out of manifestation. To forget a slight against us is *solve* as is the tendency for inner images to merge into other inner images.

In this work the mountain picture is salt and the tree with the hands is *solve* in the beginning. We start with the whole mountain picture; then the image is taken apart in little pieces and exercises are given to aid in understanding the symbol. The initial salt nature of the image of the mountain gradually becomes sulfur as it is dissolved into will forces used to do the exercises. At the same time, the images at the ends of chapters are a small portion of another picture, the picture of the tree of knowledge. In the beginning this image is in a sulfur or potential condition. We see only snippets of it, and instead of exercises there are just a series of questions. The questions lead our consciousness into pondering without really knowing. This is the technique of sulfur, or questions only. It is a healing technique for a consciousness that can only think logically. It is in the sulfur pole that the forces of the will emerge as a creative and imaginative counterpoint to the logical thinking of salt. The structure of the book then is alchemically designed to become a marriage of opposites in the soul of the reader.

The balancing of salt and sulfur forces in the soul is the first step on the path toward eventual liberation of the soul. Our age dims the creative, imaginative problem-solving capacities of human beings with an unfounded belief that more information will give us answers to life's greatest problems. To an alchemist, the most important faculty a human could develop is the capacity to sustain attention in a problem that has no hope of solution. To do this, we need to be able to visualize problems pictorially. This moves them away from the prison of logic and into the realm of the capacity for the heart to think. The heart thinks in pictures that move in our consciousness in lawful ways. We could say it is listening to the qualities of motion present in the relationships between the pictures.

A well-developed heart can ponder images for a long time without requiring an answer. It takes a long time for the heart to think through all of the possibilities present in a problem. For this reason alchemists regularly included mistakes in their formulas and diagrams to lure the unwary and the unworthy into jumping to hasty conclusions by forming a salt-like conclusion to the problem simply because their hearts were unable to stay open long enough. In alchemy it was considered an act of magical will to slowly contemplate a complex symbolic image that had a hidden or occult meaning. It was a kind of exercise of will that was not linked to an outcome or particular meaning structure. It was understood that this kind of active attention and concentration developed the will more profoundly than any other type of exercise. The development of a pictorial consciousness further enhanced the active will by releasing the intellectual mind from logical sequences of analytical thought with its limitations of only being linked to a particular outcome for a problem. We would say today that the alchemists were trying to think outside of the box in order to explore the broader and fuller dimensionality of the problem. Resonance with all of the implications of a problem and the use of parables to allow the imagination free rein in the world of the psyche were the fundament for this exploration. The purpose of this alchemical approach was to allow the heart to feel the fundament and wholeness of the thought before arriving at a conclusion. This is heartfelt thinking.

This part is designed to promote alchemically the first stages of heartfelt thinking. It will probably be less than satisfying if it is "read" in the conventional sense of that word. It is a group of exercises whose purpose is to stimulate awareness that the heart is capable of thinking and that its thinking is not abstract and logical but creative. We could even say divine in the sense that heartfelt thinking can be used to divine the deeper mysteries of life, for which the light of the intellect is miserably ineffective.

2
The Alchemy of Questions

An alchemist is a person who studies the ways things in the world go through processes of transformation. It is understood that in alchemy the essential transformation is really in the soul of the alchemist. The transformation of metals is really an analog of the great soul task of making our own lives richer and our goals nobler. The great alchemical work is work done on the soul to become a more creative and flexible person.

One of the underlying concepts in alchemy is that the processes being studied must be approached by questions that are images of the process itself. In fact, questions are the alchemist's greatest tool. Without the proper question the alchemist is left with the belief that one metal cannot be transformed into another. In old alchemical texts this is sometimes described as Oedipus and the Sphinx. Oedipus had to overcome the questions arising from the old way of seeing things in order to understand the fundamental mysteries of life.

The process of asking the proper question is a high art in which the mutual states of consciousness of both the questioner and what is being questioned are explored. The best and most creative questions really have no answer but in themselves lead to better questions. Alchemists felt that answers and information stop the creative process from proceeding further. Good questions keep the dialogue moving even if it seems that nothing is happening, because they keep us

Anonymous artist, from *The Secret History of the Rosicrucians in the 16th and 17th Centuries,* Altona, 1785.

engaged in the process of questioning and ultimately exploring the diverse levels of consciousness surrounding each question.

Viewing the image of the alchemical mountain for the first time, we are confronted with a disarming mix of metaphor and analogy. It appears to have no sense to it at all. The picture is a rebus or cipher. It is a visual question that an alchemist would use to guide our consciousness into asking ourselves deeper and deeper questions. What is an answer at one level transforms at another level into a deeper aspect that once again presents the same image transformed into a deeper cipher or symbol. What we thought we had understood soon becomes another question as we make our way up the mountain. This is the path of the questioner: the alchemy of transformation.

In the following chapters we will take a journey up the mountain together, exploring the questions that the symbol presents to our consciousness. We hope to uncover some transformative energies to take into our sleep life where the real work on transforming the consciousness resides. We will ask questions and then suggest some exercises that can be of assistance in deepening the questions meditatively.

So let's begin by asking some questions about the picture. Who are these strange people at the bottom? Why is there a wall? What is the rabbit? Why is the chicken sitting on the road? Why is there another rabbit inside the wall? And on and on. We can see that there are limitless questions about the picture, but we have a feeling that all we are gathering are the details of the picture. We have not answered anything because the elements seem to lack any inward relationship. This is how it is when we first start exploring consciousness; we have some images but no glimpse of what their relationships are.

This is essentially the character of the dreaming consciousness: many seemingly unrelated pictures. To continue listing details of the picture would yield many more pictures, but how can it lead to any understanding? An alchemist would say that to make an inventory of the images is the proper type of questioning technique for the fundamental level of understanding, the earth level. In the earth level we can make a list of the images, and with this list we have the "dust" of the whole image. But then, in order to make the dust live, we have to transform the images into water. To an alchemist this means to make them flow in our inner eye.

Let's go back to the people running around in the bottom of the picture. Place the figure on the right into your inner eye; that is, try to see the picture of the man facing the wall and running with his hands up in the air. Now make the person move and wave his hands and maybe make some sort of noise. If we do this, we can "see" the activity of the person much more vividly than if we simply look at the figure and abstractly recognize that it is a running man. Ho hum, a running man. To move the figure and move with it is alchemically to bring life to the picture, the way rain brings life to barren dirt. The perception of inner moving pictures is alchemically the consciousness of water.

As a first exercise, move with all three figures and then write a sentence for how it felt to be each figure. Then do the same water exercise with the rabbit. Try to stretch the image out and animate it inwardly. Do this exercise once during the day, preferably in the morning, accompanied by a written sentence. Then do the same exercise just before going to bed in the evening, minus the written part. Next we will look at the air level of the work.

Why is a hand coming out of the cloud and grasping the tree? Why is the tree split in half? Was it split before the hand came down or after? Is the hand trying to put it back together? What is a hand? What is God's hand? What is it with God and clouds anyway? How can a cloud stay up in the air? What is up? What does it mean for a hand to come down out of a cloud? What is down? Maybe the cloud is actually God? Maybe the hand isn't God's hand? If it isn't, whose hand is it? Could anyone else stick a hand out of a cloud? Why are this hand and this cloud on top of this tree? I wonder, how was God made?

3

Lupus the Hare

JUST LOOKING AT THIS PICTURE CASUALLY leaves us with the question, What are these people doing? We might feel that it makes no sense to us. An alchemist would call this a rebus or a cipher. It is a sign pointing to something not illustrated in the picture, but which requires us to somehow already know something about the picture. This kind of participatory consciousness asks us as the viewer to somehow enter into the picture at another level above the one that is present in the image itself. An alchemist would say the picture must be led in our consciousness into the water so that its meaning can flow to us out of its becoming. This is a strange language, but alchemists felt that language which got right to the point was suspicious and apt to lead us into a false viewpoint. They specifically made images hermetic and difficult to understand so that the whole mind would be asked to enter into the process of knowing rather than just the intellect. They did this by treating images as living questions. We get no answers from these strange people. Only questions arise from looking at this image.

In the last chapter, a process was described in which we took the images of the persons and the rabbit into ourselves and flowed along with them, or "became" them. In doing that we were entering into the processes of becoming of the people and the rabbit. Learning to enter into the becoming of a symbolic picture is a great preparation for learning to listen to others and to the deeper levels of our own psyche. Alchemists understood that the capacity to enter into becomings was the key to higher consciousness. The four-elements theory gave alchemists the capacity to adjust the questions they asked to fit the proper level of the system they were studying. If they wanted information of an abstract nature they asked, what is different? This gave them intellectual answers based on information. They called this level of asking the question "earth." If they wanted to know how the system had its becoming or how it was going to change they asked the question, what is changing? This question gave them insight into the level of the system that they called "water." In water it was possible to ask a question that lead the mind into the process of coming into being and going away, which was the main concern of the alchemist intent on transformation of soul processes.

When we did the exercise of inwardly depicting the people and the rabbit in the image, our consciousness shifted from earth into water. The water level of questioning allows the mind to participate in the image rather than being an onlooker to it. By shifting into the participatory consciousness, alchemists were able to work with a question for a long time without expecting an answer. This is called keeping the question open. Working meditatively with an open question is the doorway to higher consciousness. It is also the doorway to social transformation. Contemplating the images of the people and the rabbit in water consciousness involves the heart in the process of asking questions. Getting the heart to ask questions is the essence of the alchemical method.

If we enter into the figure on the right in the image and imaginatively run around with our hands up in the air, we get a feeling of being crazy and out of control, something we might experience if we were afraid. If we run at the wall like the standing figure on the left, we get a feeling of frustration and hopelessness. We might even get to the point that we hate the wall. If we finally spot the rabbit going down into the hole and then turn to face the wall instead of paying attention to which hole the rabbit is going into, we get a feeling of doubt that we even saw the rabbit. The rabbit, or Lupus the hare, is an old symbol for the art of chemistry and transformation of gross substances into life-giving substances. This is linked to the habit of the hares to eat certain of their own excretory pellets early in the spring to repopulate their digestive systems with beneficial organisms. This mystery appealed to the alchemists who were taking the cast-off feces of the substances of the world and transforming them into medicines – similar to inoculations today.

So in the picture are some people outside the wall of higher sight who are running into walls of hatred, doubting their own spiritual transformative capacity, and fearing life and the lessons it brings. They beat on the wall of higher sight but do not see the rabbit, nor do they see the figure of the guardian sitting in the archway of the walled mountain of higher consciousness. To see these things, they need to take their inner water picturing and dissolve the images consciously into the elemental level of air. The most effective alchemical way to do this is to think the movements of the inner water pictures backward into a state of silence and then to listen into the silent space for as long as possible without forming a new picture. This silent, empty space is the psychic equivalent of air.

Try imagining the three people running forward chasing the rabbit into the hole, and then imagine the rabbit running into the hole. Then imagine the rabbit running backward out of the hole and then the people running backward. When they reach the positions they have in the image, dissolve the images and listen intently into the silence.

4

YAKIM AND BOAZ

IN THE PICTURE THE STRANGE NAKED MAN is sitting on a stump in a doorway into the walled mountain. We would not like to run into him on a dark night, but that is exactly where we encounter such a figure. The figure is known alchemically as the Confidant Doorkeeper; it is also known esoterically as the Guardian of the Threshold. This figure begins to approach us from the other side when we become more adept at going to the air level of consciousness. When we can sustain a good air consciousness, we could be called an adept. To an alchemist, the Confidant Doorkeeper is a being that slumbers in every person. It is composed of all of our fears, doubts, and hatreds. Developing a capacity to sustain a question into the air consciousness means that we have followed the rabbit down the hole and stopped running around in the world as if we were crazy. In *Alice in Wonderland,* a strongly alchemical work, the March Hare is constantly running around in a tizzy. This is the image of the three crazy people outside the walled mountain. And we will meet the rabbit again.

For now we can ponder not only the Confidant Doorkeeper but the doorway itself. The pillars on either side of the door have names for alchemists since they represent the two polar qualities of consciousness of the person moving toward the Doorkeeper. On the left is the column known as Yakim. For an alchemist, this pillar was made of salt. It represents the curious nature of Lot's wife: she wanted answers and could not keep a question open, and her lust for answers turned her consciousness into a pillar of salt. If I ask you a question I think I already know the answer to, that is Yakim. If I ask you a question with any other motive than actually the mutual exploration of how your consciousness works, then, for an alchemist of the soul, my question is Yakim, or salt. If I expect information will come from my question or even if I expect an answer, my question is Yakim. It may seem strange that we can ask questions without expecting answers, but the path into higher worlds is directly past Yakim. Meister Eckhart, the famous mystic, calls the soul that pursues information a virgin soul, or *nous pathetikos*. It is the soul of the virgin expectant that when the beloved appears it will be made whole, but that it cannot be made whole without someone else giving it some information or insight. A soul in the realm of questions is surrounded by pathos, the biggest question being, Are you my Prince Charming? This is the mood of salt or Yakim.

According to Meister Eckhart, the other kind of soul is the married soul, or *nous poietikos*. This soul has ceased being expectant and has instead become creative. The married soul has accepted the great work on itself and seeks to approach problems creatively and openly rather than with any expectancy. The married soul is *poietic,* or full of potential, rather than expectant. The married soul is living in what alchemists would call the consciousness of sulfur, or Boaz. In the image, the column on the right hand of the Doorkeeper is Boaz. We will meet another being later at a higher doorway who will ask us questions about the qualities of Boaz in our soul. The Confidant Doorkeeper first questions us primarily about our salt nature and tries to get us to see that our expectations get in the way of our goals. It is good to have goals and to think; thinking makes humans the salt of the Earth. However, it is retarding to have expectations. Think, but have no expectations. This is the higher salt.

The Doorkeeper in reality is a part of us that is a free being who lives continuously in a timeless world. The Doorkeeper helps us to remember that we are timeless beings as well as reactive persons who run around chasing rabbits and bumping into walls. Remembering this helps us to grow. The Doorkeeper asks basic questions such as, "How did it become like this in your life?" or, "What would you wish to do better?" The Doorkeeper is there to remind us that we need to ask ourselves these questions. These questions are so big that they cannot be answered just like that. They actually do not have any answers, but the secret and profound value of such questions comes not in asking them just once, but in asking them of ourselves on a regular, rhythmic basis. This is the practice of remembering the Doorkeeper. Asking ourselves this kind of unanswerable questions rhythmically, every day at the same time, forms a spiritual practice.

Getting in contact with the timeless inner being in each one of us is a big task. The secret technique is to regularly ask significant, tough questions of ourselves as if we really didn't expect answers. Ask the hard questions regularly but do not expect any answers and do not allow any rationalizations. Unless we contact the Doorkeeper consciousness every day, sporadically going inside of ourselves can be like running around like a scared rabbit or careening crazily into walls. Through working on ourselves in this way, we can form a different, more conscious relationship to time. When things start to press hard in our lives, it is beneficial to remember that our inner being is always living in a timeless realm. If we can gain access to that realm and to that inner being, then time begins to change in our lives. Actually, time remains as it is, but we can change our perception of time to our benefit.

A few minutes spent asking ourselves what we would wish to do better in our lives can be followed by the old practice of bringing to mind a few blessings we have been given, such as breakfast or a warm bed or clean water or regular transportation or a roof over our head. When we start to count our blessings after asking ourselves some tough questions, the Doorkeeper helps us to see that running around like a scared rabbit is useless and that our lives have a higher purpose that we might be missing while we are feeling we are slighted or are out of sorts or resentful or expectant. With these two practices, the Confidant Doorkeeper can point the way from Yakim to Boaz. The land of Boaz is the lower ring inside the wall.

How do we know that this is the Sun and not the Moon? What does it mean that the Sun's corona is filled with stars? Why are some stars like the Star of David and some like snowflakes? Why are the snowflake stars shown with crosses in the center? Why do most of the snowflake stars create void spots in the Sun's corona?

5

THE LAND OF BOAZ

In the last chapter we met the Confidant Doorkeeper, the alchemical Guardian of the Threshold. This being asks us to change our thinking about how we have come to expect life to be. The exercise of asking ourselves a tough question and then counting our blessings was a way of dealing with the alchemical pole of salt, or Yakim, standing by the entrance to the walled mountain. Looking at the picture, we see that the stones in the Yakim column, on the Doorkeeper's right, are well hewn and the column is solid. This pictures the type of question that is salt. A salt question has one definite answer and that answer is intellectually cognized. From the point of view of this side of the wall, the intellect is the most truthful tool for answering questions. That is true when we only ask questions having to do with technical or physical things. There should be only one clear and irrevocable answer for the torque needed to bend a steel structural member or the dosage of a drug. Lives depend upon these intellectually correct answers.

However, when this type of question and question/answer relationship gets carried over into the interactions of human beings, as often happens, it does not allow for the truth to be approached, because the truth is much larger than only one answer when it comes to questions of destiny. The other column standing by the entrance into the higher realm is known as Boaz. In the land of Boaz on the other side of the wall, other processes of questioning need to be employed. In the picture of the Doorkeeper we can see that the column on his left hand is a bit wobbly and made of imperfect stones. This is a picture of higher truth that is not dependent upon the physical laws on this side of the wall.

To the right of the Doorkeeper inside the wall we meet our friend the rabbit once again. Here the rabbit is running free and not ducking into a hole looking for cover. This is the image of the open question, in which there is no expectation of an answer. To live in an open question requires what the poet Keats called "negative capability," the capability to remain enthusiastically engaged in a question with no hope of its being answered. This is the fundamental tool of the land of Boaz the lower level of the alchemical mountain.

Boaz means sulfur. In alchemy sulfur was a burning process in which the polarities of a compound were brought closer to each other and made more intimate. In everyday language we call Boaz "cooking." Take one carrot and one onion, chop them and put them in water, and sit down and eat. But this is not so good, you would say. Put a fire under them and cook them, that is, run them through a sulfur process and they become intimate with each other. They are now soup. Now add your salt and you have something nourishing. This is the idea behind the open question.

When facing the guardian, the column of Yakim asks us to purify our salt or change our thinking about our lives. The column of Boaz asks us to take up the task of purifying our thinking about how we impact other people's lives. We are asked to be more inwardly flexible. If we find that the questions that we put to people only have the mood of Yakim, then a fundamental humanness is being denied in our questioning process. Asking questions for information distorts the process of mutual exploration of the levels of consciousness available to humans for problem solving. We will look at this more advanced mutual process next when we look at the hen sitting on the nest. For now, the free-running rabbit asks us to begin the process by asking ourselves the questions of the inner practice of "as if."

The "as if" exercise is useful for enhancing the feeling that we ourselves are capable of living in an open way within the questions of our life. In it we are letting the rabbit of our mind run free.

a. Write down a quality you would like to develop that you feel is now not a part of your personality.

b. Try to determine what this new capacity would involve your doing or not doing. For instance, you might choose that you would like to be on time for work since that seems challenging for you. Having chosen this, you could establish that you must get up fifteen minutes earlier in the morning and that you will not check your e-mail before you leave for work. This is something that you would do and something that you would not do. It is important in this exercise to pick things that you can do or not. Do not pick things like attitudes to try to work with. Those come later.

c. Try to visualize yourself getting up earlier and then not checking the e-mail in the morning. In the visualization process there will be hidden feelings around both of these activities. See if you can get close to the feelings around each activity. If a feeling arises, simply observe it and then go back to visualizing the activity.

d. Once you can visualize the new behaviors, try the following. Think of situations in which staying in bed for the extra fifteen minutes would be just fine. Think of situations in which checking the e-mail would not be a problem. In your mind's eye imagine yourself sleeping in for the extra time and describe in a few words the feelings involved. Then contrast these feelings with the feelings surrounding getting up early in order not to be late. A strong feeling should arise in this contrast. Try to describe the feeling in a few sentences. You may be surprised at the power of some of the feelings. Don't try to rationalize or explain them but simply put them down so that they can be observed.

e. In the final exercise, try to imagine yourself existing without the strong feeling you just wrote about. In the example of lateness, you may feel a sense of rebellion in your lateness, which is appealing to you even though it causes friction at work. It is the enjoyment of the rebellion that makes it difficult to change the problem. As long as the pleasure is greater than the solution, the problem stays fixed in our personality. To heal this, try to see yourself as if you did not have the compulsion to do the activity. Could you stand not having the pleasure if you changed your thinking about this problem? You will probably feel that to imagine yourself without the problem is phony and stupid. Let those feelings arise, even write them down if they keep coming up, and then dissolve them, let them flow away. This is "as if" practice. We are setting the little rabbit of our mind free to imagine how another kind of existence might be possible for our soul. To imagine life without the problem is the first step in dealing with it.

Why is the Sun on the trunk of the tree? Why are there fruits on the tree? Why is the Sun the middle part of the split tree? Is the tree growing out of the Sun? Is the hand from the cloud pushing down or pulling up?

6

THE ALCHEMICAL DEW

IN THE LANGUAGE OF ALCHEMY *coros* means the dew of the heart. For an alchemist the heart was superior to the brain as an organ of thinking. The heart took in many images from the world and fermented them, gradually producing inner pictures or "dew," which came to the meditating alchemist like a refreshing gift of the night. Opportunities to bring about situations in which the creatively fertile dew of heart thinking can be developed are rare in the fast-paced decision-making processes of today, which are usually driven by sharing information.

We have seen that the Doorkeeper warns us to purify our thinking by making sure we are aware of our thought-forming process. Then in the "as if" exercise we entered into the process of forming questions on a different level. To ask ourselves questions that have no real answer seems a bit useless, but to spend time imagining how our life would be "as if" we were not living it seems positively senseless. However, these exercises are simply preliminary exercises to the formation of the alchemical dew of the heart.

For an alchemist the dew was a miraculous substance. It was the gold of the night or the refreshment of the stars. The stars were considered to produce the finest of substances each night and this fell to earth as a kind of manna. The manna was the dew, a holy and miraculous substance. To us in our thoroughly earthed consciousness, dew is just precipitation, a kind of low cloud. For an alchemist the dew could work wonderful transformations. It was avidly gathered and preserved for use in the highest of alchemical practices.

Since all alchemical practice is an analog of soul transformation, we could ask, what is the analog to dew? Goethe, in his great alchemical fairy tale "The Green Snake and the Beautiful Lily," would answer conversation. Conversation is not the trading of information nor is it the putting forth of conflicting statements. Interaction with statements is discussion, not conversation. Discussion is a cutting off of one another with statements. Conversation is making verses with each other. Since all higher truth can only be stated in complete paradox, only conversation can occur in the land of Boaz and beyond. Everything else is running in circles chasing rabbits.

In the picture, on the opposite side to the rabbit we see a hen sitting on a nest. This is an image of the alchemical dew of the heart. To cultivate this dew, a type of open conversation can be built by giving an image like the one we are studying to everyone as a seed (salt). Each person then sits with the image for a while until someone has a question. The person with the question puts it into the center of the conversation. But in an open conversation this question is followed by another question from someone else. And then that is followed by another question, and another. The goal is to have a conversation around the theme of the image without resorting to statements. It is said that a hen will not sit on an egg that will not hatch. In this type of open conversation, our commitment to listen to each other rhythmically is imaged in the mood of the hen.

Even though this type of open conversation doesn't seem to make any sense (there is no information or answer to anything), like the little hen we keep sitting there asking questions, because we know the egg of our mutual understanding will eventually hatch. We know that the dew of the heart will fall out of the cosmos onto our hearts in the morning, that what you have asked me will ripen in my mind overnight, and that in the morning the dew will refresh my view of what I thought I saw. Keeping the question open in this way is at times frustrating because we feel the conversation is going nowhere. The commitment we make to keeping the questioning process open is a commitment to mutual exploration of the wondrous pathways of human consciousness. We quicken each other creatively when we can speak into a nonthreatening and nonhierarchical context, when the purpose of our questions is not to get answers but to explore the activity of consciousness through dialogue.

In this type of practice awkwardness and uncomfortable silence often are followed by grace and profound silence, as people work to meet each other in new ways without the familiar patterns in which I ask a question that bares a part of my soul and then you try to fix me. The work is sometimes frustrating and exhilarating simultaneously. This type of inner work can be broadened into a weekend activity by having people continue the idea of questioning by forming questions that arose in them during the dialogue process. They can then share these questions with the whole group as seeds for further work. This can be amplified if the participants are asked to come to the dialogue with one question about what they expect to learn from the dialogue. The expectations are then compared to what actually happens.

Dialogue must be disciplined though some form of focalization. In our groups, volunteer focalizers often meet ahead of time and are given bylaws for how to maintain a neutral atmosphere through mirroring questions. The focalizers are asked to consider the proper etiquette needed to establish the freedom that allows everyone to feel comfortable with asking heart questions.

In the working groups each person is asked to form a question arising out of each session and to share the question in the whole group at the beginning of the next session. Some people may have a deep interest in one or more of the sharings, so a breakout group can be formed that repeats the process, focusing on the mutually interesting question. Once again questions should follow questions rather than statements following questions. In a final session we often have forty-five minutes for a plenum format in which participants are asked to share with the whole group what their initial questions were and what their questions are now. This is followed by forty-five minutes of free space for conversation with anyone.

The mood here is the mood of the broody hen, the alchemy of the dew of the heart.

Why is the tree in two parts? Why is the upper part of the tree growing downward? Why is the hand of God reaching down to the tree? Why is the tree fruiting above the Sun? Why are some fruits being grasped and some fruits are not? Why are some hands that are reaching into the tree grasping fruit while other hands are grasping leaves? Why do the grasping hands come from the Zodiac region below the Sun and not from the Sun itself? Why are some hands dark and some hands light?

7

DRAGON IN THE CAVE

THE ELEMENT OF FIRE IS THE SUBTLEST ELEMENT and the most difficult to understand because fire is the least physical of the four elements. It is present in all transformations at all levels. When earth transforms into water (becomes molten), it is the warmth of the fire that does the transformation. An alchemist would say that the molten rock had undergone an elemental change from earth to water. At the next level, the transformation of water into air, fire is present as the catalyst. We could say that fire is the very spirit of transformation. The fire element makes our inner work more and more subtle. Silence and patient waiting are the characteristics of this element as it oscillates between its lower chaotic nature as flame and its transcendent healing quality as the warmth within the fire. This polarity is present in the image of the dragon in the cave. The dragon represents the lower fire forces of uncognized will that rise up to cloud our consciousness when we begin to work on inner development.

The cave is the body of the alchemist with its fiery will forces leading the inner life into urge and desire. As we begin working on ourselves, these will forces become perceptible to us as hindrances to our continued development. At first they are difficult to see and do not appear to be that strong because they are so subtle, but continued inner work reveals that the dragon forces in us never sleep and are continually active within every sensation and every deed. When we become aware of this level of the will, it signals that the dragon that has been living in the cave of the body and devouring our will forces is now considered to be an adversarial being. This is the fire level of the inner work. In it we must undertake to root out desire from the soul in a kind of burning process, generally accompanied by feelings of shame, worthlessness, and hopelessness. The fire of the dragon is the burning awareness of our helpless nature in the face of deep dysfunctional patterns of will. In facing the dragon, the capacity to witness the arising of inner pictures is valuable. Through practice this witnessing capacity is enhanced into the being known to esotericists as the Witness. In Western esotericism this being is imaged in the archangel Michael. The dragon rising up out of the cave of the body is subdued by using fire, the element of the purity of the forces of thinking, to transform the fiery nature of the will with heartfelt thinking.

To cultivate fire thinking, heartfelt thinking, it is useful to stretch the vision of a problem far beyond our present life situation into the realm of the future. The rhythmic force of spiritual practice brings thinking and will together in a conscious way to cultivate a will nature that can undertake inner work without being attached to outcomes or results. The rhythmic interplay of thinking and will softens the fiery nature of the will and produces soul warmth, through which the thinking can become felt by the heart. As the rhythm of the practice ripens in the soul in the warmth of the undesignated will, the dragon of the body, which wants to drag us down into its lair of despair, hopelessness, and shame, can no longer bring paralyzing fear into our souls.

Heartfelt thinking is most effectively developed when we are conscious that we are using will forces to form our thoughts. To think with the heart means that automatic thoughts must be excluded from our thinking processes by a strengthened will. Three very useful exercises for developing this capacity and for preparing the soul for the confrontation with the dragon have already been presented in part two above. The ABC/CBA exercise for developing the fluid gaze, described in chapter three, page 99, is the basis for work in the air and fire levels of the elemental mandala. The experiment using a candle in a darkened room, described in chapter six, page 155, is a good first exercise for working in the element of fire. And the technique for developing the practice of sacred sleep through the evening backward review of the day's events, described in chapter one, page 70, prepares us for going into the dragon's cave, the descent into our life of desire.

In the dragon's lair we confront our own misdeeds without the luxury of blaming someone else. We see that the difficulties in our lives have been the source of our greatest learning. We see that the endless desires which drive our lives really are another being in us who is not us. This awakens distant memories of who we really are and who we can be when we can assimilate our desires and transform them into resolve. This is the task of the alchemist who faces the dragon. In the next level we will be approaching a second guardian being who will ask us even more intimate questions. The exercises we do at this lower level will be tools for us when we meet the higher guardian.

8

THE REVERBERATING FURNACE

WE HAVE NOW ARRIVED at the top of the middle of the alchemical mountain. In the center stands a fearsome lion, which we will leave alone for now. Instead let's look at the elements just outside the castle. On the right is an alchemist's furnace. It is a reverberating furnace used to smelt ores and represents the process known as reverberation. This type of furnace is also used for the process of whitening the ash by completely incinerating things.

It is commonly thought that alchemists were preoccupied with changing lead into gold, but a common refrain in the works of the greatest alchemists like Paracelsus and Basil Valentine is that the work on the metals is undertaken to create philosophical gold and not common or vulgar gold. The reverberating furnace was used to separate metals and to purify ash to such a degree that it would release its salt in a purified form. The material to be purified was put into a place in the tall furnace where flames could be directed upon it from below and from above. This was the reverberation. The furnace had to be tall in order to house the baffles that directed the flame in the required way.

The double flame produced a fire that no impurity could resist. Purifying the vulgar metals was research that led eventually to the development of chemistry. Purifying the philosophical metals was research that led eventually to spiritual insight. To the initiated alchemist, "metal" was a term describing a living spiritual flowing process that somehow congealed into a mass within the Earth body, similar to the process of forming an embryo within a uterus out of the flowing waters of life. The term "metal," when applied to philosophical alchemy, referred to the processes by which the fluid world of sense impressions of all kinds somehow congealed into the forms of nature like an embryo in a gravid womb. In the arcane picture language of philosophical alchemy, to purify metal meant to transform the senses. The furnace beside the castle on the alchemical mountain refers to the need to purify the act of sensation if the alchemist is venturing into the neighborhood of the fearsome lion guarding the doors to the castle. The theme of the area around the door to the castle is fire in its many forms: the fierce fire of the reverberating furnace and the gentler fire of the *bain-marie* with the Sun and the Moon in it, on the other side of the castle. These images represent two of the five major fires available to the alchemist.

In trying to make a soul experience that would be analogous to the sensory purification of the reverberating furnace, it is useful to concentrate on the two major modes of the act of seeing, the fixed mode and the open mode. Exercises for developing these modes have been given above in part two, chapter three; the method involved is repeated here in abbreviated form.

1. Observe a manufactured object in two modes.

a. Fixed gaze: Make a list of details you notice while observing the manufactured object. As each detail arises in your consciousness record it in writing, then go back to observing.

b. Open gaze: Observe the object, but focus your attention on the space around it rather than looking at it. Do not allow any thought or image or insight to arise while you are observing.

c. Modify the exercise by thinking of the sequence of details you have previously observed before you commence observing. Each time try to notice a new detail you had not observed before and add it to the list.

d. Make a model of the object in modeling wax. Describe the process of modeling, that is, where you started to form it and the last thing you added to the model.

2. Observe a natural object in two modes.

a. Repeat the fixed and open exercises but use a leaf, a twig, or a shell.

b. Repeat the modeling exercise and the description of the sequence you followed in making the model.

3. Observing and reflecting.

Modify the exercise by asking yourself, What did this object look like just before it got to the stage in which I see it now? Ask the question and then do the fixed and open gaze processes. Record any answers and share your insight with a partner.

4. Repeat the two observational modes and then:

a. Modify the exercise by trying to imagine the manufacturing stages that produced the manufactured object. Try to get a feeling of evidence that what you are imagining is true. Use the details of the observations from the past exercises as support for the feeling of evidence. Write a few sentences about this process and share this with a partner.

b. Modify the exercise with the natural object by trying to grow the object in your mind's eye. Try to imagine the exact sequences. When you feel that you can image the sequences exactly, try to describe the sequence to your partner as if he or she had never encountered this natural object before. Write a few sentences about the experience.

What does it mean to work? Is work a physical force or a spiritual force? Is anything I do with a purpose considered to be work? Does the enactment of a deed have to be difficult in order to be thought of as work? Does there have to be a reward in order for my deed to be considered work? What is the difference between work and labor? What is the difference between work and pleasure? Can work be a pleasure? If I do something I do not want to do, is that work? Can I work without knowing it? Does my work need to be connected to my livelihood? Is work in the spiritual sense inherently different from work for one's livelihood? Is inner work, work? If I benefit from my work does that diminish its importance for the world? Is toiling in obscurity the purest form of work? Does being successful diminish the spiritual dimensions of one's work? What is the significance of the lightning coming out of the work triangle? Why is the "work" triangle pointing upward?

9

SUN, MOON, MERCURY

ON THE WALL OF THE CASTLE we can see that someone has drawn the symbols for the Sun, the Moon, and Mercury. This is an alchemical graffiti that reminds us that we must become aware of the forces of these three planets in our inner life before we can safely approach the higher guardian. In soul alchemy these planets represent the metals of gold (Sun), silver (Moon), and mercury (Mercury). They are images of the ways inner pictures arise in us and how much work we need to do to bring them into balance inside us before we can approach the guardian. The three planets are three fundamental modes of inner seeing arising out of sensory experience.

The silvery, reflective Moon forces in us enable us to remember things exactly as we thought we saw them. How we thought we saw them might not be what was there, but that is the gift and the trial of the Moon for the alchemist. The inner mood of the Moon is the feeling that all things will come out well if I can control them to follow the path that I see so clearly. The Moon requires that the way it was will be the way it always will be. Think of a mirror; the image is very exact, just backward.

The creative and transcendent Sun forces in us enable us to live in the mood that all things will come out well if we can just get out of the way of the process. The Sun forces allow us to face even death joyfully because we know somewhere in our soul that all things are right with God. The solar forces allow us to get out of the tight little box of our beliefs and participate in the becomings of the world. Solar forces allow us to become other beings without endangering our individuality. Think of the endless cycles of growth and transformation; that is the mood of the Sun.

The Mercury forces in us enable us to live in the mood that all things must change. Sun gives way to Moon and then Moon gives way to Sun. Mercury arises in us when we can do things simply for the love of doing them irrespective of the outcome. Mercury forces enable us to practice paying attention to the small things in life where so much of the richness lies hidden under the veil of expectations. The following exercises address these three metals and the moods they engender in the human soul.

Working with the Moon Forces

Choose someone in your present life who seems to make you upset and confused by the way he or she acts in a certain situation. You have a clear feeling that it is a mistake that both of you are on the same planet at the same time. You might find yourself wondering, "How can that person do that? How can he be like that?" These feelings are Moon feelings tied to the past and intent upon continuing it into the future. Try to imagine that you are leaving your own body and walking and gesturing the way the other person does when doing the activity that causes you to be upset. Imagine that you are a mirror for him when he is doing his dance. You may want to actually move your limbs the way he does when speaking, for instance. Then imaginatively dissolve the movements he makes and reduce your inner dialogue to silence. Repeat this activity daily until one day the other person's soul mood in doing the activity appears in your imagination simply as a gesture or intention toward movement. You may feel what that person feels when he waves his arms when shouting or how he flops into a chair and sighs when he is about to make a scene. Whatever it is, you can mirror it inwardly without judging the other person. This overcomes the Moon.

Working with the Sun Forces

Take the same person and situation as the object of the next exercise. Imagine that the thought pattern of the other person doing what is disturbing to you could be a geometric drawing. When he answers a question or make an emotional disturbance, would it look like a spiral or a square or a set of interlocking rectangles? Would his thinking process while he was upset look like a jagged series of points or a nest of rectangles? Would it look like interlocking triangles or more like a river delta of flowing and branching lines? Try to imagine the pattern of thought of the person during the times when his thinking is upsetting to you as some form of geometric drawing. Then think the geometric pattern away systematically. That is, if a triangle is drawn with one side first, then the second and the third, when you dissolve it imagine it disappearing in the reverse order of how it was drawn. Bring the emptied imagination into complete silence. Then observe the way the person defines the space in a room he enters. Does he go straight into the room and then move in circles or does he create small arcs around the periphery and then slowly drift into the center? When he talks with his hands do they draw spirals and crazy circles or do they make straight lines? All of these things point to the activity of the Sun in the human soul, the hidden language of the forces of life moving through the soul in response to images arising in the imagination.

Working with the Mercury Forces

Through Mercury we heal the split between what was and what might have been. The rhythm of the work is most important in these types of exercises. In Mercury the focus is to rhythmically attempt to bridge the gap between two polar situations. This is seen in the exercise as an attempt to link to other souls who have passed out of this life.

1. Bring to mind the image of a departed loved one. Set yourself to wondering about what the person is doing now in the place where he or she exists. This should be done just as if the loved one were alive. In this exercise we are wondering about the spiritual biography and evolution of that individual's I Am. The loved one in turn can inform us about the life lessons to be learned on this side of the threshold as seen by one who has overcome the fear of death. Our wondering about an ongoing spiritual biography creates forces of wonder in our souls that engender trust in the processes of life.

2. Recall someone who is departed who provided an example of forgiveness for another during his or her life on earth. Select a situation in your life now where someone has done something to you about which you still feel wounded in the soul. Ask the departed to show you how to turn your soul toward forgiveness for the misdeed. Your feeling of rhythmic harmony for the departed and the way in which that soul is membered into the world soul allows the departed soul to participate in your soul life in a creative and productive way. The feeling of rhythmic harmony for that individual eventually can be transferred to another person whom we are struggling to understand. The key to these exercises is the gentle repetition of the exercise with no expectation. This allows the Mercury forces to make a bridge between the worlds.

Why is the eye connected to universality? What does it mean to be universal? Why is the central image surrounded by a whole circle of eyes? What can all of the eyes belong to? What does it mean to see? Do we see with our eyes or with our soul? Are our physical eyes the only organs of seeing? Is seeing also understanding? What is an optical illusion? What is a delusion? What is a hallucination? What is an obsession? What is an inner picture? Where does an idea form in us? Where do we see memories? What is the difference between seeing and being seen? Is knowing a kind of seeing? How is it different from seeing with our eyes? Do we have more than one kind of organ for seeing? Can I see with my hands or ears? If you and I see something, are we seeing the same thing or is it different for each person?

10

SUN AND MOON IN THE BATH

IN THE DESCRIPTION OF THE FURNACE the intense heat of the reverberation was used to separate and purify the ash. This is a dissociation process. In any healing the dissociation process must precede the synthesizing. In alchemy the term "spagyric" is used to denote this process. "Spagyric" means to take apart and put together again; it describes the alchemy of taking apart the sullied forces of the soul and its habitual use of the metals (senses) and the purification of each one separately, and then the process of putting them back together again. The reverberating furnace is an image of the taking apart and purifying. The Sun and the Moon in the bath together is an image of putting together again what has been separated.

The bath of the alchemists was known as Mary's bath or *bain-marie*. It was an example of moist fire instead of reverberating fire. Moist fire was a synthesizing fire for digesting and blending back what had been separated. The description of the reverberating furnace mentioned the separating of metals from their ores and from each other. Now the senses have been purified by the work of the alchemist who has been paying attention to the qualities of sensation that give rise to inner pictures. The inner pictures have been separated and work with a particular sensation has been undertaken. It is now time to reintroduce the purified sense activities into the warmth of the soul life. This is the *conjunctio,* the union of the Sun and the Moon in the moist bath of the Virgin Mary. Remember that the Sun is the creative forces of the soul and the Moon the repetitive forces of the soul. These forces must be brought together into a rhythmic practice that, through the Mercury forces that then arise, can unite the Sun and the Moon.

For the contemporary soul alchemist, this process is most approachable through cultivating a practice in which questions take the place of answers. This allows the soul to stay in the open question for a long period of time, bringing the attention ever again to the same image or question and experiencing it from as many different aspects as possible. The following sequence of exercises is designed to lead questioners into the Mary's bath of their own sense impressions so that the healing of the Sun and Moon can take place. The questions move through a series of steps from earth to water to air and finally to fire. This is the alchemical mandala, which, as we have seen, is a symbolic form that enables a person to go into a process of *conjunctio,* or digestion, in a conscious way.

The Alchemy of Questions

Alchemical earth: What is the difference between knowledge and knowing? Is information knowledge or is it power? Can lists of details lead to understanding? Alchemically, learning requires that there be a process of soul breathing, that is the capacity to form accurate inner pictures that we can follow as they change inside of us. The process of finding and then refining inner pictures is a form of breathing that can be cultivated into imagination.

Earth exercise: Looking at any artwork that depicts people involved in a common activity, list the objects in the picture. Then list the figures in the picture. Is there any difference between the moods of gathering the two lists? Observe a figure and make a list of the elements of its costume, then describe the posture of the figure. Is there any difference in moods in these two procedures? Look at a figure in the picture, then place your own body in the position of the figure. Write two sentences about this activity. Has it changed your viewpoint to become the figure? Share this with a partner.

Alchemical water: What is change? Questioning basic assumptions about the relationships of elements in a system always leads to change. We could ask, are the elements in the system separate things or are they participating with each other? If so, how do they participate? What does it mean to participate? On a personal level, if I participate and it changes me, how do I know what I need to hold on to and what I need to give away in order to change? If I change, what does this do to my viewpoints? Can I hold more than one viewpoint and still be true to myself? All of these questions are alchemically water; they speak of the mood of change.

Water exercise: Take tracing paper and trace around the main lines of a figure. Repeat the tracing freehand, but accent the motion of the lines and not so much the exactness. Keep repeating the tracing in a freehand way until you can feel inwardly that you can remember the motion of the lines of the figure. Form an inner picture of the figure made of the motion of the lines and try to see all of the lines being drawn simultaneously instead of one after another.

Look at one of the figures in the picture and feel in your imagination that you are looking out of your eyes at it, that you are touching it with little hands coming out of your eyes. Next, decide to slip out of yourself and enter into the figure through the hands of your eyes. Feel inwardly that your body is taking on the position of the figure as in the last exercise. The difference is that you are now doing it all in your imagination rather than putting your body in that position physically. When you can experience being with or "in" the figure, decide to come back to yourself as the observer. See yourself in your imagination coming back into your own body. See if you can determine inwardly just when you have surrendered to the figure and just when you are the observer. This process is soul breathing. Write about how it feels to shift between participant and observer. Share this with a partner.

Alchemical air: What is the fundamental characteristic of an organ? An organism? An organization? Humans organize according to fields of energies that guide the processes flowing through the whole. What is the fundamental characteristic of a field? A field is a dynamic, a living, organizing process rather than a sum of positions. The activity of the field is shared by all parts in a kind of mystical union. Socially adept individuals find that their conscious access to the energy of the total field in an organization is the hallmark of managing groups successfully. Alchemically the shift from the individually driven process to the reciprocating process arising between individuals is the consciousness of air. To some, air consciousness means losing control; to others it means realizing that no one is in control but that all is organized anyway.

Air exercise: Turning the image you have been working with upside down, on tracing paper trace the *main* motions of the whole composition. See if you can form an inner picture that is accurate to the feeling of the whole web of lines rather than picking out details. This is feel-seeing. Imagine that there are small arms coming out of your heart and feel-see the web of lines with those small arms similarly to how you worked with the hands from the eyes. Write a sentence or two about this experience and share it with a partner. Focus on shifts of moods or the arising of sudden insights.

Through soul breathing, inwardly become the same figure you have been working with imaginatively. When you are surrendered to this figure, look out through its eyes and try to see how the other figures in the group within the picture look from this perspective. Now, become the figure and look back at yourself looking at the figure. Use the arms of your heart to reach out to yourself looking at yourself. Slowly return to yourself and look out of your eyes at the figure in the picture. Write a few sentences about this experience and share it with a partner.

Alchemical fire: The fire level in this mandala is the enthusiasm of the soul alchemist to keep the process going even when there is no appreciable change in anything. This patience will serve us in good stead in the meeting with the higher guardian.

11

THE HIGHER GUARDIAN

THE IMAGE OF THE HIGHER GUARDIAN is a combination of an eagle sitting on the upraised tail of a lion guarding the door to the castle of higher knowledge. In esoteric language, initiates are known as "lions" of the people. They take a vow to serve the people of their nation. This is the message of the higher guardian. The eagle is an image of the capacity of the initiate's thinking to reach transcendent heights. In the picture, the eagle sitting on the lion's tail has upraised wings, an image of the capacity of thinking to take flight. On the left, however, sits another eagle with its wings folded. It seems to be calling to the eagle that is about to take flight. This is a symbol of the intellect, or the earthbound thinking, which cannot enter higher realms. The fundamental task of the alchemist meeting with the higher guardian is to live in two worlds at once: the lower world with all of its struggles for power and fascination with technology, and the higher world with its experiences of spiritual beings and events that have such a profound influence on our human biographies. The lion is the powerful feelings that must be wedded to the transcendent thought processes if we are to enter the castle defended by the higher guardian. The following exercises are meant to be suggestions and aids in the ongoing search for access across the boundaries of the spirit.

The lion meeting the eagle represents the condition known as simultaneous consciousness. In this form of consciousness the objective capacity of the intellect must meet and marry the subjective consciousness of the feelings. The eagle sitting on the upraised tail of the lion is an image of what is known in alchemy as the thinking heart. The heart thinks when subjective and objective meet in mutual fructification. The following exercise is useful in developing a perception of the thinking heart.

As the subjective and the objective begin to interpenetrate each other in the soul realm, a keen sense of needing to make amends arises in the soul. Here a great danger makes it necessary to balance the activity of meditation with prayer. Actually realizing the extent and weight of our errors in a cosmic time frame can create a profound feeling of suffocation and despair in the striving soul. The closer we move to the Divine Light the more we can appear to ourselves in our daily life to be simply apparitions made of shadows. This can be very disheartening. The temptation here is either to completely give up on striving to develop ourselves or to become enamored of magical practices that promise to give the student occult power and knowledge.

In the presence of the higher guardian, the soul is being asked to willingly transcend the very foundation of its conscious existence. It does not let go easily into exercises of concentration and meditation. The only thing that helps is direct experience of the transcendent so that the soul can once again feel it is participating in its life in a creative way. In effect, in the realm of Inspiration we must consciously and willingly face our own dying processes. Through Inspiration we must learn to die to self. This is the teaching of the higher guardian. The lion of the feelings must die into the light of the thinking, and the freedom of the eagle must die into the life of feelings present on Earth.

In this exercise you need to work with a group of three or more persons. Each person will need five strips of paper, each about one inch wide and four inches long. The exercise is that you are told that you must leave your home for an unknown place and you are only allowed to have one thing or one person with you. You cannot have both a thing and a person, so you must choose. Write your choice on one strip of paper. Now, since you have made a wise choice, the powers that guide human destiny have deemed that you get to choose some other thing or person to take along. Again only one choice is allowed. Write down your choice on another strip of paper. Well, it must be your lucky day, or your lucky star is shining above you, for word just came in that you can choose one more thing or person to go along. The first choice was sheer survival, the second of great import, and now this one is very nice. So please choose and write again. Now, since you have been so cooperative and capable, you get two other things or persons to take with you. These choices fall into the "very cool" category.

However, now that you have made five wise choices and they have been granted, it is time for the inevitable meeting that every human being has with the angel of death. One person in the group is selected to be the designated angel. The angel will ask the members of the group to pick one of their choices and hand it over. One of the other members will take a choice from the designated angel so that that person can participate also. After the choices are taken, each person writes a few sentences about how it feels to go through this process. Then the angel of death once again visits the group and asks for another one of the choices to be given back. Each person once again writes a sentence about how it feels to do this. Now the angel visits a third time. This time, however, the angel does the choosing and not the person. Once again everyone writes how it feels to go through this process. You are left with two of your choices. Share with members of your group what went on within your soul in this process.

This exercise puts us in contact with a reality of human existence that is very much like the experience of the guardian speaking to us about our destiny. The feelings of loss in this exercise are very close to the feelings of anxiety arising at the threshold. This anxiety is present in every meditative process. It must be overcome through the practice of dying to the self. Sharing the common feelings of this exercise with others builds community and strengthens the capacity to awaken in others with compassion.

Prayer helps us in this situation in specific ways, and knowing which mode of prayer fits which situation is the essence of the al- chemical art. Prayer can be divided into two modalities, petitionary prayer and hygienic prayer. Petitionary prayer is prayer addressed to the deity so that a particular goal is attained. This level of prayer has doubtful implications for the eventual salvation of the soul. A more effective path to prayer is hygienic prayer, in which we address the deity, but only to offer attention to another being. The intent is very strong but the content is left open. There. The simplest example of hygienic prayer is to repeat the phrase "Prayers for X, Prayers for X," over and over like a mantra, which is most effective when an image of the person is held in the inner eye and strong feelings about him or her are roused in the soul. This type of prayer can be used to flood the other person with good thoughts; we give our forces of attention to the spirit in the name of the other person. Such prayer is hygienic for both souls. The danger in praying is always that we designate what the results of our prayers should be. This is dangerous because while it is a fact that what we pray for usually comes to pass, we might not have the wisdom to see the situation clearly in the long- term view. The combination of prayer and meditation is the healing practice that helps the lion and the eagle to come together and al- lows us to enter into the holy of holies.

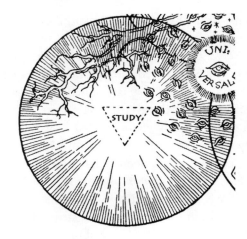

What does it mean to study? Does study change anything? Am I different when I know something than when I do not know something? How do I know that I know? How does someone else know that I know? How do I know that someone else knows? Is there a difference between information and knowledge? Is there a difference between knowledge and knowing? What is knowing? What is not knowing? When we say, "I know," is my knowing the same as your knowing? Why is the "study" triangle in the picture pointing down? Why is the "study" triangle surrounded by a radiant light? What has study to do with light? Why does the conventional symbol of the light bulb going on represent someone understanding something?

12

TREE OF HEAVEN

IN THE PICTURE WE CAN SEE that a tree is growing out of the mountain and that on the tree are stars. This is a cosmic or heavenly tree rooted in earth but with heavenly fruit. Alchemists know that there are many trees in the human being. In times past alchemists understood that the tree of knowledge was what they called Apollo's Lyre, or the nervous system. It is through the tree of the nerves that a human being comes to know the cosmos. The forms of nature play upon our nerves through light and sound, and inner pictures arise as a result of these impulses. The cosmic tree in the picture is growing on a forbidding outcrop of barren rock. The cosmic tree in the microcosm that is the human being is locked up within the very center of our rocklike skull. From there it spreads its roots out into the body. The stars on the tree are like the thoughts arising in our minds as a result of the activity of the cosmic forces present within each sensation. Light, color, sound, warmth, and movement pour into our nerves, and through them into our beings in a constant deluge of cosmic force.

Strangely, we are not aware of the cosmic nature of these miraculous forces. We see only memories of what were once marvelous forms of puddles, trees, clouds, and persons. The tree of heaven must be taken by the alchemist and transformed into a new tree. Knowledge must be transformed into experience instead of becoming more rigidified into data. To reanimate the senses and enliven them, soul alchemists must practice transforming their experiences of a deadened sense world into a participatory adventure with cosmic beings.

This transformation requires that we lose our habitual ways of being in our bodies. When we have not transformed the inner pictures, we feel that we are primarily a body. This feeling must be consciously reversed for us to enter into the message of the tree of heaven. The following exercise is designed to systematically dissolve our habitual body-centered consciousness and allow the soul to identify with aspects of selfhood that normally occur only in dream states or after death. The purpose of these exercises is to safely and systematically learn how to be conscious outside of our bodies.

Periphery/Center

This exercise can help to develop eventually a sense of the continuity of consciousness across the threshold to the next world. It begins with the inner imagination that we are in our bodies looking out at a starry sky. We imagine our soul is expanding outward in a circle toward the stars. The first part of the exercise involves seeing the circle spreading above and below and right and left from our position. This is a difficult step and brings with it some fairly unpleasant experiences, as if we were seeing ourselves become nothing. The part of the soul connected most intimately with the body will struggle to maintain the perspective in which we are the center of concentric circles. It takes spiritual will to maintain the imagination that we can expand our awareness around the circumference of a vast circle.

Once we can maintain this imagination, it is possible to feel a very complete sense of silence and peace while our consciousness is expanded along the circle. Into that silence place the image of your body and its daily consciousness waiting at the center of the circle for you to come back to it. This thought usually brings us back right into our bodies. Practice gliding back into your body while trying to maintain the integrity of the circle in your consciousness. It helps to see your body in the center as an axis or hub of the circle. As a variation try to circle around your body as you observe it from the periphery of the circle.

Once you can maintain the imagination of yourself extended along the periphery of the circle, try to hold on to the sense of having a body in the center of the circle while simultaneously imagining that your soul is extended along the periphery. Alternate this viewpoint with the imagination that you are in the center of the circle looking out at yourself as the circumference.

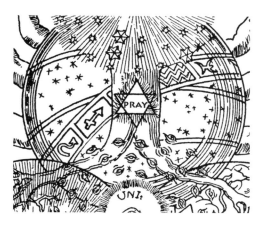

Why is the zodiac at the root of the tree? What is this tree anyway? Why does the tree have two roots, just as it has two branches? Why is the word "pray" in a Star of David? Why are the words in the other two circles in triangles and not in six-pointed stars? What are the other lines that intersect the zodiac? What does the ring of concentric circles outside the large orb represent? What has the zodiac to do with praying? Why does this picture include praying as the center of the zodiac? What does the zodiac mean, really? Isn't the zodiac a fable? Is prayer a reality or is it just a fable for persons who cannot work or study? What is praying?

13

Tree of Life

IN THE IMAGE WE SEE AN ALCHEMIST in the upper level of the castle planting a tree in the lower level. He is setting it into the *bain-marie*. On this tree are stars just like the ones on the tree on the other side of the mountain. The stars are the wisdom of the tree of knowledge. There is also a little vial on the tree, and in it is the spiritualized will of the alchemist who is giving the tree of knowledge back to the world below. In this willed deed of sacrifice, the alchemist is inheriting the tree of life that was forbidden to Adam and Eve. The tree of life is our body's blood and vascular structures. Through the tree of life we once again enter paradise, and at this stage of the work the striving is to enter paradise consciously. To participate in the planting of the tree of life, our will must be turned away from expectation and made into a spiritualized essence. The image of the tree on this side of the mountain is the image of the spiritualized will.

The Daily Will

One of the most useful capacities for establishing a regular practice is spiritualized will. The spiritualized will stands in contrast to the daily will with which we get things done in the world. In life the daily will enables human beings to do things. It is present as an impulse in the physiology, even before there is any thought of how to do what we are considering. We simply want or will to do something. Think of scratching an itch while you are reading a book. The will impulse to scratch that eventually results in the scratching is most often not in any way remotely present in the soul, which is occupied with the reading of the book. We simply will to do the scratching and then the scratching is done. This level of the will is the daily will.

The Conditioned Will

The daily will can be strengthened by paying attention to what we are willing to do. At this level we can will our mind to think about what we are doing. The will then is not automatically producing a resulting action, but when we do the actual action we usually revert back to the daily will. The higher level of will that is present when we will to do something can be called conditioned will. However, even in conditioned will, thinking about what we want to do usually follows the mysterious unconscious arising of a daily will impulse simply to do something. The daily will impulses usually originate in the unconscious far below the level of understanding available to our thinking. As a result it is very difficult to get in touch with the initial conditions that arise in the daily will and later turn into actions.

The Zone

Other soul qualities making it very difficult to understand the will are the feelings we have surrounding something we are doing. Through time our ability to do things gets filled with expectations. We usually have many expectations about results when we do something. In the daily will it is often the expectations for specific results that serve as the foundation for the will to accomplish something. The action is permeated by the feelings of expectation about the results of moving the will. But hidden in this type of will is a diminishing return. Think of eating a piece of chocolate. There is a definite expectation in the will. But the second piece of chocolate does not have the same expectation in the will as the first one. The third piece is even less interesting, and so on, until we lose interest completely. This points to an archetypal aspect of the will and its relationship to feelings of enthusiasm or expectation: the will fades away when some activity is repeated.

This has profound implications for the inner work necessary to spiritualize or reverse the will. When some action is done so often that we no longer have to concentrate on doing it or no longer feel enthusiasm for the deed, something is lost to us in our daily will. If, however, the action is something we have had to develop through practice, then the will invested in the action is not quite so threatened. We have in effect protected the will by the intensity of will developed in practicing. Athletes and artists often have access to this ardent level of will when they practice something to the point that they can actually break through the disinterest and find ways to invest the most repetitive activities with enthusiasm. When this happens it is as if the will forces in the individual are magnified beyond their inherent capacities.

At this level of will, the expectation has become associated with an outcome of tremendous enthusiasm. The forces in the will that are directed toward accomplishing a particular task are focused in such a way that the conditioning of the will is almost complete. However, this type of conditioning of the will toward a particular end result can sometimes prove to be problematic for the soul doing the conditioning. Conditioning the will to such a high level of achievement can cause disequilibrium in the emotional life, centered on power and its display. Stories of such emotional dysfunction and the temperamental displays that accompany it are well known among artists and athletes. The conditioned will, no matter how productive in the zone of virtuosity, is still not transformed or rendered fluid enough to transcend the lower impulses in the soul.

Reversed Will

Effects that impede development and transformation of the will are hidden in the everyday repetitive things we do. This is very much the case when it comes to forming thoughts about sense experiences. When we experience a sensation, our daily will is engaged for a short while. It rises to the surface of our consciousness just long enough to participate in the sense experience and then, when we are able to cognize, or recognize, the tree or the cloud, the daily will once again submerges into a dark inner space, where it lives a life hidden from our immediate awareness. Every human being must go through this fallen quality in the daily will or else we would be hallucinating all day. We would be like children unable to pass a mud puddle, which would certainly make us late for our important meetings. The will in the mud puddle would lure our own daily will into a playful dialogue, and then the sense experience of the mud puddle would become intoxicating like it is for a two-year-old. In order to pay the bills in later life, we have to adulterate this fundamental childlike and creative daily will impulse and damp the magic of the world down into more manageable units of will. As adults we must constantly say to ourselves, "This I can do right now and that I cannot do right now." This allows us to survive, but there is a price to pay in the daily will.

When we have a sensation, the magical forces present in both the thing we are sensing and the bodily response we are having to it meet in the nervous system as an inner image is formed of what we are sensing. If we have an aversion to the color vermilion, for instance, then the bodily response that is the root of the will sets up a series of images, which we associate with the sensation vermilion. We experience the association as a particular mood in the daily will. There are two basic moods: it is me, or it is not me.

Bad habits are really just associative thought patterns that run in the same tracks each time we think them. A large part of the difficulty we encounter when we try to work on changing our attitudes is the tendency for thought patterns to constantly shift from one thing to the next without any logical or objective connections between one thought and another. Often the mind touches one thought and then moves on to another thought related somehow through our personal experience. This is known as associative thinking, thinking based solely upon our *personal* associations.

In order to break the fixed patterns it is useful to think of things in ways that are not habitual. This, as we know, is easier said than done, for with every sense experience we have, a corresponding set of associative thoughts usually arises unconsciously at the same time. For instance, some people see the color vermilion, which is a warm fire-engine red, and immediately do not like it. Maybe their experience is that vermilion is the favorite color of someone who is or was unkind to them. They have learned to associate the color vermilion with an inner feeling of anxiety. Other people may have a different associative pattern and feel energized by the same color. Their association might be positive: vermilion might remind them of the energetic manner of someone they loved as a child.

In reality, a color like vermilion is objective as a sensation, but the inner response in someone who is bothered by it is not objective; it is associative. Most often associations are connected with some form of personally unique, often subtle, response patterns to objective sense impressions. This makes associations difficult to observe in ourselves and difficult to work on. They are too close to us to be seen. This is the underlying problem with habits.

In order to develop the will and transcend the lower impulses in the soul, the will must be spiritualized to function without any expectations of success. To do that, the intent must be strengthened. The exercises below, already presented in part two, chapter four, but repeated here for convenience, are aimed at strengthening intent in the will.

The Intent to See

The ability to see inward pictures has a lot to do with the intent to see them. One of the most effective ways of increasing intent is through dynamic visualization. In this exercise you are going to visualize a circle, but before you try sit quietly for a few moments and intend that you are going to see the circle. This means bringing to mind the feeling that you know the circle will appear in your consciousness. Intending to see alerts the organism that something is about to happen. Continue intending the circle until you sense it somewhere in your sphere of awareness.

If, when you try to visualize the circle, no inner circle at all arises or the image starts to move or dissolve reestablish it by drawing it in front of you in the air. If you can get to where you can imagine the circle but it keeps fading away, try to visualize the following. First intend the circle. Then imagine that when you are drawing the circle you see your hand drawing and try to hold the inner image. When the inner image starts to fade, imagine that the inner hand that drew it is now erasing it. See the circle being erased in the opposite direction to which it was drawn. After it is erased, intend to see the circle and then redraw it.

After the imaginative exercise get a large sheet of drawing paper and cover it with circles of all sizes, drawing them with a pencil. After drawing, intend to see a circle and then visualize it. With this technique you should sooner or later be able to stay "in" the circle for a minute or two, fading with it and reestablishing it as it pulsates. The inner image oscillates with the flow of your cerebrospinal fluid pulse. If you hold your breath you will most often find that the inner image stabilizes. When you breathe, your spinal fluid circulates and the inner images flow away with the current. With this exercise we are learning to anticipate this flowing away and trying to work consciously into the rhythm of the fading and reestablishing of the image. An exercise like this, preceded by a conscious period of intent, strengthens our capacity to visualize.

With this new capacity it becomes possible to find in our soul an image that comes to us when we don't want it to come. It may be a feeling for ourselves or others, or a particular innocent craving like wanting something sweet, for instance. When you feel the craving, use the strengthened inner capacity to form a picture to imagine you are seeing yourself from outside eating the sweet. Then dissolve the picture and live into the silent dark space where the picture goes when it dissolves. Now be present and watch the image of the desire for sweets return into your soul. Form the image of your eating and once again dissolve it. The practice consists in dissolving the inner image until the desire to do the activity does not return. We should then go and have the sweet.

Over time this practice develops a strong inner picture forming capacity, and the will that is normally engaged in automatic representations linked to desire patterns is released from the usual habitual pattern and is reversed and transformed into a dynamic, creative force in the soul. In this way we uproot the unconscious images hidden in our nervous system and consciously plant the tree of knowledge bearing the fruits of our transformed will. What we learn from our inner work in reversing the will pictorially allows us to bring down spiritual truths from higher worlds and work with them in this world to serve others instead of being a slave to habitual patterns in the will. The essential tincture in the little bottle in the upper branches of the tree is the spiritualized will formed by the alchemist in work done in higher worlds and brought down to Earth for the service of others.

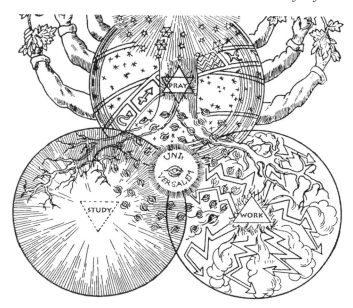

Why do things always come in threes? Why do fairy tales have three brothers? Why is the punch line to a joke always on the third try? Why do alchemy books and pictures always have three things? Why do study, work, and pray come together in a triangle of circles? If I want to do research in the spirit, which one comes first? Does it matter? Should I pray first and then study or work first and then pray? Are all three the same thing or are they different? How are they different? How are they the same? Why is pray at the trunk of the tree and the other two on the roots? Is study a kind of work? Is work a kind of study? How can I change my work into a prayer? How can I change my prayer into work? How can I transform my study into prayer? Can prayer be transformed into study?

14
THE LABORATORY
WORK AND PRAY

IN THE LAST IMAGE WE SAW the alchemist transforming the pictorial will and reversing it into what is known esoterically as magical will. Magical will simply means that the person doing the willing is aware that he or she is willing. In other words, there is more intent in magical will than in daily or conditioned will, no matter how conditioned it is through practice. In order to transform the will into a transcendent or spiritual form, a complete reversal of the impulse-ridden urge to power is required. The seeds for this transformation lie deep in the daily will related to the daily soul experiences of sensation. The tool is the reversal of the tendency of the will to fade when enthusiasm for the reward begins to wane. In normal sensation the nature of the will is imbedded in stimulus/response patterns far below the level of the awake consciousness. There is a kind of sleeping urge to power hidden in the unconscious repetitive things we do every day. This is very much the case when it comes to forming thoughts and inner images in response to the daily sense experiences we are having.

The picture of the house with the fire burning in the fireplace nestled high on the mountain is an image of the alchemical achievement of the reversed will trained to understand and meet the deep challenge contained in normal sensation. The movements and the processes of the spiritual hierarchies are hidden in sensation as an "open secret," to use Goethe's words. The flowers and the clouds are not simply sets of forces that can be analyzed and understood completely by the methods of natural science; they are a secret language of the activity of the spiritual hierarchies.

In the laboratory on the mountain the alchemist is engaged in the great work of transforming the metals of the sensations into more purified forms. That is why there is smoke coming out of the chimney. The house has many windows, just as the head has many sensory orifices. There is a serious, industrious mood to this house. It is a big house, no longer a small hut. The alchemist is prosperous but still hard at work. The mood of this picture is the mood of the old alchemical mantra *"ora et labora,"* pray and work. Do not do one without the other. The exercises for this level of work are aimed at a fundamental transformation of the dream nature of sense activity. To work on the senses means to transform the dream life in order to awaken in the place where we are normally dreaming. The most accessible dream space available to us is found precisely in the sensations that permeate daily life. However, to awaken in these sensations requires that we have access to the dreams in the day-awake state. To develop this capacity, deepen the basic practice of sacred sleeping presented earlier in part two, chapter one.

The daily review in the evening can be enhanced by paying strict attention to the silent space that arises when we finally can picture inwardly the reverse order of the day's events. The key here is not to get hung up on trying to remember the tiniest details of an event if the remembering blocks the flow of the picturing. Strive to strike a balance between remembering details and getting the inner picture to flow or glide through the day backward. A practice that can help to enhance the flow of the images is to imagine that you are sitting there doing the backward review and then remember the event right before you sat down to do the review, which was, say, brushing your teeth. At this point, instead of trying to plow on backward to the next event before you brushed your teeth, return to the image of you doing the exercise, then add the brushing of the teeth, and then add the next thing which was, say, having a cup of tea. Here again, instead of trying to plow backward up the stream from there, go forward from the cup of tea to brushing the teeth to sitting down to do the review. Then go backward from the review to the teeth to the tea, and so on to the next event in reverse. This may take a bit of time for a week or so, but it soon develops a strong will to reverse and imagine the sequences of the day. It is possible with this capacity to remember in detail the events of the day backward in a timely and enthusiastic manner without wandering and fretting. If this strong glide is developed, the image of us sitting in meditation in the morning becomes the last thing we see inwardly in the daily review – assuming of course, that we have established a practice of sitting in mediation for a while as the first thing we do upon awakening in the morning.

If a strong glide is developed in the daily backward review and we have also established a morning practice of prayer and meditation, then as we pass through this meditative space going backward we become capable of listening directly into the space where dreams transform from spiritual experiences into the language of feelings on Earth. The space just before we awaken into day-awake consciousness is the place of the dream, and the alchemist intent on transforming the senses needs to be very familiar with the ways sensory images are used by our guardian angel to help us understand the lessons we are learning in the realm of sleep. We can actually ask the angel to be there in the morning to help us understand our dreams; most likely we will be awakened at 4:30 with a mantra already going in our heads. This help is a great incentive to establishing a morning practice. The place where we were awake in the dreaming the night before in our backward review becomes a rendezvous place for us with the incoming dream in our morning practice. We become awake before we are awake, and the dream content is moved into a much more intimate relationship to our day-awake consciousness.

By consciously stretching the awake state into the dream state, we transform the dream into an alchemical tool of great value. Our sleeping is then much more restful and productive, and the rejuvenating forces of the night start to gently seep into our daily activities. This is sacred sleeping applied to the work of transforming the dream. Once developed, the capacity for entering the dream state with our waking consciousness leads eventually to the state of the continuity of consciousness. The awake state and the dream, and even sleeping, begin to relate to each other, and we experience the capacity of being aware of how inner images arise during the heretofore hidden dream states of sensory experience. This is sacred sleeping enhanced into the capacity to be in our body and out of our body simultaneously. Our work is a prayer and our prayer is our work and our meditation is done simply for the love of the deed, without expectations.

Is it okay to just keep asking questions without getting any answers or is it just stupid? Why does it matter to me if it is stupid? Am I not allowed to be stupid? Who says I can't be stupid? Why am I afraid of looking stupid? Why am I afraid of being stupid? What is being afraid? Does this train of thought have anything to do with anything worthwhile? How would I know? Why am I thinking these things? What is this picture about? Does seeing more of it give me more insight, or does it just make the whole experience more confusing? How can I distinguish between an insight and an error?

15

THE HEALING MEDICINE
YOUR WOUND IS YOUR GIFT

THE IMAGE SHOWS A SPHERICAL GLOBE with a cross sitting on it and a crown hovering above. These two symbols are discussed together because at this high level the truth can only be expressed in polarities and paradox. The globe resembles an alchemical flask, or cruet, in which essences are stored. At the end of such a long alchemical process, some sort of product would be stored in a vessel like this. The wine or oil for the sacraments in churches are stored in cruets, and the glass stopper is often in the form of a cross just as is depicted in this image. The essence is the sum total of all the work that has been done, saved as a precious substance in the hermetically sealed vessel so that it does not escape or spoil or become sullied once again with impurities. We have sealed off the precious substance of the work and can now use it for our own purposes.

This is a great gift, and it is simultaneously and paradoxically a great wound. To have such an essence at our disposal implies a great responsibility. If we have amassed wealth, we must now protect it or circulate it, or else it will stagnate. If we have amassed great knowledge, it must be given over to others, or else it will rest uneasily within our heart. If we have developed power in the world, then circumstances will constantly arise to test the power and prod us into giving it away to others. Whatever we have labored to place in the cruet is our gift and also our wound. It tells others what our issues are and where our weak places are likely to be found. To have the cruet of the magical essence is another trial. This is a difficult lesson after having traveled so far.

In earlier times the crown of the king was not simply a bauble or part of a costume. It was actually an esoteric implement, a kind of dish antenna, enabling the head that wore it to pull in the cosmic wisdom needed to rule the people according to the best principles of the cosmos. The crown represented not the power of the kings or queens but their capacity to submit their own thoughts to the higher wisdom of the cosmos. This act of surrender allowed the head that wore the crown to navigate treacherous political ground with dignity and acumen. Eventually this ancient view of the crown became politicized and then linked to military and economic power, leading to the downfall of monarchies and the rise of the modern political state. In its more esoteric form, the crown still represents the divine right of kings, which was originally a mark of service, not of power. In many ancient civilizations the king was not expected to retain power into a ripe old age. When he began failing he was killed and another was put into his place. "The king is dead, long live the king," describes the practice and is paradoxical only to a modern person who believes that rulership is a quest for power. The crown is actually a symbol of the surrender of personal power for the good of the whole. The ruler who misunderstood this was moving inexorably into peril.

What we hold on to is what imprisons us. Our beliefs allow us to develop and simultaneously limit our further development. Our enemies are our most diligent and committed teachers. To exclude them from the circle of humanity is only done at the expense of our learning. We can help the spiritual world by taking on some of the hard lessons as a part of our own inner work. Many of the exercises given in these chapters were aimed at this goal. Expectations are the snares that trap us into blaming. Expectations limit us, while long-term goals strengthen the will to prevail even when there is no hope of resolution for a problem. The poet Keats called this ability "negative capability," the ability to stay enthusiastically engaged in a problem when there is no hope of a solution. The Buddha said, "Act, but do not be attached to your action." This is a critical faculty for soul alchemists. It involves the work of putting a lot of effort into forming a small amount of essence and then letting it all go in the authentic faith that the spirit will move and we will know when we need to know. Until then we work on the essence and practice listening into the silence. Our spiritual crowns guide the right thoughts into our meditations and we are guided by a vision of Moral Imagination to seek to do the best in a given situation, especially when we feel that we do not know.

This exercise helps us to experience the degree to which our inner life is programmed to include certain people in our daily life and to exclude others. The first part is a way of experiencing how we have organized the feeling relationships around us to protect the essence from being polluted or dispersed. The second part is an attempt to visualize how turning the soul toward a broader perspective can sometimes allow even our enemies to be our teachers.

The Circle of Friends

Take a sheet of paper and draw a small circle in the center. Then draw a larger circle around that so that the two are concentric. Then draw two more circles each one slightly larger and also concentric. The circles should look like an archery target with a bull's-eye in the center. Now take some plasticene clay or modeling wax and make a small doll, which is meant to represent you, and place it in the center of the bull's-eye. The figurine should be only about two inches tall. Do not worry about details or a likeness; you know it is supposed to be you. Next make a figurine of one or two of the most favorite and trusted people in your life. Place these figurines within the next circle out from your own circle on the chart. These should be people who are so close to you that when you are together you tend to say "we" a lot. The next circle out is for acquaintances and casual friends, people who are not as close as your close friends but are still included in "we." These may be family members or just acquaintances. In the next circle out place people you know who bring up uneasy feelings in you when you have to deal with them in life situations. Outside of the circle of friends and acquaintances put figurines of the people you try to avoid, or those who bring up antisocial impulses in your imagination when you see or hear them. Take time to look at this chart and its figurines. Then try to visualize the relationships you have depicted in it. Write a few sentences about the feelings this chart brings up in your soul.

Make another chart on another sheet of paper. This time draw only the largest circle from the last chart. Take the figure of yourself and position it on the circle in the place closest to you; we will call this point south. Write a sentence about how this feels in contrast to the first arrangement. Then position the figurines from the second ring, that is your close friends, next to you on the same circle but to your right and left so that you still get the feeling "we" from the arrangement. Write a sentence about the feelings connected to this. Next place the figurines of your acquaintances at the positions of east and west on the circle. Play with the positioning at east and west and see if you can get a feeling for "we" and "not we" by moving the figurines along the circumference of the circle. Write a sentence about the feelings connected to this placement. Next place the figurines of the people who make you uneasy somewhere on the circumference, toward the position of north. Once again write a sentence about your feelings. Finally place the figurine of a person who was excluded from your previous circle onto the circle in the north position directly opposite to you. Take some time with this one. Now form an inner picture of the whole circle and then write a few sentences about how this process and arrangement is different or not different to you from the first arrangement.

Finally, imagine that the person opposite you is standing on the same circle as you are and seeing you directly opposite. Try to move yourself along the circle imaginatively until you can stand in his or her place and look back at yourself. How does this feel? Return to your own place and then look at the person opposite to you. Imaginatively try to move him or her along the circumference away from the north position and a bit closer to you. Write a few sentences about what arises in you when you imagine doing this.

Refer to this practice when new persons enter your life or when struggles with old friends threaten long-standing relationships. In the last resort, soul alchemy is the preparation we can undertake to learn to surrender ourselves into the being of another person and still maintain the integrity of who we are as individuals. In alchemy this is know as the alchemical marriage, and it represents a far distant goal for every person on Earth. The practice of soul alchemy is an initial attempt by individuals to realize this distant goal of all human beings.

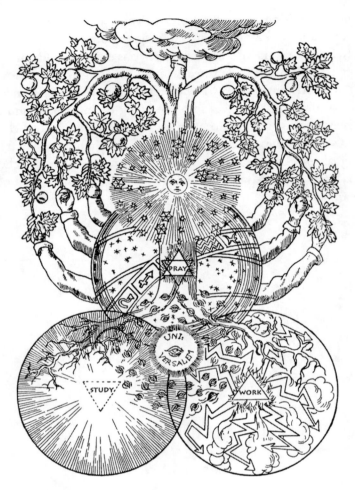

What is this picture supposed to mean? Can't these artists just say what they want to say instead of making it so strange? Is strange better than just coming out with the meaning? Why was this picture given throughout this part in little pieces? Are the sequences supposed to mean something? Is the intent of this process to make me think? Do I resent that somewhere in my soul? Can't this book give me an answer? Would getting an answer help me to think better? Would I be any better off if I got an answer? Is there any advantage to just continuing to ask questions? (Drawing by V. Weigel, *Studium Universale*, Frankfurt, 1698.)